IN MEMORY OF

Geraldine Moyemont

from

Mr. and Mrs. Steven E. Stroh

THE DWIGHT PUBLIC LIBRARY

# Loving Rachel

Also by Jane Bernstein

*Departures*

# Loving Rachel

## A Family's Journey from Grief

### JANE BERNSTEIN

**LITTLE, BROWN AND COMPANY**

BOSTON      TORONTO

The names and descriptions of some of the
characters in this story have been changed.

Library of Congress Cataloging-in-Publication Data
Bernstein, Jane, 1949–
Loving Rachel.
1. Glynn, Rachel.   2. Handicapped children —
United States — Biography.   3. Parents of handicapped
children—United States — Biography.   I. Title.
HQ773.6.B47B47   1988        362.3 [B]        88-597
ISBN 0-316-09204-5

10   9   8   7   6   5   4   3   2   1

VB

*Published simultaneously in Canada
by Little, Brown & Company (Canada) Limited*

PRINTED IN THE UNITED STATES OF AMERICA

To Charlotte,
who endured

# Contents

# Acknowledgments

Thanks to Carol Ardman for her careful reading of this manuscript; to Drs. Loren Fishman, Ronald Siwoff, Martin Diamond, and Robert Gould, all of whom took time to answer my medical questions; and to June Kaiser, Hinda Haskell, and Derry Tanner, for their patience with my non-medical questions. Thanks also to Virginia Teller, who does not fit into the story through no fault of her own; and to my agent, Lois Wallace, and my editor, Jennifer Josephy, for their wisdom and support.

Robin Fine, Florence Levine, Chris Stevens, Lourie Testa, and Karen Walsh were among the many people at Children's Specialized Hospital who worked with Rachel. I am grateful to them, to Carolyn Weil for her uncommon kindness, and to the rest of the Hospital's extraordinary staff.

Thanks to the New Jersey State Council on the Arts for their fellowship assistance, which made the writing of this book possible.

Of all that I read on blindness during Rachel's first year, nothing touched me as deeply as Selma Fraiberg's *Insights from the Blind*. I highly recommend this book.

I would also like to thank Paul, whose way is not to look back, but whose encouragement was unwavering.

# PART I

# ❦ 1 ❦

# Expectations

*August 1983*

IT IS THE KIND of summer day that New Jersey is known for, with air that is thick and still and unbearably hot. Paul comes home from work with patches of sweat across the back of his shirt, his mustache as incongruous as a fur stole at the beach. He gives me a quick distracted kiss, then edges away, hands hidden behind his back, mischief in his eyes. I cannot begin to guess what he holds, though I know he wants me to try. Blackberries? The pen I lost last year? A dragonfly?

He brings his hands forward, and what I see resting placidly upon one palm is a rat, a big white one the size of my daughter's sneaker, her fur disarrayed, her pink eyes fixed on something straight ahead, whiskers twitching. Paul calls: "Charlotte!" and drops the animal into his breast pocket.

Our four-year-old hears his voice and dashes down the steps, the first eight on her feet, the final five thump thump on her rear end. It is the age of adoration, a time in her life when she speaks of her father in religious tones. It does not matter to Charlotte that we have struggled to raise her in the fairest of homes — non-sexist, non-violent — the way she sees it, I am good at choosing clothes and making ponytails, while the earth and stars belong to him. My place is in the kitchen so that she can cuddle up with *Him*. "Where is *He?*" she asks when he is late, because life is dreary when *He* is gone. At dinnertime she stays close to the door, idly coloring or building a tower, one block piled on top of the next until the whole thing collapses, her ferocious appetite subdued during the interminable wait. "I'm not hungry. I want to eat with *Him*." She mopes around until she hears the sound of his car engine in front of the house, then races toward the door crying, "Oh Mama — *He's* home."

"Dadd-eeee!"

"I have a little something for you," he says.

The pocket shifts and bulges. Charlotte leans over to check his pants because it is here that she has found the magnifying glass, Mexican jumping beans, scented erasers. She tosses onto the floor his wallet, hankie, pens, then steps back, puzzled, near tears. The rat pokes her head out of his pocket. Her ears are like daisy petals; by any other name, she would be admired for her fine white coat. Paul puts her on the floor, and I watch the way she stands between us, and wonder again why she does not run away. Is she sick, or disoriented? Has she been bred for passivity? Charlotte presses the animal's head with her index finger, and the whiskers twitch.

"She's so cute!" she says.

"She's going to have babies any day," says Paul. "I thought it would be interesting for you to watch."

"Why?" she asks, in a way that makes me feel that answers are irrelevant. I am choosy, and will not respond to these aimless whys, but her father will never pass up an opportunity to teach.

"Because Mommy is going to have a baby."

"I *know*."

At last the animal darts across the room. I lift the *Merck Manual* from the bookcase and look up "Plague" in the index. Ah, there it is, "Bubonic Plague; Pestis; Black Death." So, it still exists.

"She's no ordinary *Rattus rattus* — she's a *Rattus norvegicus albinus,* lab bred for thousands of generations, saved from this —" finger, like a knife blade, drawn across his neck when Charlotte is distracted, for she knows that he works with rats, but not what he does with them.

When he has her attention again, he says, "She needs a name."

"Rat," she says.

"Rat?" I try to coax a new selection. "What about Whitey or Snowflake or Sigrid — Sig Norvegicus has kind of a nice ring to it."

Paul asks me with his eyes to be still, for Charlotte is still sensitive about this issue of names. We had asked her to suggest a name for her unborn sister and then vetoed Baby Cheeses, which had been her choice. She hates what we have chosen — Rachel Alexa — and tells her friends and teachers and my parents on the phone that inside her mommy's tummy resides the little Baby Cheeses.

I shouldn't be surprised by her adamance since names are such a big thing in our family. I altered my first, once Martha Jane, and will not give up the last, and have struggled to find the perfect name for each child. When I was pregnant the first time, the sex of the unborn baby was not known to me, but this was clear: The child would not be named after anyone, not after my sister, because every time I called to her, I would be reminded of my sister's early death; not after Paul, who shares his father's name, because Jews name after the dead, and it seemed a bad omen to name my child after a husband who was very much alive, and anyhow, he is the one and only Paul to me. We chose Charlotte Claire, a name like confectionary, said one friend. Charlotte, like Martha, said another — everybody's great-aunt. "A horrible name!" my father pronounced, because sixty years before he had been betrayed by a red-haired Charlotte. And now Rachel Alexa, perfect number of syllables, pleasant hushed sounds that rolled off the tongue.

Paul makes a home for Rat, a bed of cedar chips in an old aquarium where once we kept elephant fish, a grate at the top, and through a special hole her feed bottle. This he sets on an end table so that the rat can be at Charlotte's height. He uses words like "miraculous" and "wonderful" when describing to her the upcoming birth. He calls the event "awesome," and this Charlotte understands, though not in the way he had intended, because awesome has flown eastward from L.A., and is a big word among preschoolers in New Jersey.

The rat does not move much, and I understand on these hot days just what she feels. She rests, low to the ground, her sides distended, the skin stretched thin so that I can see the movement of the fetuses wriggling beneath. I sit beside the tank, thirty pounds above my normal weight, my face round, fingers stiff and swollen, calves twice their normal size. Urged by Paul, Charlotte takes off the aquarium lid to pet the animal, and upsets the feed bottle. Water drips onto Rat's fur. Charlotte lowers her finger, and Rat draws her head between her shoulders, and skitters forward and back. The finger travels a hair above her head, and I am reminded of photographs of enemy planes buzzing above rice paddies, ready to attack.

"Enough!" I cry, heaving myself up. "Leave her be!"

I go upstairs and lie so still upon my bed that I can feel the faint breeze from the open window. The birds scamper on the air conditioner. Our neighbor mows his patch of lawn with an old rotary mower that clanks and whirrs and tosses up the sweet smell of cut grass. Rachel shifts inside me. Charlotte wheeled and kicked and knocked against me, like a person who is frantic to escape from a locked room. This one stirs lazily. My due date is a week from now, and I no longer think about my unknown baby, the way I have during the nine months past. I no longer speculate about the texture of her hair, her eye color, the shape of her nose and chin, the form her certain beauty will take, the bias of her fine mind. I have stopped counting the time until she will arrive. Instead, I am holding fast, like a passenger on a raft in rough seas. Not yet, baby. The wallpaper for your room lies in tight rolls on the floor; an unfinished manuscript is spread across my desk. I've been so busy that I have not paid full attention to Paul and Charlotte and need a few more days to take them in so that when everything has changed, I will be able to recall these times clearly. The need to be twice as conscious, to make sense of things, is so strong that perhaps my body has sent Rachel this signal, for she turns inside me, like a person in deep sleep.

I sleep, too, waking only when Charlotte climbs onto the bed, and Paul sings "Supper!" in my ears — supper because to the son of New Englanders dinner is what is eaten at noon. On the dining-room table is the cold soup I made that morning, a salad, yesterday's muffins. "Look at the *nakkins!*" Charlotte says, showing me the way she folded them into triangles, her newest feat. "Just sit," says Paul.

I take my place, nearest the kitchen doorway, and sit very still while they put food on my plate and fill my glass with seltzer. I am wishing that I could freeze this frame. I am trying to open all my pores so that this tranquil moment will stay with me. I am concentrating hard on this task when Paul says:

"Mommy has the bovines."

And I say, "Moooo."

After we eat, Charlotte and I get into the bathtub together. She needs no toys because she has me. She bobbles a breast, leans her cheek against my swollen abdomen, pokes a finger to see if she can invert my navel, restoring it to its proper position, tries to work an inch-long comb through my hair — intense, breathing heavily, tongue above her upper lip.

I used to look in the mirror and/despair when I saw my image. The lady of Nizes with breasts of two different sizes, waist too high, legs that flunked the diamond test — "Your legs ought to have a party so your calves could meet." During pregnancy my despair turned to pleasure, that my body could do this, and so well! And then Charlotte was born, and loved me without judgment, knobby toes and scars and stray hairs — it was all the same to her — and in time, it was all the same to me.

While we play, I try to step outside myself for just a moment and view the two of us splashing in this old slope-sided tub, but Charlotte lowers her face into the water and flaps her arms wildly, and I must watch to make sure that she does not drown while blowing bubbles, or send waves over the side, because the imprint of the tub is beginning to show clearly on the dining-room ceiling. My little mermaid rises, hair plastered across her face, and I see the streaks of summer grime from wrist to elbow. I put aside my need to imprint this sweet moment and grab the soap.

I know what I must do, and as soon as Charlotte is in bed, I hurry upstairs to the attic, where there are hundreds of photographs stored in a carton. I carry them into my office and separate the first batch on the floor. After a while Paul joins me. I look at him in the chair across the room, then in the picture taken when we were newly married, his face naked-looking without the mustache; mine softer, less angular, my hair wavier than it is now. We set our camera on a tripod in those days, so both of us appear in every shot, entwined most often; fingers between fingers, arms around backs. We're in a canoe, we're displaying two bowls of wild berries, we're standing against a concrete house in a poor Caribbean town.

"When was this taken?" I ask, showing Paul a picture in which he and a buxom frizzy-haired woman stand in front of a tenement in New York.

Paul does not prize solitude the way I do. He likes laughter and disorder, the sound of voices, another body nearby even when he is working, and for this reason, the commotion of family living suits him well. He has come upstairs with books and computer printouts, preferring to sit beside me on a chair that hurts his back than be comfortable in the cool solarium and read alone, and now he studies this picture for a long while. "Carmine Street," he says at last. "Nineteen sixty-six. I wonder what happened to that shirt."

I no longer find it unbearable seeing him in photographs with old girlfriends, though there is still the lingering regret that for so many years he lived, loved, ate, and adventured without me. It hardly matters that seventeen years have passed since the picture was taken, that the woman beside him may be fat and middle-aged by now. She will always stand with her arm around him, laughing.

"Ancient history," he says, going back to his magazine. I am sorting through a second stack when he says: "You should sleep."

"I know," I say, poring over photographs. I should sleep, but sleep will be impossible until I can make order out of what exists. What I am going to do is arrange all of our pictures chronologically and tell our story through snapshots. First there were two very different people who met and fell in love; then Charlotte was born, sat up, cut teeth, stood, walked, charmed and annoyed us. Then you came, Rachel Alexa, whoever you are.

"It's ten o'clock," Paul says. "It's eleven o'clock," he says an hour later. "My day will be shot if I don't get to bed," he says sometime after that. He falls asleep on the chair and snores lightly, his mouth open. His gold molars gleam beneath the light.

I sort through hundreds more photographs, and when my weariness has changed to light-headedness I begin to choose the best shots, arrange them on pages and think up captions. October 27, 1979 — We carry Charlotte up to our fifth-floor walk-up . . . October 21, 1980 — We move to New Jersey . . . February 4, 1982 — Charlotte tastes her first snow . . .

It is nearly one A.M. when I decide to quit. I go downstairs for a glass of water, and what I judge at first as utter stillness of night turns out to be a range of familiar sounds: cicadas and crickets chirruping loudly, Rat scratching in her tank. A light breeze lifts the long, sheer living-room curtains. I kneel before the aquarium and see that she has heaped the shavings in one corner of the aquarium, and lies with her swollen belly against the cool glass bottom.

Rat gives birth the next day, to one, and then later, when I am no longer gazing intently over the top of the aquarium, to a mound of pink babies with smooth rounded heads and undeveloped paws. They are naked and pink and as featureless as erasers. The entire underside of the mother's body is lined with teats, two rows of them. She is truly double-breasted, neck to hips like an overcoat. When Paul returns from work, he kneels before the tank.

"Isn't it marvelous!" he says, as I try to count bodies.

Nine, no, eleven, and she has only ten teats, two of which are under her arms. When I point this out, Paul regards me for a long time, and at last says, "So are yours." Then he goes into the kitchen, spreads peanut butter thickly on two pieces of bread, and arranges banana slices between them. "Rat has gone, and so will you," he says portentously, wrapping up the sandwich and putting it into a paper bag. "Tonight will be the night."

"Come to bed early," he says later, and I remember what I have learned in childbirth class, that exhaustion is a key factor in making labor difficult. At ten I get into bed with him, and he wraps himself around me. He is rather thicker than when we first met, with smooth skin and heavy limbs. He rests his big square hands upon my belly; his mustache rubs against the nape of my neck. I have never met another person, adult or child, who can fall asleep as quickly or as soundly as he. I get up, and he rolls over and wraps his arms around his pillow, never nearing consciousness.

My bags are packed, nightgown, nursing bra, ChapStick, sour lollipop, socks, back massager, dimes for phone calls. Upstairs the pictures are spread in piles across my floor. I open a large manila envelope and see Paul as a baby, dressed in a white christening gown; Paul in a bow tie and jacket and little shorts, with the fair curls his mother clipped and saved in an envelope I have upstairs; his sister with artificially pink cheeks and extra blue in her eyes. I study these studio portraits for a long time. They tell me about style but fail to give the smallest hint of character or personality; they do not predict how troubled he would be, or suggest why an unhappy boy would want to relive his childhood by having children.

Did I know the day we met that Paul loved children? Or was it only after a week? The exact time escapes me, because the fact that he loved children was as much a part of him from the very start as his silver hair or his wild laugh. It wasn't as if I didn't like children, rather that they were never in my thoughts. I had never held an infant or baby-sat for little ones; I had no friends with babies, which from afar seemed so achingly vulnerable and demanding. The rare times I entered a household with children, the noise and disorder made my ears ring. The unending cycles of caring and cleaning, the sentences that never got finished, the poor worn women who had buried their dreams and stayed home making sandwiches while the men and children played — not me, no way. And anyway, how could either of us think of such things when we were both so busy?

Paul does not hold on to the past as I do, and says quite often, "What did we *do* before she was born? I can hardly remember life without her."

What we did was travel a lot, every three months or so flying to a small, untouristed Caribbean island. We made love a lot, ate out a lot, saw friends a lot. It was not a hedonistic life at all, however. We worked much harder than we played. When Paul stayed late at the lab where he worked, I stayed home and wrote. When he drove there weekends, he got a pass that gave me entry, and a typewriter I could use, and we worked for long hours in separate rooms. Work was our first bond; we were fifteen years apart, of different backgrounds and temperaments, but each of us had a dream. When we met I was working as the editor of a confessions magazine, and writing fiction lunchtime, evenings, and weekends, and he was working as an engineer, going to graduate school in biology, and studying lunchtime, evenings, weekends; by the time we married I had started a graduate writing program and wrote to, from, between classes and in the evenings, and he had gotten an internship in the biophysics department of the same research organization, worked brutal interns' hours and studied for doctoral comprehensives whenever he was home.

And yet Paul's love for children made me think about them. Over the next three years, as I scrutinized families, developed theories, and questioned him about his views on child care and the role of the father, the "not me, no way" softened, and I began to believe that if we didn't see the kind of family we wanted to have, we would just have to carve out something new as parents. We would be trailblazers.

When I look at our photographs from the time before we had children, I see smooth, untroubled faces — how naive and confident we were to believe that we could produce a perfect child exactly when we wanted one! But that was what we did. Five months after Paul had taken his doctoral comps, and my first novel was accepted for publication, I became pregnant with Charlotte.

Most of my friends were single, and my pregnancy frightened them. I remember an afternoon I met with two old friends for lunch, and how they backed off when they saw me. One said, "Oh my God, you're *huge*," as if my size was a sign that I lacked self-control. The other acted as if what I carried inside was an explosive device, and not a baby, and several times during the meal said, "She's going to pop, I swear." They told me a story about a smart, aggressive lawyer, on the verge of making partner, who had a baby, announced that it fulfilled her as nothing else had, and quit. Then there was the graphic artist who had made detailed arrangements for a two-month maternity leave, and six weeks after the baby was born, called up her boss, announced that "this was what it was all about," and never showed up at the office again.

Women like you, they were telling me. Women with dreams and ambitions, whose faithless hormones turned them into mothers. I laughed at these tales, and said, "You know what you're doing, don't you? You're asking me to believe that childbirth alters the brain chemistry. You're telling me that next month I'll be someone else."

When I left the restaurant, I saw them everywhere: mothers on park benches, their strollers lined up in front of them; mothers wiping sticky hands, filling buckets in sandboxes, pushing squalling babies; mothers tugging on recalcitrant toddlers. The sight of them made my head throb; by the time I got indoors I could feel my brain beating in my skull. I imagined the hormones doing their trick, shooting through my bloodstream, causing irrevocable change. An aspirin would stop the pounding, perhaps it would stem these changes, too. The only problem was that I could not take an aspirin — I could not take anything because I was pregnant.

The first inkling I had that I was no longer the master of my fate was during labor. I suppose I had known in some dark recess of my brain that labor was hard, but so were marathons, and I had completed one and gone out for an ice cream sundae afterwards. Of course I had heard about women who screamed and bit rags and tore their hair during labor — melodramatic types to whom screaming came easily. Nothing prepared me for childbirth, not exercise or inner will or my childbirth preparedness class, where the strongest word used to describe the fire and agony was "discomfort."

The sun set and rose and set again before she was born. After the delivery I slept for three hours and then walked barefoot down the corridor to see if it was true that I had had a baby. There she was, third row from the window, second isolette from the left, so incredibly beautiful. Her skin was red and parched, her head pointed, her nose pushed to the side. She had scratched herself in utero with long fingernails that the hospital would not clip "because of insurance problems," and that a nurse advised me to chew off myself.

Yes, beautiful, my beautiful little girl. I held court for three days. Friends and obscure cousins dropped by; flowers arrived from my father's customers and my mother's coworkers and the neighbors on the street where I had grown up. Her birth was written up in an interoffice memo where my father worked, and in the newsletter of the temple where I had attended Hebrew school seventeen years before. All these announcements confirmed what I felt deep inside, that Charlotte was not just my firstborn, but the first child *ever* born. And yet what did I speak of with my guests? My book, which had just come out, the nippy weather, the political situation in Bangladesh, the World Series, the price of body waves — anything but the baby, absolutely anything. There I was making pronouncements about rent control, while the whole time my breasts, as big as cannonballs, were tingling, and my ears were attuned to the squeak of carts in the hall, and the mewling of newborns. I ached to hold her, for I had trouble believing that she existed when she was not in my arms, and yet I blathered on and on. "What's more exciting, the book or the baby?" "Well . . . the book doesn't cry."

It's me, I was telling my guest. (And at the same time: Is that Charlotte I hear? Is that her cry?) It's me, I'm still the same.

Not Paul, who announced to all who asked, and many who did not, that he was transformed by Charlotte's birth. He was a totally changed person and understood life at last. He came to the hospital each night with a shopping bag filled with fruit, apologized for what I had gone through, and swore that if he had known how bad it would be, he would never have asked me to have a baby. While I ate flame grapes, tangerines, mangos, comice pears, Jaffa oranges, and raspberries, he held his tiny newborn. After I finished gorging myself, he pulled the curtain around the bed and changed her diaper. He loved to change her diaper. Every night he would lay her down on the bed, work her tiny arms through her undershirt, unfasten the diaper tapes, and hold her naked in his arms. He would look from her to me and murmur words like "joy" and "mystery" and weep.

"That's what happens when they let men into the labor room," I told a friend, who was alarmed by his weeping. "It messes up their hormones. Happy, sad — he doesn't know what he feels."

He knew exactly how he felt. Ecstatic day and night. Filled with postpartum joy. He strapped her across his chest, wore her everywhere, talked about her endlessly, showed her off to everyone. "Doesn't she have the cutest nose you've ever seen?" he asked my parents' neighbors, a couple who remembered me as the little pipsqueak who raced through the yards with their children. "And her mouth. Isn't it adorable?" They nodded and agreed with whatever he said. Yes, her nose was cute; her mouth was adorable, her hands were remarkable, her eyes perfection, her feet edible . . .

"And her asshole; doesn't she have the sweetest little asshole . . . ?"

Paul descended from his ecstatic flights, and I eventually changed. Charlotte's birth released in me a little voice meant for little people, whereas before I had no voice, and therefore nothing to say to babies. I tore diaper coupons from my dentist's magazines, read consumer guides on baby paraphernalia, collected tips on mothering, frequented toy stores and infants' departments. Charlotte nudged and pushed and kicked to make space for herself beside all the stuff in my life; as soon as she learned how to climb, she scaled the bars of her crib and joined me in my bed, as if she knew that when I was alone my dreams did not include her. My single friends were wrong. I did not exchange one love for another. I had not altered my focus, I had lost it. Now instead of one steady path I had many roads, each with many branches.

It was not just Paul and me and the baby makes three. It was Paul and me, and the high cost of child care, without which I could not work, and help! there isn't space for all of the equipment that the contemporary baby must have, and how can I carry a child and groceries up to the fifth floor? Being trailblazers did not stop us from having the same woes as millions of other new parents — loss of time to work and play and spend with our friends or each other. There was also the sudden realization that we had put a lot of effort into fulfilling our dreams while neglecting to think about money.

What's remarkable to me is not that we had the same problems as everyone else, but that for all the flux and commotion, we went from being a couple to being parents with hardly a blink, so that Paul could wonder, a month after our baby was born, what life had been like without her. All the past was ancient history, mornings in bed, weekends working together at the labs. We were parents now, and had been for as long as we could remember, and would be until we died.

Paul began ogling newborns when Charlotte turned two, and dropping hints about how wonderful babies were, how gorgeous pregnant women. We had a house now with extra bedrooms he wanted filled with little ones.

What I wanted was to have my second book finished before I considered getting pregnant again. My work had progressed slowly in the two years since her birth, and even thinking about another baby felt like a professional death wish. That didn't stop me from harboring a secret longing to have another child, a longing I knew made no sense.

For a year I protested. I withstood grandparents dropping anxious hints about how nice a sibling would be for my lonely child, and friends who asked discreet questions about my fertility. But when Charlotte turned three I began to feel that family life was so complicated that I would be old and widowed, my nest empty before there was a clear space in which to fit a new baby. And so I let the longing take over and became pregnant with number two.

*September*

Charlotte starts back to nursery school, and Rachel stays right where she's been for the last nine months. The placenta ages after term and gets hardening of the arteries, and because she is already two weeks late, my obstetrician decides to send me twice a week to the hospital to get tests that will show whether it is providing her with sufficient oxygen and nutrients. On the days that the tests are scheduled, I drag my swollen body out of bed at six A.M. in order to catch a train to New York, and then a crosstown bus to the hospital (and later, a cab to the obstetrician's office).

The serum estriol test is simple — a needle in the arm, a little of my blood from which the function of the placenta can be checked. Then it's upstairs to labor and delivery for the non-stress test, where I must lie with a fetal monitor strapped across my belly and a pen in my hand so that whenever I feel the baby move, I can draw an X on the tape that spews from the machine beside me. Rachel's heartbeat should increase when she moves, just as ours increases when we walk or climb stairs. If two accelerations are not seen in ten minutes, then more tests will have to be done to insure that the placenta is functioning adequately.

The labor and delivery area is so jammed it looks as if some freak meteorological event has caused every pregnant woman in New York to go into labor. No fetal monitors are available on my first visit, and I am told I'll have to wait. All this fuss, all the nurses in blue scrubs and shower caps, the bustling residents in green, all the women breathing huh huh huh if they took childbirth classes in New York, and hee hee hee if they came from New Jersey, while I sit in the sunroom with ecstatic in-laws and puzzled siblings and page through a week-old newspaper and wait.

A monitor is produced after a couple of hours, but there are no free labor rooms, so I am escorted to a bed in the recovery area. I change into a hospital gown, position the monitor on the apex of my bulging abdomen, and spend another hour waiting for the baby to move. Rachel never stirs. Legs peek out from beneath the partition beside mine, scrubs that don't quite cover a man's blue jeans, shower caps on his sneakers, and his soft, tentative voice as he greets his newborn for the first time. "Hello, baby. Hi. *Hi.*"

I am sorry that I asked her to wait.

Early on the morning of my fourth visit — up at six, train, bus, serum estriol, non-stress test — I realize that my labor has begun. I go through all the tests, and at the end of the day take a cab uptown to tell the exciting news to my obstetrician. He gives me a wan, sympathetic smile and says, "I hope not. Because if you are, you'll have a lot of work to do."

Could I be wrong? Could these very regular, very intense contractions be false labor? I meet a friend for lunch, take the train home, walk to my house from the station, feed my family, gather my bags and Charlotte's, pack snacks for Paul, and then drive to my parents' house, where Charlotte will stay.

I send Paul into my old room for a nap and watch TV with my mother until the contractions become so regular that I know I cannot sit around any longer. By then it's *really* time to go.

It is midnight and the roads are empty. Paul speeds into New York, getting us midtown in record time. The hospital, all lit up from within, is before us, thank God, then disappears from view.

"Just one more time around," Paul tells me.

He cannot find a parking place, and it is a matter of principle with him not to pull into a lot. I am arched in my seat with a pain of major proportions, and he is saying, "There's probably space on Thirtieth Street."

As we whiz past the hospital, I remember the charts he had made of my contractions four years ago — time, duration, subjective description ("Oct. 22nd, 1:07 P.M., 72 secs. While eating orange . . .") — and how after Charlotte's birth he had wept and said, "If only I knew how bad it would be." Now he says, "Second Avenue's usually good." Another contraction seizes me, and I freeze, half standing. "Maybe I should try Twenty-eighth."

We finally find a spot and go upstairs. Paul holds my hand, breathes with me, encourages me, praises my performance, sponges my face, warns me in sportscaster's style of the onset of a contraction. "And . . . it's a big one, a double-peaker . . . here it comes . . . one and . . . hee . . . hee . . . hee . . ."

After seven hours of exhaling, effleuraging, complaining, pushing, and a good deal of what is known in childbirth classes as "losing control," the new baby is born. She is big and plump with a head of dark, oily hair that is lighter at the ends. My love rushes in — I am flooded with love, overwhelmed by it. Also I am hungry.

Paul arranges for me to get some scrambled eggs and then phones my parents. "Well, we were up all night, but she's fine; she's lying in the recovery room eating breakfast for two . . . What do you mean *she* must be tired. *She's* in bed, *I* still have to drive home."

I share a room with a first-time mother, whose windowsill is jammed with roses, wildflowers, fragrant bouquets, rooted plants, arrangements festooned with cloth birds and butterflies, one topped with a naked cherub. Twice a day, during visiting hours, more flowers arrive, and scores of guests — her husband and family, her coworkers and neighbors. At night forty relatives arrive with champagne and Belgian chocolates. The phone rings constantly, and to each caller she relays the story of her agony and joy. During the rare moments when she is alone, she cries because she is lonely, because the baby will not stay attached to her breast, because *he* cries, because she is afraid to go home.

I lie in bed suffused with happy hormones. What sweet, simple pleasure I find in mothering this time. How nice it is just to hold her. I fall asleep and wake up wondering if she really exists, and finding her in the isolette at my side, fall back to sleep again. The happy hormones

are doing their trick, lulling me into complaisance. I feel like earth-
mother lying here, breasts swelling with milk. Born to nurture.

At last the phone rings for me. My parents want to know if Paul has
gotten any rest yet. Later in the afternoon, an old friend strides into the
room, elegantly dressed in a nubby oatmeal-colored sweater and a long,
sleek tan skirt.

She hands me two birds of paradise and looks for a vase. There are
none on the entire floor because my neighbor has them all. In desperation my visitor fills the dented wastepaper basket with water and sets
the birds of paradise in front of the blinds so that their beaks turn in
opposite directions. We walk to the nursery and look at the babies behind the glass, all of them swaddled tightly, only their misshapen heads
sticking out of the striped blankets, one asleep, one yawning, one crying.
They look like creatures from a science fiction movie; carnivorous pods
with strange humanoid faces. Rachel's hair has been upcombed at the
sides into a Mohawk. We nominate baby boy Ruben for best personality, baby boy Rodriguez for nicest eyes. Baby girl Glynn wins hands
down for most contemporary looks.

The rats have fur now, the beginnings of a white coat that resembles
a layer of talc. Their ears stand apart from their heads, their noses are
snubbed so that they resemble tiny flat-nosed sea mammals. Sometimes
they lie in a wriggling pile, a mass of undulating flesh, hearts beating
rapidly beneath translucent skin. More often when I come upon the tank
they are beneath their mother, and all I can see of them is a pair of hind
legs jutting out and kicking at the wood chips, someone else's front legs
pawing the air, a third baby's tail. It is a little like musical chairs under
there, with eleven babies and only ten teats, and at times one of them
gets cast out completely. Rat is tranquil and tolerates the scrabbling and
bickering that goes on beneath her distended body. Her offspring nibble
and she rests, only her nose twitching.

I love my own new baby; I feel perfectly content going about the
repetitive chores involved in caring for her. With Charlotte, the anxiety
of inexperience complicated my feelings; she seemed so mysterious and
complex and vulnerable. This time I know what to do. If she cries, I
can soothe her, and if I cannot, I understand that this too is part of
having an infant around the house. Rachel makes it easy for me. She is
remarkably content, nurses without fuss, sleeps soundly and for so long

that I often go into her room to wake her up. At night she wakes twice, and before long only once, and after her feeding falls right back to sleep.

"Why do you love her?" asks a single friend who comes to see me.

A reasonable question of a woman with no particular liking for children. Why, indeed? I grope for answers and find none that encompass all that I feel. Why do I love her? Because she's soft and smells good. Because she's mine. Because it's in my genes that I should love her: It is somehow encoded that when she smacks her lips, or when I hear the rustle of her plastic diaper, my breasts tingle, and the milk leaks in readiness for her.

The others do not feel as content. Rachel's presence confuses Charlotte. She is very agitated and wants only to be with her baby sister. She wants to hold her, to hug her so tightly that no one else can get near. She talks about her in a feverish voice. I had thought that I could reassure her by giving her extra love, but she is willful and argumentative and rejects my attention. It is not me that she wants. She will not take a walk with me, something she loved to do before the birth, because it means leaving Paul with Rachel. Nor will she let me put the sleeping baby in the crib so the two of us can play together. Instead she presses against Rachel's body, waking her, so that my attention goes to the crying baby. The thought of us with Rachel when she is not around is so upsetting that she begins to wake in the middle of the night when Rachel does. More than once, as I am returning Rachel to her crib after a feeding, I find Charlotte in the doorway, silent tears running down her cheeks.

I take pictures of the two of them that first week, Charlotte on the top step, Rachel in her arms, and bring them downtown to be processed. How touching they are: Charlotte, who has always seemed so small to me, suddenly grown up compared to the baby, her body tight and well muscled. The way she holds Rachel tells everything: arms wrapped tightly around her sister, and in her eyes love, confusion, envy so intense that it colors everything.

Paul puzzles me with his coolness toward Rachel. I cannot help remembering him holding Charlotte naked against his chest, a fearless Papa, sighing: "This is what it's all about." I laughed at his drama, amused that his reaction was so utterly typical of the age — a father who's into fatherhood — and yet I loved him for it, and loved the way he invested something as humdrum as diapering a baby with great meaning. The euphoria was muted by sleepless nights and the constant responsibility for this bundle of needs, and by the passage of time itself. I had looked forward to Rachel's birth as a time when he would again clutch my arms and shake the torpor from me, and say, "This is it. This is what it's all about."

If Rachel has transformed him, it is into a wearier man and nothing more. He rarely holds her or plays with her, never tosses her in the air or kisses her bare rear end or sleeps with her across his chest. I ask him about this and he says: "She's more delicate than Charlotte." He says: "I feel disloyal to Charlotte." He says: "She isn't interested in being held." He says: "When am I home?" It is true that he is gone for long hours, that the cells he grows in order to study their metabolism need the constant care and nurturing that infants do, that even the weekends are not his own. At the same time, I know that none of these things fully explains why this baby has failed to touch him.

### October

Paul comes home early from the labs one Saturday, and we drive down to the Jersey shore. It is cool and uncrowded this time of year. Rachel sleeps fully covered on the blanket beside Paul, who reads and underlines text in a heavy book. Charlotte and I sit at the edge of the water and let the silt and surf wash over our legs. The beach is all ours, but out toward the horizon are a dozen Windsurfers, their bright sails turning in the wind. Charlotte holds my hand and sings a song so softly I cannot hear the words. It is the first time since Rachel's birth that I have seen her calm and playful, and it makes me aware how a baby's arrival tears apart the neat pieces of a family's life and demands that they be reordered.

On the way back, we stop at a farm stand for corn that has just been picked and the last of the beefsteak tomatoes; and a few yards up the road buy flounder from a boy who looks to be about thirteen. Charlotte sings "Strawberry Fields" in the car, and Paul joins in. I sit with my head against the seat back listening to their funny off-key rendition. I feel as if the tenseness of this past month has been caused by the reordering, and that we are at last on our way to being comfortable again.

When we get home, Paul brushes the sand off the children and takes them into the solarium while I start dinner. Although I am not often an enthusiastic cook, today it feels like a privilege to be left alone in the kitchen, tearing husks from the corn, washing the succulent misshapen tomatoes, slicing sweet onions and garlic and lemon. For a few minutes they are so completely out of my thoughts that when I recall them again it seems as if hours have passed. I peek into the room and find Charlotte lying on the floor making zigzags with colored pens. Paul holds Rachel at arm's length — a peculiar sight, but at least he is holding her.

When I return to tell them that dinner is ready, Paul has his arm outstretched above his head, with Rachel flying belly down on his palm.

"Aren't babies supposed to track?" he asks me.

"At one month? Give her a break."

Rachel hovers above Paul until he moves her slowly to his left side. The ride stops, and she floats above him, loose-lipped.

"What are you *doing?*" I ask.

"Getting her to look at me."

Rachel does not have Charlotte's wide, round eyes. She is an Eskimo baby, narrow eyes with epicanthic folds, in a broad flat face, straight black hair that falls into points across her forehead.

"She *is* looking at you," I say.

"Now maybe. But watch."

This time he flies her until she is positioned to his right. Her eyes are not on him. She appears to be looking out the window instead. He calls her name and swivels her body so that she faces him. She looks the other way.

"Maybe she's bored," I say, reaching upward to rescue her.

He holds her more often after that, always at arm's length, always to his left side so that she looks at him out of the corner of her eye. One day he says, "She reminds me of Aunt Margie," referring to an aunt in Massachusetts, a tiny, timid old woman who rarely left her street because *they* were encroaching upon what had been familiar to her, dark-eyed, dark-skinned others from God knew where, and who never left her chair the one time we met, and sat, drawn into herself, watching me with a wary, sidelong glance.

He holds Rachel to the left and plays ventriloquist, and she is the dummy that says: "I never sore such filth in all my days."

And: "He was just like the rest of them Heinies, stubborn as hell."

And: "Well now, Billy, he always had a soft spot for the old Jew-lady."

He begins to call Rachel Suspicious Eyes, S.E. for short, and when I bring her to him, he holds her on his palm and floats her to his left, satisfied that at last she is looking at him.

At six weeks, Rachel is serene and predictable, and if she is still a sleepy one, she has at last begun to smile when we call to her and tickle her cheek. Her smiles are not big body wigglers; they are small and rather shy. We are such a boisterous crew that it is hard to imagine producing such a quiet baby — not that I mind at all. Rachel is so easy we take her to the movies and to parties and restaurants, where Paul wears her strapped across his chest, covering her head with a napkin so that crumbs will not litter her scalp. Strangers stop to tell us what a delightful baby she is, and, showing absolutely no modesty, we agree. Several friends have commented on the unusual connection I have made with Rachel, and indeed it seems to me that her serenity has made me serene, and that perhaps my confidence contributes to her easy nature. I feel very fortunate not to have a baby that cries for hours, a fussy child whose demands rock the household, shattering the peace.

Because she still sleeps for most of the day, it is easy for me to work. I have an office in the attic, a small finished room with a view of nesting birds in a tall hemlock. All the odds and ends from my former life are up here, posters and photographs from times that have passed, the little "thingies" that Charlotte loves, tucked away in various boxes — tickets from rock concerts, leather and bone hair ornaments, the pieces from a puzzle ring that I can no longer put back together, a Beatles button, a folded ticket from Santa Barbara, where I was fined for hitchhiking, a kilt pin, a flip book. Every morning I carry Rachel upstairs and set her in an infant seat beside my typewriter. She is my second born, and I know from experience that any day it will all be over, that she will rouse from her sleepy infant state and demand my love and attention.

The weather gets cold, and the last of the leaves fall from the trees. I can zip up the jeans I wore before I was pregnant, and spend quiet time with Charlotte. Only Rachel does not change — not yet.

On a cold Sunday, Paul goes to Boston for a neuroscience meeting. He does not like to travel alone and calls home every night to speak to Charlotte and me. The meeting is huge and exhausting for him, thousands of presentations, more talks than he can possibly attend, an explosion of information. Also there's the enjoyment of meeting friends from graduate school and researchers from other institutions, of being im-

mersed, with no distractions, in the work that he has chosen. It is a
new career for him, and though his day-to-day job is often tedious and
unrewarding, he still feels a young man's delight in science.

Late one night he phones to tell me about a woman who got a grant
to study vision in infants. He asked her at what age babies began to
track moving objects with their eyes, and in response, she told him
about an experiment, in which a newborn was propped on its mother's
lap while across the room objects were flashed on a screen. The woman
told Paul that if she stood behind the screen, she could tell the position
of the objects on the screen by observing the infant's eyes.

"Doesn't Rachel do that?" I ask.

"I don't know, we haven't tested her."

"Did you look for this woman? I don't understand, did you tell her
you had a six-week-old daughter? What did she say?"

"She had a poster up and I stopped by to talk to her because I thought
her work was interesting. That's all. Now go back to sleep and stop
worrying, will you?"

It is generally my policy to worry more when someone tells me not
to worry at all. I hang up the phone, take Rachel from her crib, lay her
on the bed beside me, and watch her gradually waken. Her eyes open.
She thrusts her tongue and makes her "feed me" face. I call to her and
touch her soft cheek, and when she smiles at me, I think, ah, middle-
class parents. What do we want from her, sonnets? Mathematical theory? She's only six weeks old!

I forget about the researcher until Paul comes home and has me prop
Rachel in my lap, while he sits a few feet away and moves a toy across
her field of vision. There is so much fat around her eyes that it's hard to
tell whether she is tracking. Sometimes it does not seem as if she is
following the moving toy, and that her eyes move at random, and sometimes she clearly seems to track whatever he holds.

He stops his experiment and say, "I guess she's all right." Then he
kneels in front of Rachel, and seeing how small she is, and how pa-
tiently she sits, he laughs and says with great certainty, "She's
*fine.*"

*November*

Paul and I planned to spend Thanksgiving with his parents in Florida. It seemed like a fine idea — five days in the sun, in time for my

father-in-law's eightieth birthday — and yet while we are packing to go I am seized with a great foreboding, and I cannot figure out why.

My in-laws meet us at the airport, brown people in pastel clothes, two of several who crowd the gate. I send Charlotte forward to meet her grandparents, and she edges between the white-haired crew to find them. It is forty degrees outside and my mother-in-law's pink cardigan is buttoned to the neck. My father-in-law wears the broad-brimmed straw hat he has had since moving to Florida.

Nana sees us and not Charlotte, and walks with a broad purposeful stride to Paul, who holds Rachel in the carrier. For a moment I am afraid that Charlotte will go unnoticed, but my father-in-law swoops low to hug her. Paul's mother is not content to unzip the carrier and look at Rachel's face. She wants the baby in her arms, the soft, sweet child of her son.

I remember bringing Charlotte here at just this age. My mother-in-law had rocked her new granddaughter for hours and cooed to her softly and said, "Oh! What a story!" when she bubbled or burped. Charlotte had cried a lot, and nursed so frequently that I came to the table with a pillow on my lap so that she and I could feed at the same time. I remember my mother-in-law saying, "You old cow," whenever I unhooked my bra, and how, when I woke for the six A.M. feeding, she was up, too, and when I changed Rachel on the small counter that jutted from the wall — their breakfast nook — my mother-in-law was there with a kitchy-coo for the baby. I had never seen anyone love so intensely, and I suppose it made me feel deficient, and in my inexperience, I bristled. But if Charlotte had been too new to share, this one is a gift for the grandparents.

When we're on the road Paul asks after various relatives, and his father, who is rather hard of hearing, tells us about the cement trucks that barrel down these roads and about accidents on rainy nights, sometimes talking over the existing conversation, and sometimes not. Their house is in one of the hundreds of retirement communities built in this dry, flat part of the state, where once there had been orange groves and cattle ranches. On the way we pass entrances to several of these communities — Breezy Knoll, Lake Pleasure, Monticello, Palm Hill — each a cul-de-sac off the endless Florida highway.

We pull through the gate and drive slowly to their house, passing a woman on a thick-wheeled tricycle, and a couple who walk briskly along the side of the road. The plantings have prospered: the sago palms have quadrupled in size, and the poinsettias are turning red, but these metal houses were not built to be permanent, and I can see where they have aged. Hailstones have dented a carport roof; there are rust stains on the siding beneath a neighbor's bay window. Residents call their houses modular homes because the pieces that are carried on flatbed trucks are stapled together in varying ways to give the illusion that they have been custom-built for each retiree. The state of Florida will not be fooled and requires that license plates be nailed onto each facade.

When we arrive my mother-in-law says: "What a good baby, sleeping through all this commotion."

"She'd sleep all day if we let her," I say. It is the first time I've thought or spoken these words and the sound of them makes me so uncomfortable that when my mother-in-law says, "Of course she would," I am instantly relieved. "She's a baby, and what babies do is sleep, God bless them."

And that she does, all day and most of the night. While Paul and I sit on the screened-in porch and read, and Charlotte plays at our feet wrapping Nana's beads and necklaces and rhinestone brooches around her forehead, neck, and arms, my mother-in-law paces throughout the house, wearing Rachel like a shawl. She murmurs to her and says, "Oh, what a story!" when Rachel smacks her lips, rocks her in a chair passed down from her mother, and sings her odd, atonal tunes. I have seen sepia-toned pictures of Nana when she was nineteen and a new mother herself. She was a stunning young woman, tall and slender, with the wide blue eyes, straight nose, and muscular legs that Paul and Charlotte have inherited. In these photographs she holds Paul across her shoulder and glares fiercely at the photographer, as if to say that ten feet is too damn close when this precious child is in her arms.

My father-in-law feels bad that we are just sitting around, and reminds us about the mermaid show nearby, and the upcoming citrus festival, and the restaurant they took us to the year after we were married that serves drinks in scooped-out pineapples and features a small jungle with several monkeys and a hippo. I remember well the sight of people feeding the hippo marshmallows. The great dumb beast had a tongue like a queen-sized mattress, and two teeth as flat as tree stumps. People threw marshmallows onto the mattress, and the beast clamped down its jaws, sank beneath the lily pads, and surfaced later with the same marshmallows on his tongue. You could go inside for lunch and a drink, use the rest room, have your picture snapped and embedded in plastic on a key chain, and when you dropped in on the hippo for a quick farewell, those same marshmallows would still be there.

"We're happy, Pop," Paul says. "Back home we've been going every minute of the day. I can't tell you how great it is just to lollygag around."

"You do whatever you want," he says, and he is the kind of man who means it.

"That's what we want."

And so we sit on the porch for hours, getting up once in a while for a glass of iced tea or to use the toilet, and Rachel is always asleep. Paul's mother carries in special little snacks for us, macadamia nuts, or thin slices of her rich homemade fruitcake, and when she does, Rachel is draped across her shoulder. Sometimes Pop joins us, and he and Paul try to place in time old cars and houses they owned and people they have not seen for decades, and they go at it until Paul's mother comes in with Rachel in her arms, and chides them for their obsession with the past by saying, "Don't look back, look ahead."

The fun of lying around, every muscle at rest, begins to diminish. Has Rachel been lulled into sleeping all day? Are my mother-in-law's arms a strong narcotic? Has she always been like this? The next time I see her doze against Nana's shoulder, I take her away and hold her at arm's length the way Paul does. I swing her around until my arms get tired, then set her on the carpet and tickle her feet. She kicks and moves her arms as if she likes it. Soon after I stop she begins to fade.

"It's been too much excitement for her," my mother-in-law says. "A big plane trip, a brand-new bed, an old Nana who can't keep her hands to herself. Of course she's tired."

"Charlotte didn't sleep like this when she was here."

"Charlotte was a live wire. You can't compare the two."

She sleeps and sleeps. I wake her so that she can nurse, and when she's done, I give her to Paul, and he flies her stomach down in his palm. She glides above his head, perplexed though not alarmed. He stops her when she's to his left and says, as Aunt Margie, "Kids today are just no good. Smoking marijuana cigarettes. Crashing up expensive cars. We didn't have no cars a'tall, Paul, it was just as well. A girl went out on a date, and the date was over, he brought her straight home, and that was that. Nowadays you hear about these boys, they go into the service, they come back drug attics."

My mother-in-law, not far in spirit from that fierce nineteen-year-old, sees him from the doorway and says, "What are you doing, you crazy old thing?"

"Flying her," I say.

"Torturing her — I swear, you two don't deserve to have this baby. Look, Paul, she's so tired her eyes are rolling. Don't be so mean, let her have her nap."

I stand behind Paul and see that she's right, that Rachel's eyes are rolling like a drunkard's. "All right," I say, reaching up. "We'll let her rest."

We go out the next day, armed with light deflectors and a sun hat for Rachel. The heat does not bother her, nor does the sun or our conversation. She sleeps in the car, and throughout the surprise party we hold for Paul's father, and in the carrier as we walk on the beach afterwards. She is asleep when Charlotte, ambling in the flesh ahead of us, is accused by an officer of the law of indecent exposure and warned of arrest if she tries it again, and during the long visit with Paul's nephew. Everywhere we go we hear the same thing. What a good baby. An angel. A doll. The day is so pleasant, her sleeping so convenient, I forget what worried me the day before. The next day when I wake and she doesn't, I remember.

Paul and I borrow my in-laws' bikes and pedal through the development. Everywhere we go, the houses are elaborately landscaped; vines creep up the sides of carports, squat palms decorate lawns. License plates from the home state are screwed onto mailbox posts. In front of four houses in a row are wooden ducks with wings that rotate in the wind; daisies with petals that swirl pop up from the dry lawns on three houses in a row. Paul stops in the real estate office and gets a key for one of the model homes. Ocean Breeze is open today. We park our bikes in the Florida room and step inside. It is cold and smells like a new car. Paul opens closets with particle-board doors and taps fiberglass siding and studies a very authentic piece of plastic cheese. "Jarlsberg," he says, setting it next to a rubber scallion.

The bedroom has white shag carpeting and a huge chintz-covered bed. The lamps have bases that look like giant gumballs. Paul lies down and says, "Not bad," and holds out his hands to me.

We nestle against each other, old lovers in the retirement home. Such familiar skin; my limbs and his twining as neatly as puzzle pieces. I feel as if we have been married for fifty years, part of each other's lives far longer than we have lived alone — old age is so much longer than childhood. I know his body as well as my own, the mole on his arm that made him self-conscious as a child, the blue spot where he was jabbed with a pencil, the spider veins behind his knees. I touch his old shoulders and back, rest a hand between his ancient thighs, feel his old mouth against mine. Stay with me, I think. I can't remember what it's like to live alone.

We had planned to take a late plane in order to have the day together, but the knowledge that we are leaving makes it impossible for us to do anything except ready ourselves. Hours before departure time our suitcases are lined up, and my mother-in-law is asking if I have everything.

I get down on my knees, lift couch flaps, and peep under chairs while Rachel lies in her grandmother's arms. Charlotte joins me in this game and together we come up with a doll's shoe, a broken hairband, a sock that may be Paul's, a book called *Mr. Nosy*. The whole time I look, I can feel the dread inside me, hard and rough-edged. I should have talked more and been livelier and seen the hippo. I should have shown my love, for who knew whether we would meet again next year.

Our good-byes are quick. I want to say something, but my feelings are inchoate and reside in my gut, not my mind, and when I turn back before boarding the plane to wave a final time, my in-laws are hand in hand in the distance and do not see me.

We arrive home late that night, pull the clothes off our sleeping children, and slip their rubbery limbs into pajamas. Paul runs the water for a shower, and I go upstairs to my office.

On a shelf above my desk is a magazine about child development that was given to me at the hospital. In between the ads for baby food and diapers and pictures of big-eyed babies are developmental charts. I find the one for a baby of two months and scan the columns quickly. Stares indefinitely at surroundings. . . . Fixates on one of two objects shown. . . . Follows moving person with eyes. . . .

The floorboards creak beneath me. Paul calls for me softly. There is one more thing I must check before I go down, a journal that I kept about Charlotte, a listing of conventional things, first smile, first tooth, first word. I hear his heavy footsteps as he works his way up the stairs and find "Charlotte at eleven weeks, two days . . ."

He stops in the doorway and says, "What's up?"

I read: " 'She lies beside me now, kicking and wiggling, her arms flailing, never still for a second. When she wants up, she calls out to me, arms open wide . . .' "

Paul comes close to turn the page.

" 'When I nurse her she looks up at me with those big blue eyes, and gives me a gummy, body-wiggling grin, and I love her so.' "

"There's something wrong with Rachel," I say.

The time for knowing and not knowing is over for both of us.

"Yes," he says.

# ❦ 2 ❧

# The Diagnosis

IT WAS A TUESDAY EVENING when we returned from Florida and read those entries in my journal, and now, on a Thursday morning we sit in the waiting room of a neuro-ophthalmologist who had told me three times in the course of a short phone conversation that his fee was very high (which indeed it was). Thirty-six hours have passed between the time when Paul and I were ready to know and the actual appointment.

Thirty-six hours is nothing in the space of a lifetime. But during these thirty-six hours I had the care of an infant whose eyes jittered in their sockets. Suddenly it was so apparent I could not believe that I had allowed myself to be fooled for so long. I had found in the *Merck Manual* a name for this symptom — for that was what it was — and a list of possible causes, nearly all of them dire. *Nystagmus* — "Rhythmic oscillation of the eyes. . . ." My spirits rose and fell like the waves in a rough sea. I was woozy with fear, then confident that she would be all right, then woozy again. In those hours, I nurtured some awful scenarios, most based on a listing of possible causes ("In general, nystagmus indicates . . . brainstem dysfunction. . . ."), but at the end of each one, I would picture the doctor telling me that although things had looked bad, everything would turn out well after all. He would pat me on the shoulder, and say: "All that worrying you did was for nothing," something I have often been told. It was a sensible thing for this creation of mine to say, however, because although I am an incurable worrier, I am also an incurable optimist, and he would acknowledge both of these aspects with respect.

Paul and I took Charlotte to school on Thursday morning, and then battled the rush-hour traffic into New York. The hospital was located in a part of the city where I had seldom been, and I was surprised, when we arrived in the neighborhood, at how vast the complex of large, plain buildings was: truly a city within a city, yet separate from it, the way Vatican City is separate from but contained within Rome. Paul and I parked in a hospital garage, then followed arrows to the appropriate building. We walked beneath scaffolding, and out into bright sunlight. Gargoyles on the building across the street looked down on us, their mouths in O's. The sidewalks were busy with men and women who wore photo IDs clipped onto their jackets: Everyone had two faces.

The doctor's waiting room is a dim corridor furnished with two brown plastic couches, an end table, and a pile of Yale alumni magazines that are soft at the edges from frequent perusal. A secretary with ornate half-glasses listens to Muzak on her transistor radio and types steadily. It is not like sitting in a family practitioner's waiting room, where the people around have sniffles or warts that need to be burned. Something is seriously wrong with the people who are here. I find myself speculating continually during the two hours that we wait. What is the matter with the woman in dark glasses, who keeps her fur coat wrapped around her shoulders in this stifling room? And the man, also in dark glasses, who whispers to her in German every now and then — is he a patient, too? Sitting across from us is a young couple dressed as if it were still the sixties, he in a fringed jacket, and she with a beaded headband tied across her forehead. They quiz each other for a test, breaking only for slow kisses. What could be wrong, and who is it?

We are called in at last. Dr. Hines is a tall, bony man with sleek black hair that fits like a cap and hollowed-out cheeks. He wears a white shirt, and a burgundy tie printed repeatedly with the head of a setter. He paces in his cluttered office, hands in the pockets of his loose trousers, and we pace, too. Rachel sleeps in the carrier on Paul's chest, the only one at peace.

"So she's two months old, and you noticed something was wrong when —"

"Last week," I say, "but Paul was concerned before that. She doesn't look at us or show any interest in toys. And she sleeps nearly all day long."

"We called her Suspicious Eyes because she never fixed her eyes on anything," says Paul.

The two of us laugh, eye each other guiltily, then go silent.

The blinds are dusty. Microscopes line the window shelf. Along the width of the room are bookshelves that sag from the weight of heavy brown texts. The doctor's desk is broad and made of dark wood. A leather cup holds pens; papers fill a matching tray. In a leather frame is a photo of a beautiful girl in a woolen cap, posed next to a pair of skis.

"I thought that all babies were supposed to do for the first couple of months was nurse and sleep. I mean, I have a four-year-old, but when I tried to look back, I couldn't recall her actually *doing* anything. You forget," I say, turning to the photo of the girl, with her rosy cheeks and blue ski cap. "It goes so fast, it really does, and she was so easy to be with, she fed well and slept well and was rarely fussy. But then I found a developmental chart in a magazine and a journal I had kept when my older daughter was a baby, and —"

"Give her to me."

Paul unzips the outer and inner pouches of the carrier and works Rachel out. She is asleep and remains in a fetal position when he passes her to the doctor — her knees raised, arms curled close, fists beside her face. Dr. Hines grasps her beneath the arms, and she thrusts out her lower lip as if to cry. He is a large man, and his hands encircle her body. He waits for her to rouse, and then holds her at arm's length as if to do an Aunt Margie, and spins her around the room. He leans back on his heels, and they go around and around. He is a friendly father and plays this game for fun. Do well, I think, as if she has the power to alter her fate. Do well.

Now he has a second game. He asks Paul to balance her on his knee while he flashes a red strip of fabric that has images on squares between patches of red. I strain to figure out what they are, and see . . . Mickey Mouse. Is this possible? He flashes the strip horizontally and then vertically, moving it all the while. He is a magician, and the cloth will be transformed into a dove. Dr. Hines will applaud, the dove will coo, we will say thank you and go home. "All that worrying was for nothing . . ."

Dr. Hines continues. His beautiful daughter smiles. Paul coughs.

"I need someone to hold her while I put drops in. She won't like it, but I promise it won't hurt her. Do *you* want to do it?" he asks me. It is the first time he has acknowledged my presence.

"I better," says Paul.

Her scream plunges me into ice. It goes on and on until her voice grows hoarse and wavery. The walls sway, the microscopes slide. "We're not hurting her," Dr. Hines murmurs. "We're not hurting her, she's just frightened."

The screaming goes on and on until everything is chattering inside me, teeth, heart, knees. I hold on to my arms to steady myself and feel my nails break into my flesh. I don't want to be here. I don't want to stand here, utterly powerless to help while she screams.

Dr. Hines tries to examine her eyes with an ophthalmoscope after the drops are in. His hands are big, and her eyes are small. She twists on the table and squeezes her eyes shut. He cannot seem to get the instrument in position. Over her screams he swears he is not hurting her.

Suddenly she quiets. I close my eyes and hear the whirr of the electric typewriter in the waiting room. I imagine Rachel years from now, a little girl with almond-shaped eyes, her hair still black and straight. She is bundled in a red snowsuit, and hurries past me so she can play outside. "Your hat!" I say, though it is already on her head. "Your hat!" in an angry voice, because I want to hold her in my arms for a moment, and there is no other way. I imagine her squirm while I tuck her hair beneath the brim, looking every way except at me. "Once we were afraid," I tell her. "You were very little, and we thought you couldn't see."

"Look," Dr. Hines is saying. "There's pupillary response. See how she responds to light?"

"Then that means the damage is farther back —" Paul says.

Farther back means in the brain. The bookcases sag. The desk is crowded with papers, the ceiling yellowed with age. When I think what I have wished in other anxious moments — that a boy would like me, that I might ace a test, catch a bus, get a seat in a crowded movie theater. If only I could give all that back and have my child be whole.

Dr. Hines leaves Rachel with Paul and returns a moment later with a frail young woman in a lab coat, a Dr. Somebody, barely five feet tall, with tiny hands. Rachel has stopped screaming and is gasping convulsively. While Paul holds her, the woman examines her eyes with little difficulty. She is delighted by what she sees, and though she tries to put on a somber face before us, she reminds me of a mycologist who has just dug up a rare mushroom.

"You can pick her up now," Dr. Hines says.

Paul gives her to me. Her eyes are red and puffed shut and she cannot catch her breath. I stroke her head until the gasping lessens.

I am still petting her, fully involved in soothing her, when I realize that the doctor is speaking to Paul.

"— it's called optic nerve hypoplasia. Her optic nerve has failed to develop completely."

"So she's blind," Paul says.

Blind.

"Development continues until the child is about nine months old, so it's hard to predict whether she'll have any vision, and if she does how much. She may have light and shadow, she may *not,* though the pupillary response suggests that we can hope for that much."

"Will she be able to read?" I ask.

"I didn't say *usable* vision — I said vision — light and shadow. I wouldn't dismiss that if I were you. Having light perception makes mobility far easier."

"Is it degenerative?" Paul asks.

Dr. Hines seems weary of explaining the same simple thing. He shuts his eyes and says with ill-concealed irritation, "It's a static condition that neither improves nor deteriorates —"

Nothing can be done. There are no drugs, no surgeries, no therapies, no cures at all.

"But it appears alone?" I ask. "There aren't any other —"

I am still searching for the proper word when he shakes his head and asks: "Is there anyone with visual problems in your family?"

"She's nearsighted and I'm farsighted. Other than that kind of problem, no," says Paul.

"We had an amnio —"

"It's not a genetic disorder, it's a congenital defect. Something happened during development."

"What?" I ask.

He glances at me, then turns to Paul again. "Certain studies suggest an association of maternal ingestion of quinine or anticonvulsants with optic nerve hypoplasia. Did she take any drugs when she was pregnant?"

*She.* "Nothing," I say. "Not even an aspirin."

"Any illness during pregnancy?"

"No."

"She had a cold at New Year's," says Paul, turning toward me. "You went out cross-country skiing and didn't change out of your thermals, remember?"

Dr. Hines runs a finger across the bindings of several brown books. I feel as if Paul has slapped me.

"Colds are not caused by wet underwear," I say.

Hines opens a volume on his desk. "Perhaps it was just an accident in development — these things happen." He taps the open book with a bony forefinger. Across the left page are two photographs. In one is a healthy optic nerve, pale, veined, pinkish. In the other a dark halo surrounds the brightness. He gives us figures that relate to Rachel, one-third healthy tissue in one eye, one-half in the other.

Rachel breathes lightly in my arms. Her vulnerability frightens me, and I hold her so tightly that my arms tremble. I want to ask Dr. Hines what he is talking about, but I cannot formulate the words, and he is clearly in a rush, his words running headlong into each other as if he cannot possibly finish with us soon enough. He edges us toward the door as he speaks. Perhaps it is unintentional, but it has the effect of making me feel as if my next question better be a good one, because it will surely be my last.

He tells Paul that he is going to refer us to a neurologist, who will examine Rachel and arrange for a CT scan that will rule out, one hopes, the slim possibility that a brain tumor caused her problem. At the same time she will have an evoked response test that will say whether or not we can hope for any vision.

"What can we do?" I ask, my last and most important question.

"Where did you say you lived? New Jersey? You should get in touch with a social worker from the Commission for the Blind."

He walks us to the door. "I'm sorry," he says.

Paul laughs. "Oh well, we won't shoot the messenger."

They shake hands. Paul slides Rachel into the baby carrier and leaves. Dr. Hines edges past me and takes a cassette player from a desk drawer.

"Good luck," he says to me.

I am still in his office when he begins to speak into a small microphone. "Rachel Glynn, two-month-old girl, no evidence of visual responsivity other than closing her eyes regularly to bright light . . ."

The woman in the fur coat gets up when I walk into the waiting room. The boy's eyes are red, and as I pass I see that he's been crying.

His girlfriend has her arms around him and is whispering in his ear, trying to comfort him.

He's going blind, I think as I leave. He's so young, and he's going blind.

I close the waiting-room door and find myself in a vast common lobby shared by the other physicians at the hospital. Except for a guard at the door, I am the only one. I cannot find Paul. I walk past several doors with names upon them, and find the rest rooms and a water fountain. The doctor's rolltop desk appears before me, the photo of the rosy-cheeked girl with skis at her sides, a diagnosis that was firm and clear. My daughter is blind. Other events before this one have altered my path — death, marriage, the birth of a first child — but never before have I felt with such sureness that I would from this moment be a changed person, separated forever from my past.

Paul's laughter echoes loudly throughout the empty space and leads me to him. He is standing at a bank of phones, the receiver against his ear. His face is pink from whatever joke he has heard; he coughs and laughs, and Rachel heaves against his chest, never waking. "I'd tell you if it was a problem, but it isn't. I practically pass your front door on the way home."

He hangs up and turns to me.

"That was Ron. I promised to get him some reprints."

His eyes are clear. Is it possible he did not hear what Dr. Hines just said?

"Why did you leave me?"

"Leave you? I'm right here."

He picks up his attaché case and starts to walk. "I can't believe the acoustics in this place. It's the reverb room, the reverb room, the reverb room."

I don't know which way to move or what to do, and when Paul begins to walk, I follow along behind him, grateful that he is leading the way. He hesitates at the door and turns to face me.

"What should we do?" I ask.

"Go home? I don't know. Let's not say anything to Charlotte, though. There's no sense in it, not right away at least."

"But she'll know. She'll take one look at us and see right away that something has happened."

"Don't say anything," he says, adamant this time. "Not until after the tests."

"What difference do the tests make?"

"We don't have any hard data yet," he says. "After the tests we'll have something to say."

We leave the building and turn toward the parking lot. When we reach the hill that leads to the lot, Paul shoots ahead of me, miles ahead, it seems just then. I watch the way women turn their heads when they pass, their eyes on the sleeping bundle against his chest. Ahh, so cute. He stops at the bottom of the hill and waits for me, and when I reach him he says, "Let's get some coffee."

"Here?"

"Here."

We trudge back up the incline, then walk along the avenue. Grim brick buildings rise all around us, but on the avenue are modest shops — dry cleaner, greengrocer, shoe store, bar — that give evidence to the fact that people live in Hospital City. We stop in a coffee shop, a narrow place with a counter that runs along one half, and short booths along the other. The restaurant is crowded with hospital employees wearing their second faces clipped onto their pockets. A wizened waitress in a peasant uniform with a low-cut bodice that laces to the waist, puff sleeves, and a full skirt shows us to a booth. Paul has trouble squeezing in because of the bundle strapped across his chest. "What a cutie," says the waitress, as she throws us two menus. Her breasts shiver like Jell-O.

Paul hands me a menu, a huge four-page book with ersatz leather cover.

Cool creamy sizzling baked broiled boiled from our pantry. I look at the pictures inside the menu and think of how aloof Paul has been toward Rachel, how empty his gestures seem, even now that he has begun to hold her. My hands are shaking. There's no way that I can eat. "What are you getting?"

"Coffee."

"Make that two," I tell the waitress, who suddenly appears before us.

Paul says, "Get *something* or your milk will dry up; get a grilled cheese sandwich and milk, okay?"

I think of him flying Rachel, all the way to the left so that she appeared to look at him. "Then you get something with me, because I can't eat alone. I just can't."

"But you love to eat alone, you once told me it was one of life's great pleasures."

"Today is not every day. Today I won't be able to eat unless you do. It embarrasses me to be this way, but I just know it's true."

"Two grilled cheese sandwiches, one large milk, one coffee," he tells the waitress.

"Two milks," I tell her.

"How old's the baby?" she asks.

Paul says: "Two months. Make one of those milks small, will you?"

"No, both," I say.

The waitress leans over to touch Rachel's cheek. I suppress an urge to pull her into the booth with us so that she can keep us company. But she leaves, and it is the two of us, and between us our daughter's blindness.

"Please say something about all this," I ask.

"The amnio always bothered me. I had a bad feeling when he drew up blood."

"Why did you bring up my wet underwear?"

"He asked if you were sick, didn't he? He asked and I thought hard because we've got to find out about all of this."

"My being sick didn't have anything to do with my wet underwear."

"Look: He said was she sick during pregnancy, and I remembered the time we went skiing, and how you didn't get out of your long johns and you got sick afterwards. Okay? Now here's our milk —"

I lift my glass and wait. Reluctantly, he lifts his. Only when I see his Adam's apple bob do I take the first swallow.

We linger in the coffee shop until we are the only customers. We do not want to go home, though neither of us says this aloud. Our waitress sits at the counter with a plate of rice pudding and jokes with the counterman. She is an old woman, or at least she looks old, and it seems cruel to make her dress in this peasant costume. I watch her crane her neck to catch her reflection in the mirror, and she does not seem dismayed by what she sees. She fluffs up her blonde hair, puts a cigarette between her lips, and says, "Gimme a match, Joey."

Paul pulls a pen from his breast pocket and sketches a cross-section of an eye on a napkin. He is himself again as he points out the transparent cornea, and the lens, two elements that help to focus images onto the retina at the rear of the eye. The retina contains receptor cells, rods, and cones, which sense the light, and on its nearby surface, ganglion cells, which are stimulated by them. During normal development the ganglion cells send out long, slender processes called axons that go along the surface of the retina, through the optic disk, and up to the brain. The sum of all of these axons as they pass from the eye to the brain is called the optic nerve. What Dr. Hines saw in Rachel's eyes suggested that the optic nerve was underdeveloped, and that about two-thirds of the axons in one eye and half in the other were missing. The absence of the axons meant that the information in this portion of the retina could not be transmitted from eye to brain.

The numbers stop me. If fifty percent of the optic nerve existed in one eye, why couldn't we hope for something better than light and shadow?

"The fact that fifty percent of the optic nerve is there — and that's an optimistic view — doesn't mean that fifty percent of the optic ganglia connect to the brain," Paul says. "But suppose she really had a full fifty percent. Then the question would be where the ganglia are located, and whether or not they are homogeneously distributed. Remember the Bulova sign on Times Square, the one with hundreds of little bulbs? The man climbs stairs, a watch ticks, all these different images, right? Suppose that someone took a shotgun and blasted out fifty percent of those bulbs at random. You'd get light, but you wouldn't get an image. You'd only get an image if there were a cluster of bulbs."

"She could have a cluster."

"Sure. She could have a cluster of optic ganglia in the periphery and be able to perceive shapes, but she'd have no color and no clear vision because the only spot in the retina where we have visual acuity is in the fovea, and the fovea is about .01 to .05 percent of the retina."

A man comes out of a back door with a mop and a bucket of sharp-smelling gray water. Paul picks up the check and slides out of the booth. He says that there's a book he needs at the library, and asks if I would mind stopping for a moment so he can get it. His suggestion pleases me. I would go anywhere just now except home.

We drive downtown in silence. Paul parks illegally and leaves me in the car with Rachel. I watch the activity outside, my nose against the window. Students in down jackets and backpacks made in Colorado pass in twos, their voices muffled. Only laughter works its way through the glass. I find myself thinking about my sister, who died when I was seventeen. I think about the crowd at her funeral — her friends, my friends, my parents' friends — and the rabbi going on about a candle being snuffed out, and Laura's fiancé, Howie, throwing a ring she gave him into the pit before the casket was placed beneath the earth.

Our house was crowded the week we sat shiva, each person arriving with a box of cookies or a tray of food. I entertained my girlfriends in my room by telling them bawdy stories in a soft voice so that they would sit close to me. When I saw my best friend, Hinda, grow uncomfortable, I took her aside and faked hysterics to fool her into believing that I was grieving. (I was grieving, but I did not know it at the time — I would not understand for years.) I remember leading my friends downstairs to introduce them to my cousin Herb, who owned a shoe store, because they would only wear a certain brand of loafer — absolutely would not put any other on their feet — and these loafers were out of stock in town. When Herb said he had them in his store, they shouted out their orders — cordovan, oxblood, navy, black, 8 medium, 6 AA, 9 — and my mother turned to her niece and said, "How I love to hear them laugh."

I remember the silence when the company left, how the three of us never spoke. We got up at night at different intervals, never facing the others. Sometimes when I woke in the middle of the night I would be aware of footsteps, or the reflection of a light that went on and off. I might find a glass with murky sides from the buttermilk my mother drank, or chicken bones if it was my father.

But here is what weighs the most: the low brick wall outside the high school that I sat on with my friends. We had staked it out as juniors and earned the right to claim it as ours in September of our senior year. It was our space, the surest thing that most of us knew in a world of shifting alliances. My spot was between Barbara and Robin, always, forever — until I went back to school after Laura's death and found that Robin and Barbara had drifted together, that there was no space. I had a dizzying sense upon approaching that I no longer existed for my friends.

I was right, as it turns out, and that is why, though time has turned so many of my memories into anecdotes, this still weighs. I had frightened my friends. They could not face me after what had happened; they did not know what to say. They stopped themselves from laughing when I was around, and tried to weed from their speech all offending phrases —

drop dead, I could murder you, I wanted to die — so that apart from the business of being an only child for the first time and living with parents who grieved, apart from getting used to the fact that my sister had been stabbed repeatedly by a boy she had never known was this loss of all my friends. I could be with them and be a ghost or I could be alone. I learned that year how much easier it was to be alone.

# ❦ 3 ❦

# The First Twelve Days

*8:30 P.M.*

THE HOUSE is dark when we return and has a pleasant woody smell from the shavings in Rat's tank. Paul goes upstairs to change Rachel's diaper, and I stand in the darkened foyer. I remember when we first moved in how fascinated I was with all the things I suddenly owned: drapes, windows, doors, wooden doorknobs, cup hooks, and cabinets. I had lived in an apartment for so many years that I found myself wandering around these rooms, saying, "All this is mine!" as if I were an heir to a vast homestead, instead of the co-owner of a shabby old house built nearly a hundred years ago for a working man and his family. An oil burner, all mine, a hot water heater of my own, a set tub in the basement — I had never heard of a set tub, and now I actually had one. The fascination wore off after a month, and I was left an uneasy tenant in a house formerly owned by people who had had an incontinent dog and a fondness for chrome switchplates and mustard-colored paint. With every change we made, the house became more and more ours. Now, all of a sudden, it is theirs again, and I feel as if I am standing in the darkened foyer in someone else's home.

Paul hurries down the stairs and stops before me. "You don't have to stand in the dark," he says, as if what I am doing is trying to enter the world my daughter is in. He switches on the light and asks, "Where's Charlotte?"

"At Lauren Fowler's, across town. Paul — I can't make any promises about not telling her."

"Lauren — is that the mother or daughter?"

"The child. The mother is —" Janet? Joanne? I can no longer remember.

A minute later I hear his voice from the kitchen. "Hi, is this Lauren's mother? I believe I have a daughter at your house."

I listen to him give a traffic report to this woman that we hardly know and tell her that everything is fine. Then he hangs up and leaves me.

When he is gone, I sit in the room the real estate agent called the solarium, and most people call the porch, and Charlotte has asked that we rename the family room. I put on the lamp and sit on the rocker. Windows span three of the walls, and during the day the room is flooded with sunlight. Rachel's infant seat is here, and also our plants and stereo and tape deck, and the small black and white TV that during the week I hide. In the corner is a large wicker hamper meant for Charlotte's toys — there *are* toys inside — I can see a bag of crayons, her sticker book, a small naked doll. She is a collector, like her father, and also fills the basket with champagne corks, coupons with pretty pictures, chopsticks, plastic berry boxes, gold string, deflated balloons, party invitations, rocks and leaves and flowers she has picked weeks before that are too precious to part with.

The rat regards me from a corner of the tank. I cannot help thinking of her as belonging solidly to the time before. Already I am nostalgic when I remember Paul kissing me on that hot August day, his hands hidden, the rat passive in his palms, and Charlotte racing down the stairs, filled with love and awe. I want to hold her in my arms, but I am afraid to see her, and so, while the wait seems interminable, at the same time, I hope that they will not arrive too soon.

I go into the bathroom and switch on the light. The face that confronts me in the mirror above the sink is not smiling, but that can be altered. Otherwise, I look familiar. She will be okay, I tell myself. Children are resilient — isn't that what people say? What people don't say is that her life, too, has been changed, that she has been cast unalterably out of the mainstream — just as we have.

It puzzles me that this should hurt when so many of my years were spent struggling to be different from those around me. In sixth grade, I ate dog biscuits and learned to wiggle my ears and bend my fingers in odd positions; I wrote mirrorwise so consistently that to this day I write mirrorwise as smoothly and rapidly as I write forwards; in ninth grade I wore black tights and long strands of beads and thought of myself as a beatnik, though the beats were long gone, and I was never quite sure what they stood for anyway; by the time I hit high school I spent my weekends in dark little Village coffeehouses, mooning over obscure folksingers who sang about boxcars and thirsty boots and rye whiskey. I didn't think at the time of all the thousands from other suburban towns whose way of nonconformity was just the same as mine: If someone had suggested it, I would have howled in protest, for I needed to believe that my road was a different one, that I strove in some inimitable way. Years before I thought seriously of having children, I nourished a hope that my child would be an outcast and thus grow up a sensitive human being. Being a mother changed that — seeing Charlotte pushed in the playground, or shunned by another child for the crime of wearing boys' (i.e., navy blue) pants made me realize instantly that being an outcast hurt, and that what I really wanted was for my daughter to fit right in, to be comfortable, to be in the mainstream, to be saved from as much suffering as possible.

And there she is, racing through the front door, spaghetti stains on her shirt, lunchbox thumping against her knee, a handful of drawings and notices that I must look at right that very second. I hurry to her, and kneel for a hug, and I cannot tell her, I cannot bear to hurt her.

"Hello, sweetie," I say, greeting her as I always do with a hug and kiss.

She is stiff in my arms, her exuberance suddenly gone. She is too young for concrete fears, yet somehow she knows.

"Charlotte —" My heart is a hammer, cracking at my ribs. "Rachel cannot . . . see."

"But we're going to make a great life for her, aren't we?" Paul says. "We're going to teach her all about the world, and when she gets a little older she'll play and swim and go to school with you, and have friends, and be happy . . ."

"I need cookies," my daughter says.

Cookies? Why does she need cookies? I have to figure this out quickly or she will think that I have forgotten her. Already she has backed away, and chews on a lock of hair. Cookies, cookies . . . For school, yes. It's our turn to bring the snack.

I am so relieved I begin to laugh. "We'll get cookies, don't worry. I'll buy them as soon as you go to bed. Nothing will change, honey, I promise. You'll get cookies."

"And no brown ones," she says as she walks off.

*What do you do? What next?*
You have something to eat, look at the newspaper, brush your teeth,

go to bed. (And isn't it amazing — your daughter is blind, and you are reading an article about James Watt in the *Times*, actually absorbing it, word by word, though slowly, because your brain is split, half of it taking in the utter tastelessness of his remark "two women, two Jews, and a cripple," while in the other half the scene in the ophthalmologist's office replays, and you see again the picture of his pretty daughter, and hear his irritable voice tell you, "I didn't say *usable* vision . . .")

In the morning you wake up, and before your eyes are open, you remember that your baby is blind, and because you are so vulnerable at this hour, you have no way of diverting or protecting yourself. Your older daughter comes into the room, and so you get out of bed and get her dressed, and when she gives you a very hard time because she wants to wear a short-sleeved dress, and it is only twenty degrees outside, you squelch the urge to put your hands around her throat and scream, "Shut up, you twit, I cannot be bothered with this!" and you let her wear the summer dress . . .

"What I want — " I say to Paul at breakfast, and then I am stopped by the flood of desires in my mind. What I want is for Rachel to be un-blind. "What I want is to have a normal life anyhow, I really mean this."

He dips his head in what is half a shrug and half a nod.

"People get swallowed up by things like this; they get obsessed, they stop laughing —" and I remember my mother's story about a woman across the courtyard of their garden apartment in Queens, who "ran from doctor to doctor" looking for someone to give her hope for her daughter when in reality there was none. "I want to take Charlotte to the zoo and go on vacations, and start back to work — if I felt that work was taken away, too, I couldn't take it. Promise me we'll try to get on with things."

A ridiculous request, I realize. But he looks up, and I see that his eyes have filled. "We're going to make it, I tell you —"

He holds me in his arms, and I feel a surge of hope. We're going to make it, yes. We're going to find pleasure wherever it exists, and enjoy Charlotte, and make sure that Rachel's life is rich. We're going to con-tinue with our work . . .

"And have more children," he says. "Promise me we'll have at least another two."

I cannot think about another baby, not with Rachel so young, and in need of so much nurturing. I want him to stay with me a while longer, and so I say, "Two, three, twelve, anything you want," just to keep him.

It does not work. He breaks away and looks at his watch. I follow him while he collects his jacket and keys and attaché case and tell him about Annie, a blind girl who had the same piano teacher as me, and how independent she was, and what an incredible family she had. Annie had a checker set with square and round pieces, instead of black and red ones, and cards with Braille in one corner. She rode a bike through the park behind her house, and at her birthday party, to which I was invited, there was a treasure hunt, which she won. She went to the prom with Billy Russell, and had her picture taken, which most of the kids thought was very strange, and then went to college, and . . .

Suddenly he is gone, and it feels so final, door slammed, glass panes rattling, car motor revving, not to return for ten or twelve hours, leaving me with *her,* she is mine alone, my sightless child, my problem. The end to the Annie story floods my mind the moment he leaves, the part that I wanted most to tell, how when mainstreaming took effect she transferred to my high school, and I would see her every day in the halls, and remember the shoofly pie her mother made for us, and the fun we had playing together. I yearned to say hello and never did, because I did not know how to do it. For two years I waited for the courage — *courage!* — that's what I felt it took to say hello to a blind girl who had been my friend. I never did.

*And then?*

You call the hospital and find out when her CT scan and the evoked response test have been scheduled. When you get the date — December fourteenth — you hold tightly to it, and hope that time will pass quickly. The tests are the next step; they will yield some further piece of information; they will help you figure out what to do. All you have to do is get through the next eleven days.

*December 3*

I am adamant about telling my parents about Rachel and Paul is adamant about not telling his. First he says he doesn't want to say anything until there is something more definitive to say. Then, after an appointment has been set up, he says that he wants to wait until after Christmas. We are both vehement about our positions, though I know, and I suspect that he does, too, that reason lies on neither of our sides. My argument — that it is wrong to hold back such an immense piece of information, how I hated whenever it was done to me as a child — is not untrue; it merely camouflages the real reason, my childlike need to tell. Mommy, I have hurt myself; Daddy, fix my boo-boo. Paul says that I have no idea how important Christmas is to his family, and that it is unfair, when they live so far away, to tell them. They will only worry and fret; his mother will get hysterical. What's the point when there isn't anything that they can do?

True, true, but even so, I call my parents. When I hear my mother's hello, I breathe deeply, and say, "I have something to tell you both —" and ask that my father get on the other extension so that I will not burden one with the chore of having to tell the other. I am okay until I say, "Mom? Dad?" at which point I begin to weep for the first time, and with such force I feel as if my insides will come out, that the sheer physical force of my crying will invert me, leaving my guts on the outside, like some poor bashed cat on the road. After this I understand what Paul is avoiding, and that he knows in some way that all his well-learned training not to gripe or complain will not serve him here, that despite years of independence, all he will have to do is say, "Mom? Dad?" and not be able to stop what comes next.

And so I tell my parents, and my mother must be thinking of all the years she put Band-Aids on little scrapes and kissed away tears, because she says, "Oh, I wish I could *do* something, I wish I could make it go away."

For a while no one speaks. I listen to my father breathe on the up-stairs extension. We are all reminded of other wounds — I can feel it in the silence, and so I fill the silence by telling them that the doctor who saw Rachel was an expert in his field, that we could not have gone to anyone better, that the condition is static, and not degenerative, and that we plan to help her have a good, full life . . .

My mother says, "Just because the doctor was a big shot doesn't mean he couldn't have made a mistake," and the Band-Aid is stripped from my skin. In its place are a mother's words to a child who wakens from a bad dream crying. Don't fret, it was only a dream . . .

She says: "I don't give a damn that he charged you four hundred dollars for forty-five minutes, he still could be wrong. Look at Dottie —"

a neighbor whose glaucoma surgery was botched, and at the very same institution.

There was no mistake, and for me to pretend that there was would be infinitely more painful than this slow process of knowing. "He looked in her eyes and saw," I say. He saw it, and he called in someone else, and she saw it, and then he showed us a picture, and we understood how easy this deficit was to see.

After I hang up I begin fully to believe the diagnosis, and the pictures I did not realize I had created so vividly of my bright, beautiful, healthy daughter are gone. In their place are resurrected memories of every blind person I have ever seen, beggars mostly, blind men with eyes that roll in their sockets that terrified me as a child and terrify me now. My daughter, my child. And there is nothing hopeful I can conjure, nothing at all, and I say this to Paul, so great are my fears.

He says, "I don't want to talk about her, okay? Because if I talk about her I think about her, and it's counterproductive to think about her, especially now, before the tests, when we don't even have any hard data."

How can he *not* think about her?

"And when you get her in the morning? When you lean over her crib and hold her in your arms, will you not think about her then?"

"Is this getting us anyplace?" His voice is brittle. "Tell me, is it getting us anyplace?"

"It isn't getting us anyplace, it just *is,* and I *can't* stop thinking about it."

What can I say? That he *should* think about her and be as shaken as I? It's what I want, though. For him to share my misery. And yet when he turns away from me — and why not, we have nothing more to say — and I see his unhappiness in the slow way he plods up the stairs, it breaks my heart. I call his name and he turns and comes back down the stairs and holds me, just what I have needed. "Let's not fight, okay? Not now. Not now."

*December 4*

We have told four other people, who, unbidden, have passed the word, and now the phone rings day and night — cousins, and cowork-ers and friends we have not seen in months calling to offer their condolences. When Paul is home, I hide in the bathroom or the basement, or hurriedly unsnap the flap of a nursing bra, and put Rachel to breast — anything to avoid taking these calls. Paul handles them all with utter grace, giving the bad news, sweetening it right away, changing the subject when he senses the caller's discomfort, his voice so cheerful that it seems as if he has hardly been shaken, that the news that his daughter cannot see is no more distressing than if she had broken an arm or been nearsighted.

When he is gone, I try my best because I am touched by the awkward effort of cousins and friends (all of them thinking of dogs, canes, tin cups full of change), who tell me that they are sorry, sad, grateful for the health of their own children, who remind me of Charlotte and all the ways that we are lucky, and pass on word of medical miracles — mechanical hearts, cornea transplants, children diagnosed as hopeless who are going on for higher education. Everyone knows someone who is blind and a success. I hear of a blind pianist, a blind sax player, a blind singer, and nothing about a blind girlfriend, a blind mother, a blind friend. I say thank you when I am asked if I would like to meet the blind musician, "Thank you, maybe in a few weeks —" because I am grateful that someone out there is trying to reach me.

The house is very still after Paul and Charlotte leave, and it frightens me, though I have always been a person whose need for solitude has been great and whose work demands long hours alone. As soon as I hear Rachel stir, I stand beside her crib and wait for her to rouse. I watch her lips begin to move — she has puppy dreams of mother's milk and suckles the air above her. I take her in my arms, my big, chubby baby, with skin so soft, and dark smooth hair, ten fingers that flex when she nurses, ten toes that curl. When I hold her, I know, though I do not fully believe, and so I let myself slip into the delusion that nothing is wrong.

Then the phone rings, and the dream is shattered. Speaking about her takes my breath away. I describe her condition and my heart begins to hammer at my chest, because I hear what I am saying and for that moment I believe it. I have learned to pick up — in the conversation or the silence — the time when I must do my job to ease the awkwardness, and I tell my friends just then that Paul and I are committed to getting on with life, and that I have not given up work (a wish more than reality). I tell them about the dozens of conversations we have had in the past — what would you rather be, deaf or . . . visually impaired, and how I always said that I would rather be . . . visually impaired because it does not cut you off as much from the mainstream. I tell them how I feel I have more to offer to a child who is . . . visually handicapped than I would a child who is retarded (I wouldn't begin to know what to *do* with a retarded child) or one who is deaf because after all, I'm so verbal. . . . I tell everyone that I have already gone to the library and taken out both books on children with . . . visual problems, and how I called the Commission for the . . . Visually Impaired, and that a social worker was coming over to teach me everything I needed to know as a parent of a child who is . . . visually impaired.

Anything but the word, any euphemism that will sidetrack me from it. Even when I want to say it, I cannot get my lips together to form the initial *b* because hearing the word would make it far too real.

The word stays locked inside me, and my fears spill over. I hear Paul's key in the lock and what I want is to greet him with kisses, and give him entry into a happy home. I rush to the door and think: Don't say a word about Rachel; just let him be. It is not his way to wring his hands and worry aloud. Say hello, tell him you missed him. Let him hang up his coat and sit for a while.

He steps inside and I put my arms around him. His body is rigid and his hug so distracted that I forget my promises.

"Rachel slept all day. I couldn't keep her awake no matter how hard I tried . . . ," trailing him into the bedroom, where he sits to unlace his shoes. "She sleeps like that because she's been deprived of stimulation. I read it today. It's the biggest danger visually impaired babies face, because if they aren't stimulated, they sleep all day and then grow up to have serious psychological problems. But I can't stimulate her. She keeps falling asleep."

"Who called?" he asks.

Now I cannot stop myself. He is my husband, my companion. We have shared our stories, and taken each other's enemies as our own. He has never mocked my concerns, never turned me away, never failed to be a comfort, and though he is not a man who unburdens easily, he has allowed me, far more than in our early days, to do the same for him. I tell him that I feel as if my life is over — in the house all day long with her, never a moment when she is not in my thoughts. And how today

I read that a visually impaired child needs to be oriented, and that wind chimes by the front door are a nice way of letting the child know where she is, and that I want to buy wind chimes . . .

He walks past me into the kitchen, and stares into the refrigerator for a while. "Did anyone call?"

Who called? What did she say? How did he find out? This is what he wants to hear, this man who has never been interested in the he said/ she said stories, or the small insults and minor events in lives outside his own family.

Who called? Was it a denier, a believer in medical miracles, a look-on-the-sunny-side type who tried to convince me how fortunate I am that Rachel is not hideously deformed? Did we get another blind musician story? These last have become a joke between the two of us, our only one. Little Rachel Wonder, Rachel Charles, José Rachel Feliciano. What will we do if she's tone-deaf like her dad? I will tell him, but first —

I search for his hand, his gaze, for an expression that I can understand. "Can you *say* something, please? Hello, how are you? I need to know that you're alive."

"Wind chimes sound like a good idea."

I follow him into the dining room, and watch him cut two slices of bread and open a tin of brisling sardines. Silver tails peek from the edge of his sandwich; gold droplets of oil spot his plate.

"Today I kept thinking about an article I read last year about how people fear being blind more than anything except cancer. The blind themselves inspire fear. I keep worrying that when people come close to Rachel and see her eyes roll, they'll back away. I'm afraid she'll be unloved."

At last he looks up. "What is the point of all this?"

"You don't think these things?"

"No."

"Never? Then what do you think?"

"Nothing; I don't let myself. Look, she's a beautiful child. Her life can still be rich."

His mind does not play tricks like mine; he does not have images that come upon him without bidding: his daughter with her hands held out in darkness, his daughter with a cane, his daughter unloved, his daughter rocking, poking at her eyes, separated from the world.

He says: "It's all noise —" this favorite phrase from his days as an engineer. Noise — I'm extrapolating on noise. "It's a waste of time inventing these possibilities when you have no idea what she'll be like or what the world will be like in fifteen years."

"I don't invent them — they come upon me."

"Well, it's noise," he says, abruptly getting up.

The phone rings, and Paul is nowhere in sight. It's Joseph, a good friend of ours; with his wife, the only two people we know from Siberia. How the hell did he find out? I mean to ask, but he has already begun a long story about a famous man from his country. His accent is rather thick, and I am too agitated to listen closely. Terrific, I am thinking as he goes on with the biography. A blind *Russian* musician, just what I want to hear about.

I stop him before the story ends. "Excuse me. I don't think I can handle another story about a blind musician."

There is a lengthy pause — a bad connection, a delay caused by different cultural references? "Mathematician," he says. "He's a mathematician."

Paul appears, and I hand the phone to him, and because I am interested in who said what and found out where (and always have been) I hover close.

He talks for a while, mostly science, and just when I am about to give up says, "I'm going to ask them to do a brainstem when she goes in for the CT scan. I'm not sure that she can hear."

A brainstem? She does not hear? I start to tremble all over, and grab on to my own arms, though I know by now that I cannot stop myself from shaking no matter where I clutch. Why is he saying this? And to Joseph, not to me. He's asking them to do a brainstem (whatever that is). He isn't sure that she hears? He thinks that she is blind *and* deaf?

"Why did you say that she was deaf?" I ask when he gets off the phone.

"I didn't say that she was deaf, I said I thought she might be."

"But *why?*"

"Because I'm not convinced that she can hear. Look. Let's not worry about it until the test results are in."

Let's not worry about it. Just like that. Blind and deaf. From Stevie Wonder to Helen Keller in one dizzying instant. Already I rebel against the stories I would hear, and think: Don't you dare tell me about this singularly remarkable life, this one person among all the miserable, helpless blind-deaf people who ever lived. Don't tell me about miracles — miracles don't happen in New Jersey. Not to us, anyhow.

We stand together. I must stop telling him about my visions because he cannot stand to hear them. I must stop or he will turn and go up the stairs without me.

"Life isn't worth living deprived of so much," I say.

I cannot help it; I am out of control.

He nods and says, "If it's true, we'll let her die. I'll do it myself, I swear to God."

*My* baby? Something rises within me to shield her, some unknown animal thing that springs from within the mother to protect the child. My body encircling hers, my body protecting her from the enemy. If she is blind and deaf, I do not want her to live, but I would kill anyone who touched her.

### December 5

As soon as Paul and Charlotte leave, I take Rachel upstairs and set her in a patch of sunlight. I speak to her in a soft steady voice — me, Mommy, the one who loves and feeds you, I am the one. Sunlight, soft voice — and in my mind, the unthinkable possibility that these things, and most of what I know, might be meaningless to her.

Rachel? Baby? I kneel beside her and call her name. What do I expect? For her to look at me. I know that she cannot see at all, but that does not stop me from putting my face near hers and expecting that she will look up with her dark eyes and reach out and wiggle with joy. I wind a music box and she seems to respond, kicking vigorously. When the music stops she lies still upon the blanket.

I take off my shoe and slam the floor, and she startles, arms flying out — no question about it. The test is one of life and death. My chest aches so much I can hardly repeat it. Here goes — the music first, the squeaky toy, my voice calling her name, over and over.

"Watch," I tell Paul when he returns from work.

We stand on the loose attic floorboards outside my office, several feet from Rachel. Her diapers rustle; her tongue thrusts from between her lips. I could almost laugh. I stamp my foot quite suddenly and she startles, not as dramatically as earlier, though it is clear that she has tensed. Again I repeat it.

"Is that supposed to mean something?" Paul asks.

"Didn't you see her tense when I stamped?"

"It could be from the vibration for all you know."

"She does it when the phone rings, and there isn't any vibration then. She tenses and blinks."

"She blinks, great. How many times does she blink every minute? Ten? Twenty? Don't make me tell you how terrific it is that she blinks when the phone rings."

"She startles, too. Arms flying, the whole thing. Why can't you believe me?"

"Because I didn't see it, and I can't believe something that I don't see."

"You don't trust what I tell you?"

"Trust has nothing to do with it. I'm a scientist. I've been trained to believe what I see or what can be proven and nothing else."

The phone rings just then. Paul turns to get it, and Rachel startles, just as she had earlier. His skepticism shakes me, but I am determined not to let it weaken my belief that she hears.

"It's for you," Paul says.

"Hello!" I tell the receiver cheerfully.

It's Linda, friend, screenplay collaborator, and former neighbor. She asks me how I am, and I say, *"Good."* It's true, isn't it? "The social worker is coming on Wednesday."

The social worker, yes; my savior — *she will tell me what to do.* I will wash my hair for her and tidy up the house. I cannot wait.

"You sound *too* good," she says. "You're allowed to cry, you know."

"I do cry. I cry whenever I talk to my mother."

"You can even scream and yell — I won't think less of you or hang up or stop calling."

"Eeek," I say.

She will not laugh.

I promise to remember her when the time comes that I break, and then I get off. I think of all the stories I have heard — women whose screams echo over the oceans, women who take to bed and never get up, who tear their hair, who cannot eat or love, women who languish until they die. I see not the tragedy in these lost lives, but the relief that madness must be. I wish I could scream and tear my hair so that the ache would be released from within me, for the truth is that I am no more resilient than they, nor is my will stronger. It is just that my way is to grieve politely.

*December 6*

The social worker from the New Jersey Commission for the Blind and Visually Impaired is young and newly married, with waist-length hair and big tortoise-shell glasses. Her name is Sharon, and she wears a fisherman's sweater, blue jeans, and an ornate diamond ring, which she twists as she speaks. She describes the agency to me, and tells me apologetically about the papers that I must sign. When I give her Rachel's history, prenatal to present, she listens attentively until I am finished, then slides off the chair, and crouches before her. Is someone in *her* family blind, I wonder? Mother, sister, husband?

"She's adorable," she says, stroking Rachel's cheek.

I agree. (She's adorable and will never know it.)

She takes out a small thin flashlight and flicks the beam of light on and off across Rachel's face. She sees my obvious disappointment when Rachel does not respond, and says: "Sometimes vision is slow in developing."

"Dr. Hines says development continues for nine months."

Less than seven are left for Rachel.

"It can take children a lot longer to learn to use what they have. I have a three-year-old who's just starting to distinguish shapes. We didn't think he had any vision at all."

She hunches forward and arranges herself in a good listener's posture. "Do *you* have any questions?"

Of the endless number I have, one obsesses me: Why did she take this job?

I ask her about Braille reading, mainstreaming, sports for the blind. (*Who in your family is blind?*) We talk about blind skiers for a while. I tell her about the inordinate number of blind musician stories we are hearing, and she laughs, which pleases me. She obliges me with little-known facts (total blindness — no light perception — is extremely rare; most "blind" people have some degree of limited vision) and numbers (only seventy school-age Braille readers in New Jersey; just over five thousand in the country).

"Are there any blind children nearby?"

She opens a notebook and leafs through a few sheets of paper.

"There's one little boy, but he's very low-functioning . . . And a six-year-old in the next town, an adorable kid; he's got some neurological problems, but he's doing really well."

"Anyone with optic nerve hypoplasia?"

"Kristin Peters. She's sixteen now and was mainstreamed into the high school a while ago. She's doing okay, but she's lost a lot of time because she has a seizure disorder that isn't under control, and she has seizures nearly every day . . ."

I learn two things right then: One, that blindness is a "low-incidence" handicap. (In my town of thirty thousand, there are two other blind children, both multi-impaired.) And two, like the kids in town, the majority of blind children have other problems. Eye infections that years ago caused blindness are now treatable; congenital cataracts and opaque corneas can be helped by surgery. That still leaves infections such as cytomegalovirus and toxoplasmosis, genetic and developmental causes, accidents and diseases. There can be problems with the eye itself — congenital retinal disease, for instance; or failure of the optic nerve to form fully (as in Rachel's case); or the eye can be perfectly healthy, with damage at the visual cortex, in the brain itself, interfering with processing. Advances in neonatal care have enabled more and more premature infants of extremely low birth weight to survive, babies at high risk for developmental and visual problems.

The social worker asks if I would like to be put in touch with any of the families. "Kristin's mother is really wonderful — the whole family is. I know she wouldn't mind if you called."

"Sure," I say, though I am not ready to call anyone.

She is so sweet sitting there at the edge of the seat, twisting her diamond ring and waiting for me to blather on, that I cannot help but blurt: "Is someone in your family blind?"

"No-o-o." She is smiling now.

"How did you get into this?"

"I worked one summer at a camp for blind kids, and I really enjoyed it."

"Oh," I say.

"Did you want to ask me anything else?"

"What can I *do* for Rachel. There must be something."

She tells me about a program called "infant stim" at Children's Specialized Hospital for babies with developmental problems. The idea of

the classes is to accelerate the baby's development by working on problem areas, and to give therapy while the parent is there so that parents
can be trained as their child's therapists.

Sounds good, but . . . "Anything I can do *today?*"

Again the amused smile, nothing mocking in it. "She's just a baby,
love her the way you'd love any baby — hold her and talk to her —
she'll be fine."

This is not enough. I must feel as if I am *doing* something at this very
moment to help alter her fate. Isn't there a book, a technique, a toy? I
press the social worker until at last she makes several suggestions.

As soon as she is out the door, I call Children's Specialized Hospital
and speak to a woman named Mrs. Kaiser, who tells me that Rachel
must be evaluated by the staff before she can enter the infant stim program. She sets up a date in January, and when I count the days until
then, the panic wells up inside. What will I do for the next forty-three
days?

*December* 7

I buy baby oil so that I can give Rachel a massage, rubber dog toys
with squeakers inside, a plush mouse with a rattle in its belly, a plastic
ball filled with marbles . . . I speak as I approach her, play vigorously
with her, buy a penlight like the social worker's. I make tapes of clas-
sical music, which I set up in her room, though I cannot bring myself
to put her in the crib except at night. It seems like death to leave her
in this back room that is so still. Instead I take her upstairs to my office,
and set her on a mat beside me, so that she will be close to me while I
work, and surround her with toys that will honk, squeak, or buzz if she
brushes against them.

The silence frightens me. I am afraid if I leave her she will fall down
a long dark hole, and so I talk like a madwoman. "First I'm going to
find my notebook. Notebook? Oh, notebook, yes, here you are with
your nice canvas cover and brown leather corners."

To work is to shut up, and to shut up is to leave her in darkness, and
that I cannot do.

"I'm going to sharpen my pencils now, all twelve of them, and it
makes a lot of noise, so get ready. Here's the first, into the hole. Don't
cry, darling, don't be frightened."

She does not cry, because she is asleep. She sleeps most of the day, a sign of my failure. She is not interested enough to stay awake — she lacks sensory input and will have ego development problems and become autistic. She will belong to the one-third of all blind children who fail to be fully functioning adults, the children no one speaks about, who live in houses like ours, in similar towns, and have parents like us.

*December 8*

"We have to laugh," I tell Paul as we are undressing for bed. It has been seven days now since Rachel has gone from being a sweet, fat, placid baby to a sweet, fat, placid baby who is blind. "Promise me that one day soon we'll start to laugh."

"We'll laugh," he says, balling up his socks and throwing them one, two into the wicker hamper across the room. The second one hits the rim, and lands in the corner.

"You believe that?"

"I wouldn't tell you if I didn't. Now get under the covers, will you?"

He leans across the night table, and switches off the light. While I sit at the edge of the bed in darkness, he shifts beneath the blankets. After eight years of marriage I have grown used to certain things. His weariness when he comes home from work is familiar to me; his way of sleeping, the foods that he likes best, the things he cannot tolerate, the texture of his skin, his habit of tossing his clothes into the hamper and leaving the missed shots on the floor forever — or until I pick them up. Although I do not live inside his head, I have always found him easy to read. His eyes, the set of his mouth, the way he walks — I could always sense his mood. These days I look at his face and there are no signs of sorrow or stress, no clue to what he feels, and it unnerves me. I am reduced to saying things like: "What are you thinking?" something I swore I would never ask another human being.

"I'm thinking that if you lie down, I'd get some sleep."

It is only ten o'clock, and our daughter is blind and possibly deaf. "How can you sleep?" I ask.

"How? First I close my eyes and get into a comfortable position, and then I think about a deck I'd like to build in Maine. I make a few calculations, and when the figures get to be too complex to handle in my head, I fall asleep. You need to sleep, Jane. If you're exhausted all the time, everything looks worse."

I lie down beside him. The room is so dark that at first I can see nothing at all. Will this be what it's like for Rachel — this utter nothingness no matter how much I strain to see an image? Or will it be like this (after my eyes have begun to adapt), still dark, the bureau and bookcase blacker than the space around it; the doorway lighter? I try to think about building a deck on our cottage in Maine, which after all would be very nice, but linger instead over words like red, blue, near, far, and wonder how, when she has no vision, I will ever learn to describe the world to her. Paul snores lightly.

The phone. I lie in bed, my heart throbbing. Paul picks it up on the third ring, and after a pause says, "Maura! How are you."

Maura Regan, a friend who lives in Massachusetts, our seventh call today.

". . . Yeah, well, it was just one of those things — an accident in development, we were told . . . No, I don't think so, Maura, because her *eyes* are fine, it's her optic nerve that didn't form properly." He turns from me, and props himself up on an elbow. "Yeah, I *know*, I know that's true, but the optic nerve is in the brain — it's just not feasible to think about brain transplants. The good news is that it's a static condition, and she's fine in every other way — you ought to see her, she's a great little kid, if I do say so. Lots of black hair tinged with blonde. At the hospital nursery they combed it into a Mohawk for Jane . . ."

"Maura Regan," he says after hanging up. "Heard it from Glenn. Don't give up, there are always brain transplants."

He curls up and falls back to sleep.

A deck, I think. One that looks out onto the bay. Something with rails that have closely spaced slants. In nice weather I could plug a long extension cord into a socket and take my typewriter outside. I could watch the herons perch at water's edge, and the cormorants line up on the island that disappears at high tide, and the lobster boats idle while the men pull up traps. Herons, cormorants, lobstermen, traps. Things drop but do not disappear, rain falls from the sky, you have ten fingers and toes, my darling; Charlotte is the one who drags you across the room, Mommy and the breast are one.

*December 9*

Sharon visits again. I show her the carton I have — every toy on the market that rattles, squeaks, rings, buzzes, and plays music. She laughs softly and twists her ring and says, "Blind children enjoy toys that don't make noise, too."

*December 10*

Charlotte has learned the word "blind" and uses it with comfort. I am told that understanding what it means is far too abstract for a child of her age, though the word itself has taken on a meaning — *something is wrong* — but not with her sister, whom she straightens in the infant seat so that she may watch "Sesame Street." Blind means that something is wrong with *us,* that despite all our smiles and assurances, we are unhappy. And why shouldn't she feel this — she lives with us. She knows that we use up all of our cheer on her; she hears us on the phone. She sees me at the end of the day, weary and preoccupied. She stands in doorways wide-eyed and silent and watches me cry.

*December 11*

Dr. Hines's report arrives this morning. I take it upstairs to my office and read it several times, stopping to look up unfamiliar words and make notations in the margins. It is midday before I figure out that my difficulty in understanding it has less to do with the jargon than the fact that the letter was undoubtedly typed directly from his recorded words the day of the examination and is filled with fragments and run-ons, and a syntax unlike any I have ever seen.

We brought our two-month-old because of her "history of a minimum of two weeks of a tendency of her eyes to be conjugately deviated to left or right side." Her eyes were dilated with Mydriacyl and examined. "Moderate optic nerve hypoplasia was observed, the basis for visual deficit of some more than likely significant amount although not absolute considering the reliable closure of her eyes to bright light and presumably related rovinglike oscillation rather than an ocular motor defect, although uncertain."

A CT scan has been arranged in order to rule out a congenital tumor and "septo-optic dysplasia, absent septum pellucidum, which often necessitates supplementation of growth hormone."

The tumor had been mentioned, but this last thing — septo-optic dysplasia — is new to me. A septum is a membrane or dividing wall, according to the dictionary. Dysplasia is abnormal growth or development. *Gray's Anatomy* describes the septum pellucidum as "a narrow partition between the two lateral ventricles." In a drawing of the "median sagittal section of the brain," I see that nearby this septum are the hypothalamus, optic chiasm, and pituitary. Is septo-optic dysplasia as remote as the tumor? Should I be upset?

I read the letter to Paul that evening and wait for his response. "It would be terrific if they could get an image," he says after a few minutes.

Image as in NMR (nuclear magnetic resonance), or MR image, because, he says, CT is good at distinguishing between bone, cartilage, and soft tissue, but NMR, which is also a non-invasive technique, is better at showing up differences between soft tissues, tumors, and fat, and would, therefore, be better at distinguishing between septums and tumors. The procedure is not FDA approved for babies, however.

### December 12

We wake, and dress for work or school the same as we would any morning. Paul eats breakfast while I make lunch for Charlotte. He gets up with his empty bowl and cup just as I am ready to join him at the table. "I'll be late tonight," he says, and his mustache brushes against my cheek. He leans over to hug Charlotte, then picks up his briefcase and coat. Charlotte follows him, waiting on the front steps in her bare feet until his car is out of sight.

Today I am going to work, I think, as I prepare her breakfast. All I have to do is revise one chapter each week, and I'll be done in February. If the manuscript were accepted, it would not soften my sorrow over Rachel, but it would be something to hold on to, something more concrete than the hope or fear that shapes my day now. Charlotte eats while I clean up from my own meal; brushes her teeth while I tie her shoes; uses the toilet while I change Rachel's diaper. I linger too long at the changing table, and she positions herself in the doorway and says, "Come *on,*" and drags me back on track.

Hinda calls, and we talk for a moment. She is my oldest friend, my surrogate sister.

"I can't believe how you're handling this," she says before she gets off.

"I'm not handling it. It's happening to me. I'm just going with the flow."

"Please," she says, in an exasperated voice that I have known for twenty years. "Most people would just fall apart."

I hang up, pull jackets off hangers, hand Charlotte her lunchbox, and take Rachel in my arms. I step outside myself just long enough to watch the way we go about our chores, all of us part of the same, well-oiled machine. I think of Hinda's words and wonder if perhaps I have some part in these ordered days. For the first time I am able to imagine a time when my thoughts will be my own, and the hammering in my chest will have ceased.

I walk Charlotte to school. She does not like me to escort her into the classroom, so I station myself at the end of the corridor and let her walk in alone. She hangs her coat on a rack in the hall, and gives me a little wave. I have just turned to leave when I am approached by a little gnome with platinum pigtails that sprout above her ears, and immense green eyes that overpower her slender face. She walks beside me, silent until I look down.

"Your baby's blind," she says.

"That's true," I say as I hurry down the steps.

I'm going to work today, I think. I'm going to work.

When I get home I carry Rachel upstairs and set her on her back in the middle of the mat. Surrounding her, in a large circle, are the toys that will rattle, squeak, ring, buzz, or play music if only she would reach out. She has no vision to stimulate her, no field of beautiful, shining things that might be nice to touch or mouth. But if she brushes against these toys enough times she will learn that a world exists within her own grasp.

I tickle her and kiss her all over, stroke her cheeks and call out to her until she gives me a shy sweet smile, fly her on my palms, and swing her in the air. She falls asleep soon after I stop, so I get up. I walk in small circles until I remember my resolution. Today is the day. Today I will work.

I take my manuscript from the shelf and find the chapter I had been revising when we left for Florida. The typescript on the page is lost amid handwritten stuff that snakes between lines and fills all the margins so that in order to decipher my changes the page has to be held at all angles. Where was I? I have been away from this for so long that it is hard to reenter this world that I have put together. Even my handwriting is inscrutable. I sharpen three pencils, and read the chapter through. When I am done, I pick up the shortest pencil and write until the side of my hand turns slate gray. I stop to take a sip of tea and then look at the paper to see what I have written:

raw clams
unwashed vegetables
amniocentesis
LSD taken in '67
tap water
tonic (quinine?) at G.'s reading
wet underwear

Rachel wakes up, and by the time I finish nursing her, it's time to get Charlotte.

Megan the gnome spots me as soon as I get to the nursery school. She races down the hall and follows me into Charlotte's classroom. Her black sweatshirt says "Thriller" across the front.

Charlotte stands in the play kitchen, dressed in a velvet cloche, a long sequined gown that bunches on the floor, and red patent leather shoes. She is making tea for a bear.

"Hello, Megan," I say.

She gives me a crooked little smile, and then says, "Your baby's blind."

"She is, but she's a very nice baby. Would you like to see her?"

I get down on my knees and take off my jacket so that Megan can see her asleep in the pouch. Megan touches Rachel's cheek, then tries to work her finger into Rachel's fist. She is very gentle, and I am pleased. I feel as if I am doing a public service, that I am giving this little girl early exposure to a blind child so that she will not grow up and be terrified. See? I think. She's just a baby with soft skin, and a little mouth, lips parted while she sleeps, lashy eyes shut.

"She's sweet, isn't she?" I say.

"She's blind," says Megan, walking off.

*December 13*

Charlotte gets home from school and says: "When I have my birthday party, and we play pin the tail on the donkey, Rachel won't have to wear a blindfold."

"That's right!" I say, hopping up to kiss her. I cannot stop laughing. "That's exactly right."

She knows, and she does not seem to care. Rachel is blind, but she is still our baby. I imagine Charlotte walking in a field with Rachel and picking flowers for her to touch and smell. Buttercup, yarrow, orange hawkweed, the flowers we have in our yard in Maine . . . I don't mind that the image is trite, it brings me such joy that when the phone rings, I answer it with a chipper hello.

It is my mother. She says, "How are you, honey?" and I begin to weep. "Paul thinks that Rachel's deaf!"

I never cry when friends call, though at times my body feels as if it might break into pieces. Yet my mother calls and says, "How are you honey?" and I start sobbing. The worst of it is seeing Charlotte stare at me. History repeats itself: She is the living child, and Rachel the dead. She will suffer the burdens of trying to be everything for her parents, of making up for their heartbreak. She will try, and feel that she has failed, and her rebellion will be joyless.

"I'm okay," I say to both Charlotte and my mother. "I'm okay, I really am. Just give me a second."

I want to tell her how many articles I have read, and how prepared I am to help Rachel. I want to tell her how much I love Paul, and how determined the two of us are to make a good life for our family. I inhale deeply in order to catch my breath. "I'm being swallowed," I wail, and it is true just then. I am drowning, I am sinking, I cannot get free.

"I know," she says. Her daughter has died, and so has the healthy daughter that I had envisioned. She has been where I am now and says: "Some days are worse than others — who knows why. Maybe you saw another baby, a healthy one. Maybe it's the weather. Or it was just a bad day. Just believe me, Jane, one morning you'll wake up and you won't cry anymore."

"Never!" I sob.

"You have Paul and Charlotte. You can't let yourself get so wrapped up in the baby that you forget them. Marriages break up over these things."

"I don't cry," I say, my breath short and sharp, like Rachel's after Dr. Hines had put the drops in her eyes. "I really don't cry."

When Paul comes home from work I meet him at the door, dry-eyed and smiling.

"Listen to this one," he says. "In my department there are two men named Ross, two men from Taiwan, two men who are bald, and two fathers of blind children . . . Hey, you wanted to laugh, didn't you?"

I follow him into the kitchen, where he peels a banana and devours it in three bites.

"Who else has a blind child?"

"Michael Leahy — she's fifteen, though. She was a preemie, I believe."

"Ah, retrolental fibroplasia. Too high concentration of oxygen in the incubator damaged the immature retina." I cannot believe all that I already know about blindness. If only I were still ignorant. "What did he say?"

"Nothing."

"How did you find out then? Did someone else tell you?"

"Michael came into my room this afternoon."

"And —"

"He started to cry."

Oh my God, I think. She's fifteen years old and he's still crying.

# ⚓ 4 ⚓

# Hospital City

PAUL TAKES OFF from work the day that Rachel is scheduled to go into the hospital. He has breakfast with us, but when I return from walking Charlotte to school, he is asleep with a pillow wrapped around his head. I squelch the urge to wake him, and go upstairs to my office.

We have no idea when Rachel is to be admitted, only that someone will call sometime today. When that sometime arrives, we will gather the children and our bags and drive to Hospital City, where I will spend the night beside Rachel. Paul will continue on to my parents', where Charlotte will stay the following day.

The phone is silent all morning long, and he never wakens. I am not surprised. Ever since the diagnosis, his sleep has been disrupted. He falls asleep easily enough, but wakes in the middle of the night, has a snack, watches television, or works on the computer. In the morning, I find banana skins and crumbs, knives with peanut butter on them, the down jacket and slippers he wears to keep warm during these late hours when the heat is low, a stack of spectra, graphs of high-energy phosphates obtained from cells by NMR spectroscopy. On workdays, before he leaves the house, he often stretches out on the floor, fully dressed in jacket, gloves, and hat, and catches a ten-minute nap, but whenever he has time off, he spends hours with a pillow wrapped around his head. The fact that he sleeps so much on weekends alarms me. I know that he needs it, and that despite his optimism ("Her life can still be rich!"), he is depressed. One look at him now — eyes closed, ears muffled by foam — confirms that. And yet seeing him this way reminds me that I could lose him. He could die in an accident, become chronically ill, contract a rare disease. Anything can happen, and has.

I am still working on the same chapter that I started to revise the week before we left for Florida. As I look through the pages, so defaced by multicolored scribbles that I can barely decipher them, I feel like Joseph Grand from *The Plague,* who spent a lifetime perfecting a single sentence. It feels ridiculous climbing the stairs and sitting in my office each day when I do nothing more than shift a word here or there, but I am like an old milkcart horse, who only knows one route.

I read several paragraphs, make new pencil marks above one line, flip over the paper, and continue to scribble. When I regain my here and nowness, I find that I am reading an article about sensory stimulation. I have no idea when I went from one to the other, only that here I am with the article on top of my manuscript, and the phone has not rung.

The article is written in non-sexist language. Instead of using he or she or he/she, it says, "your visually impaired child." My visually impaired child may have no sense of body definition. I can aid in teaching this by tying bells around the wrists and ankles of my visually impaired child. This is also a good way for my visually impaired child to learn that she can activate sound, that is, that she can cause things to happen. Without help, she might not understand this simple phenomenon for a long time.

I must have these bells immediately. I race downstairs to tell Paul about the bells and find him still asleep with the pillow wrapped around his head. I push him back and forth as if he were a rolling pin, but he does not rouse. If I leave the house, Rachel could cry for hours, the ringing phone go unanswered, the hospital bed be filled by someone else. Still, I must have the bells. I drag the phone to the bedside and turn the volume to its highest, strap the carrier on my chest, and leave with Rachel.

It is cold outside, and the sky is the color of dishwater. Rachel's body is warm beneath the layers of corduroy; her head is covered with an angora cap that keeps slipping over her eyes. Except for a great deal of traffic going in and out of the supermarket parking lot, the streets are quiet. Stylized Christmas trees have been mounted every few yards, and the green synthetic stuff they are made of shimmers in the wind. The shop windows are white in the corners from artificial frost.

The sewing store does not have bells, and neither does the 5 & 10. The only bells stocked in the children's store are attached to little screwtop cylinders meant to encase a child's shoelaces. The saleswoman asks why I want bells, and I tell her I want to tie them on my baby's ankles and wrists. "Isn't that a clever idea!" she says. Then she crouches low and opens my jacket. "Beautiful!" she says.

Blind, I think.

I understand Megan at last. I have avoided using the word for so long that I feel swollen from keeping it inside. I feel as if I will burst if I continue walking around, passing her off as a sighted baby.

"She doesn't know where her feet are," I say.

"Of course not."

She strokes Rachel's cheek softly with her index finger, a gesture so tender that I lose myself in her admiration, in the fantasy of happy mommy and her happy baby. This carries me until we reach a new store where cleverly packaged and utterly useless things are sold.

I do not want an applause box that claps for you when you open it, a footstool mounted on two large stuffed sneakers, a mug with a feminist message. Bells are what I want, and I find them in the back of the store, with the ribbons and wrapping paper — brass jingle bells with a loop to slip string through. I take a dozen to the counter, and the saleswoman packs them in a Chinese take-out box (also available in ceramic). "Frou-frou?" she asks.

"*Frou-frou?*"

"Fine," she says, as she fills the box with colored excelsior.

I am waiting to cross the street when a large van pulls up beside me. The door slides open and a pregnant woman waves. Two children sleep in car seats in the back; the one in front twists a play steering wheel mounted to his seat.

"You're Charlotte's mother," she says, as she edges out of the van.

She has long dark hair that is pulled away from her face. Her skin is flawless; her lips upturned, her expression strange and beatific. I recognize her after a moment as the mother of Charlotte's classmate Nicholas, who has chewed off the hands of his He-Man doll.

"How's the baby?" she says.

"Fine." Has she heard? Hasn't she? Is it necessary for me to say something to a near stranger?

"There was a reason for her birth," she says.

Ah — so she knows. "We were thinking it was the clams," I tell her.

"Perhaps God brought a special baby into your family because He knew that you could bring her a life of joy."

Her voice is like velvet, her smile saintly. I think of her son chewing off the hands of his doll and go over her words: *God brought us a special baby.* I want to tell her that I don't think there's anything special about being blind, and that God does not exist, but suddenly I am no longer sure.

She says, "There is a reason for everything."

"Thank you," I say.

I run all the way home. The bells clank dully, muffled by the frou-frou; Rachel bounces against my chest. *Oh God, oh God, oh God.*

Paul is on his back in bed. His eyes are open.

"Tell me the truth. I know you don't believe in God, but what about in times of stress, like when you got that chunk of steak caught in your throat, and you couldn't breathe, and you thought you were going to die. Did you think — please, God, don't let me die?"

"If I did, it was only a figure of speech."

"Do you ever believe?"

"It's like saying 'fuck you' to a truck driver who cuts you off. You don't actually mean that you are interested in fucking him, or that you care anything in the slightest about his sex life. You learned somewhere that when you're angry you say 'fuck you,' so that's what you say."

I tell him about Nicholas's mother, with her smooth skin and her Mona Lisa smile, and how she said that there was a reason.

"There is a reason, and it's the amnio, I'm sure of it. They stuck you three times before they got fluid. One of those times they introduced a virus intra-utero, I'll bet you anything."

When five o'clock arrives and there is still no call, I phone the neurologist. His secretary tells me that we should leave right away.

It is pouring outside. Paul and I each grab a child, and race into the car. All day, all that edgy waiting, and only now am I nervous. About what? Paul hates the idea of Rachel getting general anesthesia — he would do anything to prevent it, if it weren't for the fact that she had to have the CT scan. For me, the anesthesia is not the issue, though I know it has its risks. The septo-optic dysplasia does not worry me because I don't fully understand what it is, nor does the possibility of a brain tumor, because I had detected in Dr. Hines's voice how remote the chances were. It is the evoked response test that makes me tremble, when I allow myself to think of it, because it will tell us whether or not any information is getting from Rachel's retina to her visual cortex. She will see, she will never see; and with the brainstem evoked, she can hear, she is deaf.

It is rush hour when we arrive in Hospital City. We pass the eye, cancer, brain, and main departments, and follow the arrows for the tall tan building where rooms have been set aside, like lifeboats on a sinking ship, for women and children. Everyone we pass works in Hospital City. They empty bedpans, measure blood pressure, check reflexes, examine stool samples, prepare meals, polish floors, counsel the families of the dying, teach interns, fix boilers. Your Ailment Means Our Employment.

The rain is still heavy. I leave my family in the car and race into the building. A receptionist beside the entrance asks for my name, and I stumble over my own before I remember to use our family's last name. She tells me that there is no bed upstairs for Rachel or me and that we should come back in a couple of hours. I have waited all day long, and I am incapable of waiting any longer. There will be a room. There will be a room if they have to build one for us. I say nothing to the receptionist.

I run back outside and get into the warm car. The rain has seeped through my shoes and my toes are numb. I say good-bye to Paul, and all that comes with it. Try to get to sleep early, drive safely, see you tomorrow, I love you. Then I climb over the seat to sit in the back beside Charlotte. She will not look up at me. I murmur words of love, and she riffles through a log-shaped bag where she keeps the small doll I bought her when Rachel was born, its clothes and shoes, and all the appurtenances necessary for the contemporary doll. She is so absorbed by the contents of this bag that it is easy for me to believe that this parting, which after all is for only one night, means nothing to her, and so I say, "Have fun at Grandma's."

Her fingers stop moving. She looks up for an instant, then plucks a tiny shoe from her bag and struggles to fit it on the doll's foot. Fun! She has seen me cry, she has stood by while Paul and I tell the same story over and over to our callers. She lives in a house where Rachel's eyes are a family obsession. And now I am leaving her. When I decided to stay with Rachel, it made perfect sense. I could tell Charlotte that I would be back, whereas Rachel would wake alone tomorrow morning if I were not there, and have no way of knowing it would be for just one night. She might wake and cry for hours and reject the rubber nipple because she has had only me. Only now do I realize that just because Charlotte has language doesn't mean that she can understand.

The halls of pediatrics are decorated for Christmas. Glittery balls dangle from the ceiling; a Christmas tree is trimmed with stars made of painted tongue depressors glued at angles and cut-out Santas with cotton-ball buttons and beards. A child screams continually.

It is true that there is no bed for Rachel, but a minute after I arrive a stainless steel crib mounted on tall legs is wheeled into the room where we will sleep. It looks so much like a cage that it hurts me to put her inside. I pull back the curtain that separates her cage from an empty one, then open the nightstand drawer, and the narrow locker, as if this is a motel, and I might find a menu for room service and picture postcards of a turquoise pool out back. There is a large, ugly Naugahyde chair and a window across the room, and when I draw the vertical blinds what I see outside are the tall buildings that make up Hospital City.

Rachel falls asleep, so I take a walk. I find an ice machine and the patients' bathroom. The desks behind the nurses' station are empty, and a little girl, parked in a stainless steel crib, stands and complains. She is loud and so articulate that it seems as if she is saying something very sophisticated in another language, but upon closer listening, it turns out to be gibberish. Her hair is blonde; her two-toothed smile charming. She has no fingers on one of her hands; her feet are clubbed. I round the bend, past a playroom filled with stuffed toys, and a locked schoolroom. Inside the TV room a bald child in too-big pajamas flicks stations via remote control. Charlotte's birth set us outside the childless world of morning sex, late-night parties, friends with *objets d'art* on low tables: Rachel's birth has set us here.

She sleeps on her back with her arms above her head and her legs bowed. I cover her with an extra sheet and unzip my overnight bag to look for something to read. I have plenty with me — *Insights from the Blind, How to Raise a Young Blind Child.* Also there are two autobiographies of blind men who were not musicians and several reprints from journals.

A man walks by, pumping his umbrella. Droplets of water fly into my room. "Boy, is it raining," he says. A nurse enters with a box of diapers and disposable underpads. "It's raining," I tell her.

"April showers bring May flowers," she says.

"In December?"

She lifts Rachel by the ankles and slides an underpad beneath her, and I say: "Those are handy." I'm a little desperate for conversation.

"So take some."

As soon as she leaves, I shove all of the underpads except two into my overnight bag. In order to get the zipper closed, I have to sit on the side of my bag. There I am, knees up to my chin, bouncing on my suitcase, when the pediatric resident arrives to examine Rachel. I pop up to say hello.

The resident's face and the one clipped onto his jacket pocket are quite different. "You shaved," I say, and he touches his chin. He unsnaps Rachel's stretchie, and attempts to get her arms free. He is not adept at this, and her body twists into an odd position. She wakens and scowls. When at last the suit is off, he puts the cold stethoscope against her chest and she begins to wail.

Over her crying, he asks, "When did you first notice that she was, ah, that she couldn't, ah —" He's as bad as I am.

"That she couldn't see? Well —" I am so experienced at telling this story that I no longer need to listen to myself. I tell him that Paul started to be concerned when she was just a month old, and that we called her Suspicious Eyes, and how an entry in my journal convinced me that something was wrong. I tell him a little about the appointment with Dr. Hines that led to the decision to arrange tomorrow's CT scan.

"Who's the neurologist?"

"Dr. Klibansky. We haven't met him yet."

"Klibansky!" Eyebrows raised.

"He's good?" I ask.

"The best, but . . . difficult," the resident says.

He listens to her heart, looks into her eyes and ears, takes her by the fingers so that she'll sit, pulls her higher so that she stands on wobbly legs. It's her eyes, I want to say. Her eyes are the problem. What is he looking for?

"My husband thinks she might be deaf," I say.

He steps to her side and claps his hands sharply, and when she startles, he says: "She can hear."

"And in other ways? Does she seem okay? Dr. Hines said there wouldn't be other complications."

"She *seems* fine; her muscle tone is good. Beyond that I really couldn't say."

Linda calls and asks if I want company. I am too emptied out to know what I want, and so I say, "I'm all right," which I suppose is true.

"Did you eat? I could bring you some food."

I still cannot figure out what I want, so I say that it's an awfully long trip up here, and that the neighborhood is bad. I'm not climbing the walls, screaming, weeping, tearing at my hair. I'm just waiting.

"Are you telling me that you *don't* want visitors, or you do, but you're playing hard to get?"

Or what? Maybe I cannot say yes to what she offers because I don't want to put her out. Maybe it's that being needy embarrasses me. If she comes, I would have nothing newsy or cheerful to say to her. I might sit across the room, mute and emptied out, the way I am now, or I might suddenly break, which also happens these days, one minute fine, the next weeping wildly. If I have failed to carry on many family traditions, there is one thing that has been firmly impressed upon me. Don't complain. *You know what happens if you're a complainer, don't you? After a while, when your friends see you coming, they'll cross the street* — this inheritance from my mother, via her mother.

"Has it occurred to you that I *want* to come, that it makes *me* feel good to help a friend?" Linda says. This twists things enough so that I believe that I will be doing her a favor if I agree.

It is not until she arrives, lugging a large shopping bag, that I realize that I am pleased to see her. I close the pamphlet that I am reading and say: "Blind girls have to be taught to cross their legs when they wear skirts."

"Must I laugh?"

"You don't *have* to."

"Good. Is there someplace we can sit?"

She takes the bag and follows me down the corridor. I babble as we walk, hoping to distract her from the possible horrors. The place seems very benign now. The TV room is empty. Linda pulls a pint of cider from the bag, cheese, apples, a container filled with rice and soybeans, a large square of corn bread. She lines up the food on a broad piece of masking tape that runs diagonally across a glass table, and says: "Eat."

My appetite has always felt like a creature that lives within me, a large, insatiable one that struggles for dominance over my will. It has always been this way. Even as a child I could be delirious with fever, and seeing angels above my head, and still make it down for meals. But the creature is dormant now. The smell of food, which intellectually I know is good, makes my stomach churn. Linda seems not to mind. "You can eat it later," she says.

She reaches into her bag and pulls out an issue of a stylish downtown magazine that is chock-full of interviews with stars. I start to put it aside, and she motions with her chin for me to open it. I spread the magazine across the glass table and turn the pages. All the ads have models with spiky hair in odd colors, shoulders like linebackers, fluorescent anklets.

Halfway through the magazine, I find a full-page photograph of a hot young star named Matt Dillon. His hair is styled in a flattop, lip curled in a half smile. Though his look is tough, nothing he does can disguise the smooth skin and clear eyes, the innocence that overrides his pose.

Eight years ago, when Linda and I were working as talent scouts for a friend of ours, we found this boy in a junior high school in Westchester. We had been wandering through the halls all day, and peering into classrooms in our search for the new James Dean. We had already plucked a dozen kids from their classrooms — each one attractive and lively — pulled them into the hall and fired questions at them (*Who's your best friend? What makes you mad? Have you ever been in a play?*). We were tired and ready to go home, and then the bell rang, and the halls cleared, and *he* sauntered around the bend, tough and pretty all at once, with an edge, an artifice, that all of the others lacked. He was chosen for the lead role and starred in our friend's movie and then in a succession of other ones. His brother became an actor. Another sibling recently expressed interest.

What if Matt had been in class, where he belonged? This is all I can think about whenever I see his picture. What if Linda and I had turned a different corner, or gone home a moment earlier? It was not as if he had a singular talent that sooner or later would have been recognized. It was a look we liked, a pose that we wanted, and that was all.

"Does he mention us?" I ask.

"Read it and see."

I tuck the magazine into the shopping bag. Linda brings me news of mutual friends, of films she has seen and possible jobs, and gossip about Matt's career. I listen and listen and hope that she will never stop.

The bald child, a teenage boy, I realize, returns with a redheaded girl dragging an IV pole. They sit across from us and turn on the TV. The girl flips channels with the remote control while the boy plays around with the color control until the faces are purple and the eyeballs are blue. The redhead takes a cigarette from her pocket that is bent like a chimney pipe and says, "Got a light?"

"Please don't smoke," I say.

My request has nothing to do with my air rights as a non-smoker. It is a mother's plea, and she takes it as such. "You can leave if you don't like it," she says.

Linda puts the food back into the bag and we go into Rachel's room. There is a ledge against the window that is wide enough to sit on sideways. For a while we just look outside. At first what I see is my own reflection, the dark, sad eyes, a mouth so downturned it would be comical had it belonged to someone else. Then I notice how vivid the city is outside, as if the rain has washed away all the grime. The road glistens like patent leather; the cars form a bright ribbon with no obvious beginning or end. We begin to talk, and the sad face goes away, and the city vanishes from view. Now it is just us: two soft voices in the dark room, nostalgic talk that is compelling and painful all at once. She remembers meeting me for the first time, how cheerful and funny I seemed to her; I remember how confident she appeared, and how she rocked forward and slapped her thighs when she laughed.

For years we knew the same people, but not each other. Our mutual friends were always saying, "You two should meet," and so one day we did. She found an apartment for me across the hall from hers, and we began to collaborate almost from the start. Eleven years ago we wrote our first script for a company that made sex education films. Next were two scripts that no one wanted, then a fourth that we wrote for a studio that had financial troubles and could not pay us for a second draft. This work, which we slot between family and paying jobs, is the basis of our friendship, for we rarely see each other unless we are working, and even then find little time to speak about ourselves. Now we are in this cool, dark room transported by our words.

We still talk about men, even though I haven't dated in eight years, and my stories feel threadbare from being retold too often. It is painful discussing the past, for I end up unearthing the part of me that I feel has been buried by all this grief; at the same time I want to hold on to that self. She likes men who are inaccessible and aloof — superstars. The most constant man in her life lives with someone else, two thousand miles away. I like warm, tender men who love me to distraction. She feels as if she has been the architect of her life, and I feel like a leaf, blown here and there by the wind, my life no longer in synch with the way I imagine myself.

The overhead lights are turned on just then, and we are plunged into brightness. Two nurses wheel in a full-sized bed, and place it parallel to the cage. Someone is in it, moaning in a deep voice. It is a man, for God's sake; they are wheeling a dying man into my room.

"Excuse me, I believe this is pediatrics," I tell the nurse who draws the curtains.

"It *is* pediatrics," she says, leaving with the empty cage.

"Ohhhhhhhhhhhh," the man moans.

Linda and I wait. He stops. A second later he begins to retch. It sounds as if he has pebbles in his throat. Rachel begins to cry, so I take her in my arms and leave the room.

We are walking down the corridor in search of an empty room when a huge nurse in a short uniform and knee-high hose accosts us.

"Gimme that baby, that baby ain't been bagged yet," she says.

"*Bagged?*" I see images from the Vietnam War, pieces of G.I.'s returned home in sacks. I see a Hefty bag with a twist tie, and my daughter trapped in darkness inside. "Absolutely not."

"Her urine got to be bagged tonight. Got to be. Just look at that hour, will you?"

It's two A.M. I give Rachel to the nurse and take the elevator downstairs with Linda.

The main entrance is locked. We try the door several times and then stare dumbly at it until a guard appears and gives us complicated directions to the emergency room, which is open at all times.

We go down a flight of steps, and walk from building to building through adjoining basements. The trip, through hallways cluttered with broken plasterboard and spilled nails, seems endless, a joke played on us by a hostile guard. Then we come upon a room filled with the wretched, slumped in molded chairs. The door is open.

The rain has ended, and the air is damp and cold. I wait with Linda for a taxi, and when several minutes pass and none arrives, I walk her to a police car and ask the driver to take her to a safer place.

The cop agrees without hesitation, and I am so surprised I feel as if I have cast a spell. Linda slides into the back seat and waves good-bye. On the long trek back to Women and Children, I think about that small unlikely moment and wish that there were magic for Rachel, too.

When I get upstairs to pediatrics, I hear the scream. It seems like the same cry that I heard when I arrived earlier, and I am amazed that I have blocked out this sound of agony for so many hours. I am walking toward our room when it occurs to me that it is not the same cry; it is a child the same age as the first. Barking dogs sound different, but all crying babies are alike; each newborn exactly like the next, each four-year-old calling "Mommy" in the supermarket a voice like my four-year-old. My breasts tingle, my body tries to tell me something. I race around the bend and the sound gets louder and more pitiful, until at last I stand in front of the crying baby, and she is mine, dressed only in an undershirt.

The nurse stands over her, jamming a catheter between her legs. "She went and took the damn thing out —" she says, roughly lifting her out of the cage.

How newborn Rachel looks, wrinkled and red, her legs so much thinner than her torso. I remember when she lay upon me, newly born, her umbilical cord a deep crimson, still uncut, how red and wet she was. The nurse pushes her into my arms and storms off.

Rachel quiets right away. I walk her back to our room, my hands on her warm bare skin. "Ohhhhhhhhhhh," moans the man when we arrive. I hold her against my chest and she begins to breathe regularly. Her heart beats against mine. Ah, so soft and warm, and I am . . . wet, I realize, when I find that she has peed all over my shirt.

*4:00 A.M.*

It is ridiculous to think about sleeping in the same room as a moaning man, so I have taken my bag and gone into the TV room. Inside it is stale and smoky, and when I lie on the couch, the odor that emanates from the cushions frightens me.

Rachel will probably wake in two hours and Paul will arrive for the CT scan an hour and a half after that. It seems a waste of time to try to sleep. I take out all my books and pamphlets, then suddenly realize that

I cannot bear to think about Rachel's blindness, not now, when I am all alone in a foul-smelling room at an hour which is neither night nor morning.

I find the magazine Linda left with me and turn to the interview with Matt. For all the splashy graphics, the editors of this magazine have not figured out a better way to catch a person's opinions than through the question/answer format, and the interview is very straightforward. *What are you working on now, what's in line next . . . ?* As I read I get the sense that he sees himself the way his fans see him, a star from birth. I can't get out of my mind the fact that one event, beyond his control, totally changed his life. *What was your favorite role, are you seeing anyone special, how did you get your first break . . . ?*

"Well, I was cutting this class one day, I don't know, something really boring, you know, geometry, some kind of crap, and there were these two guys . . ."

Guys!

What are you talking about? Guys! Us. Linda and me. You would be languishing in high school if not for us, you fool. Where is Linda's name in all of this? Where am *I*, for God's sake?

Here! I think, as I draw a little caret, and insert it above the line. And here in the margin . . .

And here, in misery city, having just received word after a two-hour wait that the CT scanner is down. Estimates regarding repair range from ten minutes to a week. The waiting room in this subbasement several blocks from where we slept is filled with the able-bodied. I recognize two people from pediatrics. One is a pretty young woman with a long, elaborately blown hairstyle, whose daughter is so large she barely fits into a stainless steel cage. The mother of the child with the deformed hand and feet sits utterly grim-faced reading *Truly Tasteless Jokes*. The corridor is jammed with bodies that two hours ago were so still they looked dead and now have begun to stir and moan. Near me is a man who upright is probably handsome and dignified. His teeth have been taken out. "A little higher, please," he says with perfect diction to no one in particular. "Thank you; ah, thank you kindly, my dear." He sits up a bit. I imagine him standing, draped in his white sheet, and directing the other bodies to follow; I see a dozen ghosts rise in their flowing gowns to storm the closed doors where technicians and doctors hide.

Paul and I don't know whether we should continue to wait here or take Rachel upstairs for the evoked response tests. The obvious thing is to contact Rachel's neurologist; however, neither of us wants to make the call. We begin to argue so vehemently about who should contact Dr. Klibansky that I wonder if we are the ones who have caused the bodies to stir. It is ridiculous to quarrel when we need each other's comfort, and yet the longer we go at it the more I realize that one of us must talk to this man, and I don't want it to be me. We are string savers, both of us, dragging in everything we possess in order to persuade the other to do the job — who changed Rachel last (I did); who held her until she fell asleep (he did); who slept worse (I did); who missed breakfast (he did); who usually makes calls (I do); who usually deals with doctors (he does); who does the most housecleaning and cooking, who puts the winter clothes in mothballs, who agreed to have a big wedding (me, me, me); who gets Rachel every morning, who drove here at the crack of dawn, who desperately wishes that the other person would for once in her life show some consideration (he, he, he).

We are recalling favors of five years past, visits to obnoxious relatives, presence at holiday services conducted in a foreign tongue, messy changes from Charlotte's infancy, when Paul raises his hands like a referee and says, "All right." Instantly I relax. "Odds or evens?"

"Paul, this is ridiculous," I whisper.

His face brightens. "Odds or evens?"

"You can't do me a *single* favor — one lousy time. I understand that you're hungry and tired. I feel for you. But you didn't have to share a room with a dying man."

"Ready?" he says, shaking his fist.

"All right. Evens."

"Once, twice, three . . ."

He'll show one, he always shows one; no, he'll show two because he usually shows one, and I know that he knows I know it and therefore has to change; no, he usually shows one, and he knows that I know it, and he knows I'll think that this time he'll show two, and so he'll fake me out and show one. I put out two.

Even at times like this I love to win. I am childish about it, and present him with a big fat raspberry. Paul reaches in his back pocket for his handkerchief and blows his nose.

"Two out of three," he says at last.

"Cheat!"

"Shush, sweetheart," says the man without teeth.

"You lost fair and square, so go."

The game is over, all laughter gone. Paul thrusts his jaw forward and gives me a look that is so ugly it is hard to believe he has ever loved me. "It was your idea," I say.

He turns and leaves, and my stomach twists. I work my way down the corridor to wait among the ambulatory. The baby in the cage behind Rachel's whimpers and her mother gets up to cover her. Curled up, she barely fits across the mattress.

"How old is your baby?" I ask.

"Four," says the mother.

She is not a baby. She is a little girl Charlotte's age, with crayons, a Sesame Street coloring book, and Cookie Monster slipper socks. It is the baldness that has confused me again. The mother tells me that she noticed a bump on the child's eyelid one day, what looked like blood vessels. The bump turned out to be a kind of tumor called a neuroblastoma, which had started in her gut and spread. The little girl had chemotherapy and radiation, which made her terribly sick, but seemed to have shrunk the tumors. At her last checkup the doctor found new tumors outside her skull. She wasn't afraid of the hospital in the beginning. "Now she begs me not to take her anymore."

I listen to the mother's soft recitation and wonder when she bought her pink shoes, and how she manages to fix her hair so well. Her little girl raises the arm that's been hooked up to an IV, and moans. I leave the waiting room, but I cannot escape the coloring book, the girl Charlotte's age, the mother's sad smile, the fact that people here are too worn out to weep. The lead pendulum swings in my chest, battering me. Heartache. And I had always thought that it was just another trite expression, meaningless from overuse, a word from an era when the heart was considered the seat of all passions. It is as real as a toothache.

Paul comes hurrying down the hall to keep pace with a small, stooped man with a headful of wiry gray hair and a scowl across his face. The tails of his white jacket fly. What's his rush? I think.

"Dr. Klibansky," says Paul.

I extend my hand, for no reason at all, apparently.

"Where is she?" he asks, eyes above my head.

"No one knows what's happening with the machines, so we're going to take her upstairs for the evoked response tests," Paul says.

Dr. Klibansky hurries past me to Rachel, who is lying on her back in a T-shirt stamped with the hospital name. Without a word he takes her hands and pulls her to sitting, taps her knees with a little hammer, tickles her soles — a playful man, one might think — the whole time asking us the questions that we have gotten so good at answering. Paul and I narrate The Story in two-part harmony, expecting the same kind of reception we get when we tell our favorite tales at dinner parties. Dr. Klibansky stops us and pushes hard for specifics I can no longer recall. It is not good enough to say that Paul started to worry about her in the fall.

"When in the fall? The fall is a long time," he asks. "September? October? November?"

"What do you mean, her eyes went to the side — both of them? Only one? Did they stay to the side? Which side — was it only one side?"

"She sleeps a lot? What's a lot? Sixteen hours a day? Twenty?"

I am failing; I cannot remember a thing. Sweat trickles down my sides.

Klibansky produces a tape measure, which he wraps around Rachel's head, and then around her chest, and then from head to toes, as if he plans to quarter her.

"What caused her problems?" I ask.

I can feel the heat of Paul's body as he works his way between me and Klibansky. He says, "Dr. Hines told us it was unknown."

I ask a second time, and as I do I understand just then that unknown is not enough and that I will continue to ask until I find an answer.

"Accident in development. Virus. No one knows for sure."

"How many children do you see with optic nerve hypoplasia?"

"Two or three a year, maybe fewer."

"And it appears alone — I mean, assuming the CT scan rules out the tumor and the — uh — septo-optic dysplasia, will the visual problem be all?"

He places one hand on Rachel's chest and whirls to face me. What makes him so angry? "Who told you that?"

"I don't know. I thought that's what Dr. Hines said."

"A whole host of things can show up. What we see most often are seizure disorders and intellectual deficits —"

Intellectual deficits? Exactly what does that mean?

"Can you give me numbers?" I ask. "I'm not holding you to anything, I just want to know what you mean by *most* often."

Is he annoyed because I have asked? He turns from Rachel, and glares at me, his forehead corrugated. "This is an exceedingly rare condition we're talking about and samples are collected randomly. Children without related problems tend not to show up. Of those that we have records on, we see a significant number with seizure disorders and various intellectual deficits. Your daughter looks fine, but that's no guarantee that problems won't appear at a later time."

I am watching his coattails fly when I remember the rest of my questions. What is a significant number? Twenty percent? Ninety? I want to weigh the odds, to have a sense of what her chances are. Intellectual deficits — is that a euphemism for retardation or is it something else? Seizures, as in epileptic seizures? He is gone, and there is no one to ask.

# ❧ 5 ❧

# God

RACHEL IS BEING WIRED UP when I begin to think about God. She lies in a deep, sedated sleep while the technician attaches the electrodes to her face and scalp. He is young and gentle and looks like a rock star, with his droopy mustache and shoulder-length hair. He hums a lullaby as he covers the electrodes with collodion and gauze and dries them with an air hose. The collodion has the seductive-dangerous smell of airplane glue. While I stand over Rachel, Paul studies the machines that surround the examining tables. He touches dials and meters and asks questions non-stop. I cannot take my eyes off my daughter, wires flowing from her scalp, beneath her eyes, attached to her earlobes. Baby Medusa sleeping soundly, knowing nothing.

Two tests are to be taken: the visual evoked response to test her vision, the brainstem evoked response to test her hearing. Each sensory system will be activated when the test is conducted, and we will know the absolutes: She may see, she will never see; she may hear, she will never hear.

The technician puts on headphones and adjusts several dials. Paul goes on looking and poking and asking questions as if all this is merely of intellectual interest, until the technician puts a finger to his lips.

He does the test for her vision first. A strobe light flashes rhythmically on Rachel's face — *click, click, click.* The recording is scratched onto paper with long sensors. She sleeps, her head and face covered with wires, her bare body utterly perfect, and I imagine once again that this is a frightening experience that will end well, and hear myself relaying the details months later. "You can't imagine how frightened we were."

Already the technician knows something, but he is not permitted to interpret the results that are being etched onto the paper. The strobe clicks away. He will not say anything to us, but what of his face? Will we be able to read what he cannot hide? Your child will never see. Your child will be locked in darkness. "If she is blind and deaf, we'll put her out of it," Paul had said a second time. "I'll do it myself, I swear." I look at her under all those wires, and she is so pretty. Her small chest heaves, her toenails are like the polished slivers of shells that wash up on the beach. *Please, God. I know I haven't believed before . . .*

Paul takes me aside and says: "You can go."

"And leave you?"

"I'm all right. Listen. I could really use a coffee. Cow's milk, no sugar."

"You still love me?"

"Of course I do." He kisses my forehead, as if to confer a blessing.

"Linda brought food."

"Great. Bring that, too. We should eat, I guess."

He looks at his watch. It is two o'clock and he has not had anything yet. He puts his arms around me and tries to steady the quaking.

"You're sure you're all right?" I ask.

"Sure. Get me the coffee, and I'll meet you here later."

This building is several blocks away from the one where Rachel and I spent the night, connected by a basement passageway. I'm afraid that I will get lost if I try to find it, so I go outside instead, where there are signs to guide me.

The sky is too bright; the crisp air makes my throat ache. Jackhammers break up concrete, horns blare. The sun feels like daggers in my eyes. I work my way through the crowds like a swimmer through strong currents. Everyone is talking and laughing. Strangers pass, showing their teeth. Isn't it enough for her to be blind? Does she have to be deaf and retarded, too?

By the time I reach Women and Children, I have begun to barter. All right, she's blind; I accept that. Suppose she were to come out of this with her hearing intact and her intelligence normal, what would I be willing to trade? Would I give up an arm, a leg, my work? It is essential that I be honest about this, to be prepared in case a bolt of light cuts through the lobby and a voice says, "Her hearing will be fine, start saving for her higher education."

*Okay, I'll give up my work.*

I see myself burning my notebooks and scripts, turning my office into a family room. The image is so clear it feels like prescience. (I am walking slowly down a street . . .) No one else knows or cares that I have stopped sitting upstairs and weaving tales, a job that so often has seemed purposeless and infantile. (Why am I so breathless and logy?) I have time to make a decent home, to patch the leaks and pretty up the rooms, and make my family meals from scratch. I see myself waking with a dream still drifting through my head, placing my feet firmly against the floor so that the dream evaporates, as dreams so easily do. Before me is a day like those before and after this one. And what of the moments that manage to rise through the chaos and fill me with their poignancy? If I could speak what I felt, I would not need to write, but words get caught in my throat; words do nothing to soften the knot of love or fear that sits within me. I know what would happen. I would walk around with that knot; soon I would learn not to recognize those poignant moments, for there would be nothing I could do with them.

All this may be true, but it still hurts me to know that I cannot make this sacrifice for my own daughter, that in this hypothetical situation what I have chosen has been my own well-being over hers. What *would* I do? I can tithe a tenth of my time to the needy; I can promise never again to lie or steal. Not that I routinely do either . . . I cannot think of a lie I have told, though I know in a gut way that I can be untruthful; nor have I ever stolen, even in my adolescence when doing the "five-fingered lift" was as popular as the twist. What kept me home while my pals pocketed bangles and padded bras was not a higher moral sense: It was simply cowardice.

The guard sees the sticker on my sweater and lets me inside. I crowd onto the elevator, filled with resolutions I know that I can keep.

As soon as I get to pediatrics, I can hear the crying. I hurry around the bend in order to get Rachel. My body is so heavy it takes forever for me to reach our room and to realize that the crying child is not my own.

The dying man that shared my room sits in the bed near the window. He is sixteen or seventeen, with dark eyes and curly hair, and a face so finely sculpted he looks like a beautiful Greek boy whose marble body has turned to flesh. He has a boy's self-deprecating manner when he averts his eyes and says: "I'm sorry about last night. I guess the general gave me the pukes."

"Oh, hey . . ."

Handsome boys make me as uncomfortable as they did when I was fourteen. Then I blushed and stammered as if my wishes showed. Now I am reminded that I am not twenty-five, as I am in my own imagination, but ten years past; a mother of two kids, way out of the competition.

I take my suitcase from the locker beside the empty crib, and pull out the underpads that I had swiped the night before. I am not destitute; I will not starve or die without these. Yesterday's underpants fly out, and then a wad of tissues, also swiped, which present me with a curious dilemma, since they are of no use to anyone now. My neighbor watches with unabashed interest. I grab the panties, make a neat pile of the underpads, smooth out the tissues, and leave. He is still watching when I dash back a few minutes later for Linda's food.

An orderly is wheeling Rachel out the door when I return, a half hour later. Her hair sticks up in gummy tufts, and her skin is mottled from tape marks and flecks of glue. She sleeps soundly because of the sedative — or because what she does most often is sleep.

"The CT scanner is working. Klibansky wanted us to get right over," Paul says.

"Did the technician say anything?"

"There wasn't time for the brainstem. We'll have to reschedule."

The brainstem is the hearing. I don't know whether I am relieved or disappointed.

The elevator doors open, and we barely fit in. The orderly is whistling through his teeth.

"And the other?" I ask.

"He couldn't say — you know that."

"His expression, could you tell anything from that?"

"Not a thing." He cranes his neck to catch a glimpse of the paper bag in my hand. "Is that my coffee?"

We are walking at a fast clip through the subbasements of each building, but this doesn't stop Paul. He pulls his Swiss Army knife from a back pocket, takes the bag from me, extracts the coffee, and without breaking stride, punches a small triangle in the plastic lid. Then he asks me if there's milk in it.

"Do you know how many years we've been married?" I ask.

"Yes. Is there milk in my coffee?"

"Don't you think after all the cups of coffee I've fetched for you that I know how you take it?"

The orderly winks at me.

"You still haven't answered my question," Paul says.

"There's milk, there's milk."

He takes a sip. "And you asked specifically for *cow's* milk?"

"I asked for cow's milk."

We wend our way through the bodies stretched out in the corridor, straight into the back area, where Dr. Klibansky introduces us to an Indian anesthesiologist in a shower cap and scrubs, a bag of clear glucose in one hand. The anesthesiologist describes what will be used on Rachel, and how long she will be asleep. I have no idea what he is talking about; nonetheless, I nod when he recites the names of these drugs.

Paul says: "Take care of her, please."

"Of course," says the anesthesiologist, with a slow nod.

Dr. Klibansky starts away.

"Is it okay that I nursed her an hour ago?" I say, just to say something.

Chaos. Everyone is furious. The anesthesiologist gestures in my face with the bag of glucose and curses at me in Hindi. Klibansky tears back over, coattails flying, and starts by saying, "I told *you* not to feed her," and does not stop.

"No one said a thing," I tell him.

"You should have known . . ."

I should have known, but why didn't someone tell me?

"We have to inject iodine into her veins," he says. "If she doesn't quiet, we'll have to repeat the procedure."

"He didn't tell me not to feed her, did he?" I ask Paul after she has been taken from us.

"Forget it."

We sit in the waiting room and listen to her rattling scream. It no longer matters whether anyone told me not to feed her. I listen to her scream, and when she stops, I listen to the silence. Paul hands me a tissue and I blow my nose.

"Let's eat," he says.

I look at him, and he looks at me, and I recognize my own fatigue in his face. On the table between us is a breast self-examination pamphlet. Concentric rings are drawn through the breasts so that they look like targets. Arrows aim at them. Below it is a pamphlet entitled *Frank Talk about Testicular Cancer,* which I toss to Paul. We read it together and laugh and then cannot stop. The laughter is involuntary, like a hiccough, and like a hiccough it becomes unpleasant, and makes my back ache. Across from us are two old women in black coats and velvet hats and space shoes, and I start to worry that they see us laughing about testicular cancer, and that one of their spouses is here with the same disorder. The woman on the left knits a long scarf; the other one is a classicist and twists a handkerchief. Next to them a young woman scrutinizes her blemishes in a lemon-shaped mirror. The pretty mother of the girl with neuroblastoma sits with her hands limply on her lap.

Paul puts an ashtray on the floor and takes Linda's food from the bag. He splits the cheese and corn bread in half and hands me a spoon for the rice and beans.

"You first," I say.

Paul says: "You are the firehouse, and I am the engine. Open up, here I come . . . wah-uh-wah-uh-wah —"

A chunk of corn bread lands on my tongue. Its gritty texture registers, but the taste is lost to me.

"Don't laugh at me, Paul. I made a promise that I would be good if Rachel is okay."

"Aren't you good already?"

"Really good. Decent, moral, honest. I'm not going to ask you to bring things home from work for me."

"What do I bring home — pencils?"

"I'll buy my own pencils. I don't want to steal anymore. I want to live a decent life."

The girl looks up from her lemon mirror and fixes her eyes on me. When I went to high school there were rah-rahs, boppers, and creeps. She would have been a bopper with her bouffant black hair, the dark rings drawn around her eyes, the leather jeans.

"I'll bring them home without your asking," he says.

"Don't."

"*I* didn't make the promise."

"You made some kind of promise, didn't you. Please tell me what it is."

"I promised not to complain about my reading."

A promise that touches me deeply since he is dyslexic and reads with such strain.

"To God?" I whisper.

"To myself."

We finish all the food. Paul balls up the foil and tosses it into a metal wastebasket across the room. He tries again with the waxed paper from the cheese, but it's a wild shot, and bounces off the knitter's left knee. The woman flips up the end of her coat and checks for damage. "Excuse me," says Paul. This gives me the giggles, so I go outside. Paul follows.

More bodies have been wheeled out and the corridors are jammed. Paul and I are speculating on the relationship of the old women in space shoes — sisters? friends? lovers? mother and daughter? — when Klibansky flies toward us. My bones start to rattle. I am like Pavlov's dog: At the sight of this man I start trembling.

"She's quiet now," he says. "The warm lights sometimes do that."

"She was already sedated," I say.

Paul starts to ask a question about the CT scan. Klibansky cuts him off and says, "The results of the VER came down, and they were fine."

The VER, visual evoked response, was fine. *Presence of vision.*

Paul throws his arms around me and begins to weep. His hair is like silk and his neck is hot. He holds me so tightly I am afraid that my ribs will crack. I don't know why I needed him to cry so badly, why I let the jokes and hearty laughter fool me into believing that he did not care about Rachel. He does care. Now that he is in my arms I feel as if we can shelter each other, that we will make it through even this.

He is still weeping when Klibansky says, "That doesn't mean she's going to see."

His harshness stuns me. "He knows," I snap.

Klibansky hurries off. Paul and I walk back to the waiting room. Our seats are still empty. Paul dips into one and sits with his palms over his face. "Never" has been taken away and we are cast back into the realm of "maybe." Rachel may see light and shadow, perhaps more. She may also have seizures and intellectual deficits.

The companion of the knitter clears her throat for such a long time that I look up at last and see her pointing to Paul. "Go into the office, they'll give him an aspirin," she whispers.

"Aspirin won't cure this headache," I say.

Years of indoctrination have had their effect on me. Even now, exhausted, my ribs sore, I remember my manners. "But thank you," I add. "I appreciate your suggestion. You're very kind."

*   *   *

My father pours me an inch of Scotch, brings Paul a beer, and then sits beside my mother on a green love seat and listens.

"More grief per cubic inch than anywhere on earth," Paul says.

"People were sick," I say. "And I'm not talking tonsillitis and nose jobs. I'm talking big sick like cancer and kidney failure and major deformities."

The Scotch stings my sinuses. I have always been led to believe that Scotch — like abstract expressionism, escargots, and atonal music — is something that only mature, sophisticated people can appreciate, but I am mature and sophisticated and I hate the taste of anything brown and alcoholic. What I appreciate tonight is its quick giddying effect.

"So then they put her in this little stainless steel crib —" Paul is saying.

"The cage —" I add. "No one told me not to nurse her. They nearly killed her, I swear they did. And Klibansky, what a mean motherfucker."

My mother arches an eyebrow, a technique she spent hours perfecting when she was young. My father stands, links his fingers, and cracks all his knuckles. "You must be bushed," he says.

I remain for a while longer on a wing chair that was once so big for me I sat cross-legged in it and pretended it was my throne. Now it is just a chair. Paul beckons to me and I follow into what was once my room. The two beds are still there, separated by a night table. Charlotte sleeps in the one that had been my sister's. She is sprawled on her back among the rumpled sheets, an arm flung over her head, her nightgown hiked up to her waist, a long bare leg draped over the bed. She looks like a model for Kiddie Porn. Paul puts his arm around me, and together we stand and watch her sleep. I am filled with love and regret, for I know what it is like to be lost in someone else's tragedy. She is the whole child, as I was the living one, and I have broken my promises and forgotten her.

# ❧ PART II ❦

# ⚮ 6 ⚮

# Sometimes You Just Go Crazy

*What next?*

YOU PHONE your closest friends and relay the news that your daughter does not have a tumor or septo-optic dysplasia, and that the evoked response test suggested that she might have vision. You are careful not to spread the misconception that she will see, because by now you have learned that vision can mean light and shadow and nothing more. Nonetheless, they congratulate you as if you were a gold-medalist, and you understand that despite your cautions, they are imagining a world of faces and flowers and birds for your child.

You take it all in, and love them for their concern, just as you love being the messenger of good news. But you cannot free yourself of the neurologist's words about the high incidence of seizures and intellectual deficiencies among children with your daughter's disorder. Your husband does not want to hear these words — he will not allow himself to worry about unknowns. You do not want to worry either, but the words are as tenacious as her blindness, with you every moment, so that although you can be distracted by the mundane and the amusing, you always come back to them.

And yet you want so badly to be done with the grieving, to have back in your life all the ordinary, unspectacular moments that your family had before the diagnosis. You want to enjoy a snowstorm, a bath with your older daughter, a walk downtown to have bagels for breakfast, a day where nothing much happens, but with such tranquillity and good spirit. It occurs to you that these things have not vanished; they are a part of everyday life, and when you are in good spirits they are life's pleasures, and when you are not they are its burdens, and the only thing that holds you back from happiness are the words. You decide that although you cannot make the words go away, you will grab on to these moments, stay with them, wring pleasure from them.

You get into bed after the tests and say these things to your husband. You say, "We are going to hold tight through all this," because this is what he said to you the day after the diagnosis.

*We are going to turn toward each other the way we always have in the past.*

You try to tell him how much it meant being able to comfort him when he cried, how close you felt to him just then.

*Kisses, yes? Give me a kiss.*

*I love you . . .*

*I love you, too . . .*

"There's no reason that her life can't be full," Paul says. "She can't work in a lab, but she could be a theoretician, a historian, a lawyer, a teacher —"

*And if she's retarded?* Don't say it; don't start now.

"— a classics professor, a cultural anthropologist, a mathematician, a speech writer."

"She could be a musician," I say apologetically.

He laughs and says, "Well . . . she could."

"I bought those Suzuki tapes. 'Twinkle, Twinkle, Little Star.' 'Mary Had a Little Lamb.' The theory is that if she osmoses these simple tunes now, her musical gift will be developed early. I can't imagine any kid of ours having a musical gift, but you never know, she could grow up and be —"

"Come snuggle up," he says. "We have to start getting into bed earlier."

"You're the one who's out almost every night."

"Let's not waste time talking about who did what when. *Tonight* is a start, okay? Let's get into bed earlier starting tonight. Do you have something to read?"

Nine years ago, on a small Caribbean island, Paul flipped over the handlebars of a borrowed bike. He was cut and bruised, and could do no more than rest in bed. I lay beside him in the cool stucco room that was ours for the week and read *Farewell, My Lovely* aloud. In the years since, I have read him books, journal reprints, newspaper articles, and mysteries — the two of us a perfect match, a ham with a strong voice, and a dyslexic with superb aural skills. And now I say, "Oh, wait, I just got this in the mail —" and lean over to find on my night table shelf, " 'Imagery in the Congenitally Blind: How Visual Are Visual Images?' Ginger gave it to me."

"Don't you have a mystery?"

"It's only thirteen pages, and there are a whole bunch of graphs, so it's only about ten pages of actual text, nine and a half maybe."

"Let's save it and start a mystery," he says. "I need to escape."

"It's got a great first sentence; I don't think it'll be hard going at all. Listen — 'Congenitally blind persons possess a wealth of knowledge about the visual world.' Interesting, huh?"

He turns from me, and reaches for the light.

"A mystery, okay. Give me a second and I'll get one."

I go upstairs, where there is a stack of books my mother gave me, and pick one at random. When I get into bed, I turn the book over and read him the blurb on the back cover, and the rave reviews reprinted from obscure newspapers. Then I open the book and wait for him to read the chapter heading because that's the way we always do it. He reaches out a hand and snares his glasses, and when he puts them on, he reads, "Book One."

Then it is my turn. I am a page into the book itself when his breathing starts to thicken. I ask if he is falling asleep, and he denies it. I read on. He is warm and still. His eyes are closed. When I get to the third page, I give the characters fanciful new names and insert the last stanza of "Invictus" into a dense piece of exposition about mercenaries in Angola. He never budges. I reach for the article on imagery in the blind and read it until I get sleepy. Then I switch off the light and curl up beside him.

*And so you hold together and give comfort to each other?*

Sometimes you do . . .

### Christmas Season

Everyone we know seems to be having a party this year. We go to a grog party, a dinner party, a Chanukah party, a celebration in honor of a new Ph.D., where some of the guests cannot bring themselves to talk to us, and others rush over to tell us how well we look. What discomfort our presence arouses among those we know! We are no longer two people who have come to a gathering with our interests and opinions ready for whoever wants them. We are The Parents of a Blind Child, and the guests who stand beside us at the banquet table, or sit on the adjoining cushion of a living-room couch, vibrate with unspoken questions. I have been on the other side and, confronted with someone else's hardship, wondered: Should I say something, is it better to avoid the subject altogether? Is it insensitive to speak of other things, or would it be a relief? In truth, it's a no-win situation, for when nothing at all is mentioned, the unspoken words overpower all that is said, and Rachel's blindness clouds the air around us, and when we are asked to relay our tale, which we tell so dispassionately, and so well, and I watch the curious edge toward us, I feel as if we have become our story and nothing more.

Paul and I have always been a gregarious couple, good minglers in noisy rooms, but at these parties we hold hands, and sit together in a quiet corner, something we have not done since the very early days, when a minute apart was agony. We eat hors d'oeuvres and laugh at jokes and try hard to shift the talk to other things. By the end of the evening, there is always someone who says, "I can't believe you two. You're doing so *well.*"

We are, aren't we?

He steals kisses like a new lover, and searches for my hand when we stand side by side. At night he sleeps wrapped around me. He calls from work each day and when there's nothing left to tell, he says he loves me. He comes home from work so that I can run, even when it means that he must drive back later in the evening. This is who he is, a man who takes my work and my pleasures seriously.

I meet him at the door in my yellow running suit, kiss his cheek, and start out. He stops me to ask: "Did you nurse the baby? Did you pump extra milk? Where's your vest?" I am amused by his concern and assure him that Rachel has been fed, that there is a bottle of mother's milk in the fridge, and six more in the freezer. Then I slip on my reflective vest and take off.

I run down winding suburban streets, beside a long narrow lake in a county park, through a golf course. The night is clear and crisp, and I feel like a thoroughbred as I take the hills. Running gives me dream time. When I am out on these streets my mind fully clears of all the domestic have-tos that clutter it day and night. Even now that I have lost the capacity to dream of anything except Rachel's future, it is still a relief to be out on a cold starry night like this one, and I return home filled with a sense of well-being.

As soon as I open the door, I hear Rachel's rattling scream. Paul is sitting in the dining room eating a sandwich and reading the newspaper, and Rachel is upstairs in her room. He has put her in her crib and left her to scream; she lies in the darkness, flushed and wet from tears.

She starts to comfort when I pick her up, but her chest still heaves against mine, and she cannot catch her breath. I carry her downstairs and stand beside Paul. He flips the page of the newspaper without looking up.

"Why did you put her upstairs?" I ask.

"She was crying." The pages snap as he turns them.

"You never left Charlotte screaming in her crib."

Never, not one time, and she was a long-distance type, who could carry on for hours. I remember him pacing through our small apartment with Charlotte yowling over his shoulder, or wearing her against his chest, and all the nights when he tucked her into bed between us. Even when we realized that holding her did no good, and that it was just as well to let her cry it out alone, he could never bear to leave her. And here he sits, blithely eating a peanut butter sandwich and perusing the news.

"I don't understand," I say.

"There's nothing to understand. She was crying, and I put her in her crib."

"For so long? She was soaked with sweat."

*Don't you care about her?* I do not say these last words aloud, for just then I see in the set of his jaw that he is barely repressing a deep and dangerous rage. About what? What did Rachel do other than cry, which is something all babies do? He was fine when he came home, sweetly concerned, or so I thought. What happened between then and now?

My deepest need is to ask these questions, to clear the air immediately, right this second, because I cannot live like this, it is absolute torture. But I have been married to Paul long enough to know that when he is in a state like this he has no words or reasons, only rage. I cannot mediate these moods, for he has confessed during tender times that when these black spells come upon him, he cannot bear to have anyone close. To probe now is to pick a fight that will not be resolved, and so I think: Okay, he let her cry, big deal. Generations of babies were left to cry — you were left to cry, and somehow survived. Wait until he has cooled off. He will tell you why he was upset, and life will go on.

He gets up from the table, sweeping a toy from his path with the side of his foot, and climbs the stairs alone. The bedroom door slams shut, then opens a moment later. My shoes fly out. I leave him undisturbed in the alcove off our bedroom, his office since Rachel's birth, to scrutinize a column of numbers on the computer screen.

I read Charlotte her bedtime story alone. Little Sal and her mother. Blueberries dropped into the little tin pail, kuplink, kuplank, kuplunk. Little Bear and his mother, munch, munch, gulp. Paul's stormy eyes, his clenched lips, his body, turned away from us and hunched over the screen, the seesawing inside me: Leave him alone, demand he explain; leave him, demand, leave him, demand.

He climbs into bed while I am brushing my teeth and is asleep by the time I am beside him. Sometime during the night, he rises and wanders through the house, leaving a trail of crumbs and flatwear and paper clips, his jacket and down booties on the couch where he finally collapsed.

He goes to work the next morning, dons a white coat, greets his colleagues, works in the lab. I stay home, convinced that I will work. Instead I worry about Rachel when she is awake and read about blindness when she naps. The morning passes, and Paul does not phone.

His daughter is blind and he's upset, I think. Just because he does not announce that he is hurting does not mean that he is well. Why should his laughter at parties fool me? Don't *I* laugh at parties, too? Why should I assume that because he tells The Story so well, he can as easily say what he feels? The Story is a set piece that we can recite while thinking of what we might cook for dinner.

His daughter is blind, and he does not love her, this most affectionate father, most contemporary man, who wiped my brow during labor, massaged my crampy calves, held his slick newborn in his arms moments after her birth.

He does not love her.

I, who held her in my arms, nursed her, cared for her, took such pleasure in her soft sweet babyness, could not understand why he showed so little interest in his lovely child.

Now when I think back the signs that in my serene oblivion I could not see are very clear. The baby did not look at him. He waited for her to meet his eye, and when she wouldn't he flew her at arm's length, positioning her at just the right angle so that her eyes would be on him.

He played this game obsessively without ever knowing how much he needed her to look at him.

I scramble through my stack of papers and find the ones that seem crucial now.

Here's one. Eye contact is the most primitive signal system between parent and baby. And this: Parents of normal infants reported that their first feelings of love toward their babies came about when the babies met their gaze and smiled. (And hadn't I written exactly that about Charlotte? ". . . she looks up at me with those big blue eyes, and gives me a gummy, body-wiggling grin, and I love her so . . .")

If the baby is blind, this communication is lost. Blind children do not look up at their parents or smile readily, and the parents often feel unloved and unrecognized and play less with them. The babies, cuddled less, become more passive and seem so self-sufficient that they are left alone for longer periods of time. They live in a sensory void and risk suffering from severe emotional problems. "In our consultation work we see blind babies who have spent much of the first year in a sensory desert — babies who have worn a groove in their crib mattress, babies who make no sounds, who rarely smile and who spend most of their twenty-four-hour day in sleep." ("An Educational Program for Blind Infants.")

Oh poor darlings, I want it to be right for both of them. If only he knew how much I loved him, how hard I'll work to make things better.

I phone him at work and his voice is clipped and distant. Before I can say anything kind, he tells me that he cannot talk, and that he'll be home in time for me to run.

I am filled with hope and reassurances, ready to throw my arms around him when he returns home. As soon as I hear his key in the lock, I rush with Charlotte to the door. Paul passes us without a word and goes upstairs. Though I feel too weak to run, I dress quickly and hurry from the house.

My bones ache, my body feels heavy. Miles pass and I cannot seem to stretch out. Then halfway through the run, I start to forget.

Rachel is screaming when I return, great rattling cries that fill the house. Charlotte is in her room with her hands over her ears, while Paul drinks a glass of milk. I carry Rachel downstairs and stand before him. I do not care what he suffers, not at all. Even the memory of my compassion for him has vanished.

"She's your daughter. How could you do this to her?"

He takes his dishes and pushes past me to the kitchen, and I follow him, whatever kindness I have felt gone, whatever caution I might have shown buried beneath my own fury.

"Look at her!" I say, holding her toward him, for she is still breathless in my arms.

"Don't leave her with me," he says. The plate and glass tremble in his hands.

*He* goes off to work each day, closing the front door and leaving us behind. I work at home, and share my room with Rachel. She is with me all day long, in my mind every minute. I have no work anymore except to think of her. Suddenly the weight of all the days since her birth, and all the days in the future, is too much for me to bear. "How can you tell me not to leave her with you? How can you say it?"

"How? Like this —" as he hurls the glass against the wall. "DON'T LEAVE HER WITH ME. Do you understand? Don't do it."

"*You* clean it up, *you* do it, you!" I cradle the baby's head in the palm of my hand and race up the stairs. Oh, how I hate him, always have, always will. Selfish, childish — take your tantrums somewhere else, the thought of you makes me sick.

I put Rachel to sleep and lock myself in my own room. I do not venture downstairs until nearly midnight. Paul is sound asleep.

You are her father, I think, as I watch him. Her care rests with you, too. There is no one else, no trusted caregiver, no time, except when I run, when I am without her.

Although I rarely run three days in a row, the next evening, as soon as he comes home, I edge past him, out of the house, and through the streets. All the houses are so beautiful, wreaths on their doors, windows lit with single candles, Christmas trees glittering behind sheer curtains. Happy homes, everyone is happy. My throat gets scratchy; my chest aches.

It is impossible to cry and run at the same time. Crying tightens your chest and makes your breathing jagged, and because you cannot run in this state, you have no choice except to give over to the grief or let it go. Since for me, the habit of running is stronger, my body automatically takes over.

The farther from home I get, the more the anger dissipates. He tries to be cheerful and to forget, but he is hurting just as I am. My hurt comes out in tears and his in rage against me, against Charlotte and Rachel, and inanimate things that get in his path, shoes, toys, dishes, socks. He is the victim of his rage, completely out of control. How can I be angry with him?

And then, when I approach my own front door: How can he be so awful to me when I am hurting, too, miserable, selfish man, who rocks the household with his moods, why do I live out my days with him?

Just as I walk up the front steps I hear the scream. I burst in to find Charlotte and Paul rolling on the floor. He is tickling her, which she loves more than anything, and her screams are from joy. I go upstairs to take a shower and when I come down they are lying in each other's arms.

"I'm sorry about yesterday," he says when the children are asleep. "I have to put Rachel in the crib when she cries like that. If you don't want me to put her upstairs, then you can't ask me to stay with her. Please understand."

"Don't you love her at all?"

"Of course I love her, she's my daughter. But it seems as if the second you step out of the house, she starts in and doesn't stop, and I can't take it. I just can't take it. Now can we talk about something else? Or read? Why don't we get into bed early so we can read."

We pick up the book we started a few nights before. It does not engage me, and I get drowsy after a chapter and am ready to stop. He begs me to go on. If I read one more page, he will give me the good pillow; if I read six more he will get up when Rachel cries; for twelve pages he will get Charlotte dressed in the morning. It is a game we have been playing ever since I started reading to him aloud.

I refuse to read a single page more, and end up reading twenty. I switch off the light and Paul tells me that he loves me, and that his life would be nothing if I left him. He falls asleep with his arms around me, belly to my back.

The day that Dr. Klibansky's letter arrives, my own craziness is set in motion. It starts off with the results of the visual evoked response test ("intact bilaterally") and a reminder that these intact responses in no way guarantee useful vision. Then come the results of the CT scanning of her head ("normal except for a cavum septum pellucidi, or septum cyst, a common anomaly that does not advance a diagnosis of septo-optic dysplasia.")

The details of the neurologic examination are reported next — head size normal, limb activity, tone, and reflexes all normal, head control when lifted from supine excellent, cranial nerves intact except for the optic nerve. In short, she would be perfect if she were not blind.

It is the final paragraph that I cannot stop rereading, the one in which he says to Dr. Hines (for the letter is addressed to him and a copy sent to me) that he felt compelled to remind the parents of the significant association of intellectual deficiency and seizure disorders with optic nerve hypoplasia. "Nonetheless, the studies done were normal, and the exam was normal, leaving room for some optimism."

I put this letter into a file I call "Rachel" that is already three inches thick, and several times during the day I retrieve it. Each time I study the letter I come back to the same sentences. "I felt compelled to remind the parents of the significant association of intellectual deficiency and seizure disorders with optic nerve hypoplasia. Nonetheless, the studies done were normal, and the exam was normal, leaving room for some optimism."

What is a significant association? Twenty percent of the children? Ninety percent? Why *some* optimism? *Some.* My friend Hinda, a speech therapist who has read many physicians' reports, assures me that it was dictated to a secretary (as Hines's letter had been) and that he undoubtedly had neither the time nor inclination to scrutinize each word the way I do. My mother tells me that I am looking for trouble. Paul scans the letter once, picks out "no abnormalities" in the first paragraph, "no deficits" in the second, and the two "normals" in the third.

"He said she looked fine," he tells me.

I remember these words, and also the ones that followed. "That's no guarantee."

Instead of playing with her, I test her, waving toys around, making them squeak or rattle, calling her name from across the room. She does not move or play or cry — she does little besides sleep. I know that it is crazy to expect much more from a baby that is only fourteen weeks old; I also know that blind babies are passive, because I have read more about blindness than I ever wished to know. And yet to see her like this . . . She seems not just passive, but . . . retarded. She's retarded. My daughter is retarded. I can't have a retarded daughter. How can anyone raise a retarded child, a retard — scorned and lonely? How can you raise a child who has no future — no work, no love, no friends, no place on earth?

I sit at my desk to work and end up reading the *Merck Manual.* I study the section on managing chronic disability in children, and the ones on developmental problems and learning disorder. I go over the text under the subheading "Mental Retardation," and one on chromosomal abnormalities — all things that I have read many times before. I find no word that will either confirm or allay my fears. I am reviewing the material on Dandy-Walker cysts and the Arnold-Chiari malformation when I hear Rachel coo. I sit beside her and watch her chew on a toy, and play with her hands, and then slowly lift herself up on her tummy, grunting, and she is so beautiful, so utterly babylike that I wonder why I am torturing myself like this.

Nonetheless, I cannot let go. Like a Talmudic scholar, I spend a week on this one word alone. Why would he say "some optimism," this man who was so impatient with vagueness, so intolerant of estimates and qualifiers and words like "seemed" and "thought." If he was asked when something occurred, approximations would not do, the exact date and time of day were what he was after. I do not know where he lives, if he has a family, how he votes, what he does for pleasure, only that he barged into an emotional moment in order to get the facts straight. "That doesn't mean she's going to see." And in the letter he reiterated these words. "The . . . responses in no way guarantee useful vision." A man like this would not use "some" lightly. He used it to tell us that although nothing showed up as yet, that something might, and that his optimism, and ours, should be guarded at best.

I am driving myself crazy with my fears, and taking those I need most along with me.

Why am I being so negative, my mother asks. Why won't I look at the good side?

The exam showed no deficits, Paul says. Can't I believe that instead?

"Take one day at a time," Hinda tells me. My mother says, "Take one day at a time." "Look, you've just got to take one day at a time," says Paul.

An acquaintance I meet in town pats my shoulder and offers her sage advice. "Take one day at a time."

"Thank you. I appreciate your concern. I *promise* I'll let you know if there's anything you can do . . ."

WAIT! — I've just thought of something. *You* take one day at a time. You take one goddamn day because I simply cannot do it. I am psychologically incapable of putting out of my mind the possibility that my daughter might be retarded. It's not as if I've been wringing my hands and mourning each brown hair that turns gray — it's my baby, her life, her future. Why is this being asked of me? I'm a human being, aren't I? I can be distinguished from the lower orders by my opposable thumb and upright stance and by the fact that I think and plan. Stop telling me to take one goddamn day at a time.

While steady Jane worries away at her word, like a dog with a raw-hide bone, Paul's spirits soar and plummet with such dizzying speed that none of us knows just what each day might bring, least of all him.

Sometimes he is up early, just waiting for me to share the glorious day, as playful as in the old days, when he would pounce on me if I tried to sleep past eight and blow the whistle I wore late nights in bad neighborhoods, and call, "It's activity time, it's activity time!" until I got up. Only now he starts the day by whispering, "We'll make a good life for her, we will."

Sometimes he twitches in his sleep from violent dreams, wakes with fantasies of retribution, body rigid, jaw jutting, everyone or everything a potential enemy — a child, a shoe, a careless driver, his fury so palpable that I warn Charlotte to stay away from him and I steer clear myself because he could kick me as easily as an old shoe. He hates me on these days. He hates my mother, he hates that I leave my shoes in every room, he hates my friends, my eyeglasses, my choice of words, the life that I have trapped him in, the child that I bore (and even so, remains cheerful on the telephone).

Sometimes he is *such* a daddy, assembling a small, low desk beside his own so that Charlotte can keep him company. I wake and find them side by side, alike not only with their blue eyes, fine, straight noses, and muscular, well-shaped limbs, but in their love of push pins and pens and containers of all kinds, their stacks of paper and cans of sharpened pencils, both of them busily solving puzzles at seven A.M.

Sometimes he is *such* a daddy, throwing a mug at me when I tell him about another baby Rachel's age, bubbly and gurgling and batting at toys, and yells, "I don't want to hear it, goddamn it." The mug flies out the door, bounces down the stairs, and lands miraculously unbroken, so much sturdier than I. The next morning, this man, who disapproves of adults who hit children and has never touched his own, whacks Charlotte across the face when she fusses over what to wear, with such fury in his blow that a woman in our car pool takes her aside and begs her to tell what happened, and getting no answer, calls us to find out if she has been abused.

Meanwhile Rachel goes about her business, totally removed from the chaos that she has caused. She nurses, sleeps, gurgles, grunts, plays with her fingers — she even smiles when we work hard at it by tickling her cheek and showering her with endearments. I scrutinize her constantly, searching for change, but the truth is that the only way she has changed is in my eyes, one day a plump, pretty, perfectly healthy child, normal except for her vision, and the next day retarded.

I suppose she changes like this for Paul as well, for it seems implausible that all these ups and downs are a result of air quality or barometric pressure.

Sometimes I bring it on by telling him my visions, airing my fears endlessly and obsessively, forcing him to face Rachel's blindness, which is the one thing he cannot face at all.

Sometimes when I start to cry over something stupid (for the world is filled with reminders of her blindness), and I try to hide from him, he finds me, and takes me in his arms, brushing the sweaty hair from my cheeks and brow, beseeching me to tell him *why* I am so bereft.

Why? Because a stuffed bear arrived in the mail (soft baby toy, symbol of innocence) and she will never *see* it. Because I'm depressed.

"Maybe you're getting your period," he says to this last complaint.

My tears immediately dry up. "My daughter is blind and may be retarded and you're suggesting I'm depressed because of my *period?*"

Sometimes we are so normal I can hardly believe it, but not very often.

Sometimes he loves his family and wants nothing more from life than to be with us night and day. During one of these happy times we go out, and as soon as we step from the house, we find ourselves holding hands and nuzzling, and we decide it must be the house itself that makes us quarrel, scene of so much unhappiness. An acquaintance gets up the nerve to approach us at a gathering to which we have been invited and says in a nervous way that we are inspiring. We try to be modest, but we both feel pretty incredible at just that moment. We go home and make love, and when I wake up there are four of us in bed, Rachel bobbling on Paul's stomach, Charlotte curled up beneath his arm, and he turns to me and says, "I love it, don't you?"

He asks if I will make my special pancakes, the ones with buttermilk, and sesame seeds sprinkled on the griddle, and of course I agree. A morning when we eat pancakes is a rare lazy morning with nothing pressing upon us, no plans other than being together.

While I am curling deep beneath the blankets, foolishly seeking another minute of sleep, Paul slips on his terry robe and down slippers and goes downstairs for the heat and the newspaper. When he steps outside, he sees that a demolition crew has begun to raze the old house across the street. He hurries back upstairs and pulls the curtains from the bedroom windows. The sun is so bright that even with my eyes closed, I can see its red heat.

With the children, we kneel on the bed and gawk at this most amazing sight for the next hour. First the porches are ripped off, then frontloaders batter the sides of the old house, where once a senator lived with his wife and children, until the whole thing weaves and topples over. A cloud of dust rises, and the insides spill out, bits of rooms, pipes, plaster, wooden flooring.

All of a sudden I can't bear to look anymore. A house, I tell myself. It is only a house. Why should it stir up all the grief inside me?

I leave the others at the window and go downstairs to start breakfast and shake free of these feelings of despair. As soon as I switch on the kitchen light I see dirty dishes scattered across the counter, a cup stained with tea, a sticky knife, a plate with tea bags in it, crumbs on the counter.

Charlotte walks into the kitchen and Paul follows behind, sneezing spasmodically. He straps Rachel into her infant seat while I imagine silver picture frames, flowered wallpaper, a tortoise-shell brush, velvet drapes, a clock upon the mantel, a Boston fern, everything blown into the air, turned to rubble. The only thing I have the words for is the dirty dishes that he left all over the counter last night, always leaves, though there is a dishwasher in easy reach. The dishes, the dishes. I am so upset you'd think I just found his lover between my sheets, and all he can say is, "Get off my back about the dishes, for Christ sake."

I am so distressed that I do not see it coming. All I know is that I am standing in the middle of the kitchen still griping about the dishes when he whirls, grabs a broom, and starts to beat the stove.

Rachel cries, Charlotte watches, wild-eyed and passive, the way she stands whenever I cry. Paul throws the broom into the dining room, dials the police station, and starts complaining to the desk officer about dust from the excavation getting into our house, bitches and threatens into the receiver like a crazy old codger, then hangs up, decides that it's the rats and not the dust that make him sneeze, and drives them back to the labs, where it's off with their heads, quite literally.

He leaves the four of us alone for the day — me, Charlotte, Rachel, and the blindness. For a moment I stand in the middle of the kitchen trying to figure out exactly what happened, to assign and admit guilt. I cannot do it because I can no longer picture myself, or who I was before the diagnosis, and I can no longer remember Paul's former self. It was true that I have always worried and he has always been moody, but we are so grossly twisted out of shape, so utterly deformed that we are hardly recognizable.

When the crying awakens me that night, I am so disoriented I cannot figure out who it is or where I am. Oh wait, yes, I'm home, it's Rachel, she's blind. Where is she?

I jerk upright in bed and check beneath the blankets. Then I climb onto the floor to search beside and beneath the bed. She is nowhere, and I cannot figure things out. I find her at last in the crib. Even when she's in my arms, I cannot get my heart to slow down. I feel as if the floor has opened up and between the wooden planks is a gaping hole. Keeping the back of my hand across her head, I walk her carefully into our room. "Get her OUT of here," Paul says.

"You get out," I bellow. "Get the hell out, go sleep somewhere else. *She* lives here."

He takes his pillow and goes upstairs to my office, and I nurse her and fall back to sleep.

When I wake next it is morning, and Charlotte is beside Rachel, and Paul on the other side. I remember the day — only three months ago — when they sent me upstairs to nap, and how they jumped on the bed to wake me up and called "Supper!" in my ears. And I realize that we are taking our marriage, this lovely thing that we shaped and formed and fit ourselves so neatly inside, and shattering it, and that we are unable to stop. And it is so unfair, not just Rachel's blindness, but the mess we are making of our lives, that I begin to cry. "I'm sorry," Paul says to me. Then I see Charlotte raise her head. "I'm sorry," I tell her.

*January 5*

A date with Sharon. I straighten up the house, shower, wash my hair, floss my teeth, dress in clean corduroy pants, put on contact lenses, a little mascara and blush. And then I wait.

She whips out her penlight when she arrives and shines the narrow beam of light across Rachel's eyes. No response. She is not at all dismayed. I am.

As soon as she is through with Rachel I ask about the high-school girl with optic nerve hypoplasia, careful, conversational questions, since I understand that for professional reasons, she cannot give me the gossipy kind of stuff about friends and boyfriends that I want. From her responses, I learn that Kristin has minimal light perception, that she can tell if she is standing by a window, and nothing more. She also has a serious problem with seizures. She goes to public school, reads Braille, and likes computers, is very charming with adults, though often immature with kids her own age. She loves babies, and has been nagging the social worker ever since her marriage to hurry up and get pregnant.

I could weep as I listen because it sounds so normal. I know then that if I could decide my daughter's fate, without question I would sacrifice her vision for her intellect. Since I have no control, and cannot get used to the not-knowing, I begin to play around with probability. If there is a significant association of intellectual impairment with optic nerve hypoplasia, and Kristin is bright, what would the likelihood be of the only other child in the area (Rachel) also fitting into the minority? I think next of the researcher who wrote: "It is difficult to find intact blind children," and the social worker saying, "Most blind kids are multi-impaired."

Sharon encourages me to visit Kristin at home. She says, "The whole family's really great; I know you'd like them."

A really great family. A family that has been through all of this crazy grieving and lived to tell. Is it possible to be happy after all of this?

I call that afternoon, and introduce myself by saying, "Hi, my daughter Rachel has optic nerve hypoplasia."

"Oh, *yes,*" says Mrs. Peters.

"And I'd like to see — to meet Kristin."

*Why?*

We set up an appointment for Wednesday afternoon.

On Tuesday Lindsey comes over to clean the house. Lindsey is sixteen, wears four earrings in each ear, and is a true believer in nail art. Today her nails are polished red with gold diagonal stripes across each pinkie. On her left foot is a red high-top sneaker and on her right is a white one. She goes to the same high school as Kristin Peters, so I ask if she knows her.

"You mean the blind kid?"

"What's she like?"

"A real *mess.* She can't see, she drags a leg, there's something wrong with her face. And she's so *nasty,* I can't believe it. A friend of mine tried to help her in the hall one day, and Kristin goes, like, 'Get the hell away.' Somebody should tell her you can't, like, walk *through* people. Because I don't think she knows."

In the morning there is barely an inch of snow on the ground. I call up Mrs. Peters and cancel on account of the weather. I cannot do it, I simply cannot see them now.

I've probably driven by Children's Specialized Hospital on hundreds of occasions since moving to New Jersey. Every time I passed, my eyes would move from the signpost near the road, up the steep hill, to the elegant old house flanked by Ionic columns, and the long, modern wing attached to it. Even when the buildings were far behind me, the same question always lingered in my mind: What kind of children were there?

The infant stim room, where Rachel is to be evaluated, looks like Santa's workshop — dolls lined up on the window ledge, the cubbies filled with clear boxes of toys. There are tigers and clowns, a life-sized bear slouched in a corner, a play kitchen, complete with dishes and flatwear piled in a sink, and beside it a small table and chairs. Push toys, pull toys, riding toys; a ball that is as high as my waist, a boxful of smaller ones; and this is only the start.

On a mat in the center of the room lies a girl with dark eyes and shiny black hair. She is dressed in pink quilted overalls and a blouse with puffed sleeves. Someone has tied ribbons in her hair and polished

her nails pink. She is as big as a three-year-old, but her body is utterly
limp, legs bowed, soles inward. Only her eyes seem alive. A young
woman sitting beside her runs a jar beneath the child's nose, and calls,
"Katie!" in the kind of soft voice that mothers use to wake their napping
young. "Katie — mmm — *chocolate!*" she says.

She screws the top back on and takes another of these small brown
jars from a tray that holds a dozen. "Katie!" she calls in her wake-up
voice. "*Lemon!*"

What luminous eyes the child has; huge, lashy black eyes. Though
she seems to be watching the young woman, she does not respond to
the scents passed under her nose.

"We're here for an evaluation," I say.

"Oh, you should have said. Let me get Mrs. Kaiser."

She gets up. The child does not move. There is no emotion, no fear
or disappointment, no smile; no attempt to follow her across the room
with her eyes. I try to imagine her mother going into the children's
department to buy this lovely outfit for her daughter, then waking up
this morning in time to polish Katie's nails, and tie her glossy hair in
ribbons, and I cannot understand how she does these simple things.

A woman with close-cropped hair and large clear-framed glasses strides
into the room and introduces herself as June Kaiser. "Hello, sweetheart," she says when she strokes Rachel's cheek. Close behind are four
others, all of them bright-faced and casually dressed, and of an age that
makes it easier to call them girls than women. Each wears a tag that
states her position: occupational therapist, physical therapist, speech
therapist, social worker. Mrs. Kaiser leads us over to a mat near the
windows, where I place Rachel on her back. The women crouch, kneel,
sit cross-legged around her.

"She's adorable, isn't she," says an O.T. with freckles across the bridge
of her nose.

"Look at that little cupid's mouth —"

"Bracelets," says another, touching her chubby wrists.

"You don't feed her very well, do you?" says a P.T., her cheeks dim-
pling.

Paul carries a tiny chair and sits in the circle with his knees to his
chin.

"Ammonia — oooooh!" croons the therapist across the room. "Isn't
that just awful?"

"Can you start by telling us something about the pregnancy?" Mrs. Kaiser asks.

A deep sigh, and the floor is mine. Normal pregnancy, normal vaginal delivery, everything was fine until . . . The therapists scribble away in notebooks. *Glynn, Rachel Alexa . . .*

"Does she smile?" asks the freckled O.T.

"Oh yes, she smiles a lot now, doesn't she?" I ask Paul.

He brushes a finger across her cheek and waits. I try next.

"She's tired," I say when I am unsuccessful.

"Will she smile without being stimulated tactilely?"

"I think so." I look at Paul, who shrugs.

"Try," Mrs. Kaiser tells me.

"Rachel, Rae-Rae!" Paul calls.

"Rachel!" I chime in, my voice the same as Katie's therapist's. I am another mother trying to wake her child. "She's usually napping now. We had to get her up, so she's probably completely exhausted."

The therapists turn their bright faces toward me, and the questioning begins again.

"Does she respond to voices?" they ask.

"To color?"

"Does she roll over?"

"Does she move around a lot?"

"Is her cry different when she's hungry than when, say, she just wants to be picked up?"

I see Paul shake his head, and listen to my own answers. No. No. No. No.

Squeaky toys are squeezed above her face; crocheted balls with bells inside are shaken. A porcupine with soft rubber bristles is brushed against her hands. Mrs. Kaiser produces a jar of soap bubbles, kneels beside Rachel, and blows columns of bubbles into the air. When I was a child, soap bubbles made me cry. I swear, I learned about death by seeing how lovely and short-lived they were. When my mother sang "I'm Forever Blowing Bubbles," I hid my face so that no one would tell me how ridiculous it was to feel such sorrow. The bubbles float above Rachel's head, burst on her cheeks and overalls and hands, and I feel the same ridiculous sorrow inside me.

When the evaluation is over, Paul and I sit on a bench in the hospital lobby so that I can nurse Rachel. I think of the retarded boy — a tall, dark-haired teenager — who rides through town on a rusty bicycle, scaring children because he is so big and manlike and has such a childish way of calling out to them. I think of the teenagers who gather in front of the ice cream store laughing and flirting, the friends I cannot call because they do not know about Rachel and there is no way I can tell them; the friends whose letters I will never answer because I cannot write the truth, yet it is too great a thing to be omitted; I think of Saturday evening, when we took Charlotte out for pizza and sat at a table beside a couple with three children. The youngest watched us steadily from her high chair while her family and ours ate. "How old is she?" Paul had asked. What big eyes she had, eyes that devoured us. She could not get enough. "Four months come Monday —" Rachel's age minus two days. Rachel sat with her head bowed, her hands in fists, while this one took in the whole world. I think of all that is lost to Rachel and to us and say: "I don't think she's going to see."

"She isn't."

I had only meant to test him, to prick the thick skin he hides beneath. Who knew how much I had come to depend upon his infuriating denial? Now it is real. She's blind, she's blind.

"The social worker sees a child with optic nerve hypoplasia who has tunnel vision," I say.

"She won't have tunnel vision."

"Why not? She's got almost half her optic nerve in one eye."

"We've already *been* through this."

He gets up and peers into the long fish tank beside the bench. Angels and gouramis swim by, a treasure chest bubbles open and shut. A pearl shines inside a fake oyster.

"Look. We're both tired, we've been working hard. Let's hold it together, okay? We got a raw deal, but she's a beautiful baby, and she's going to make it."

"She'll never marry."

What I am thinking is that the cycle has been broken; children are born, grow up, marry, have children, and their children marry and have children. I never thought about this until Rachel's problems began, and I understood that some people are born, make no mark, and die, that their stay on earth is no more meaningful than that of a garden annual.

"Blind people marry," he says.

"What about intellectually deficient ones?"

"Jesus, why do you say things like that?"

"Why? Because she stands a good chance of being intellectually deficient. Because she doesn't recognize my voice, or play with toys, or care enough about the world to stay awake."

"It's noise," he says.

"I didn't make it up, and I wasn't looking for trouble. I asked a question, and I got an answer, and I don't know what to do with it. It used to be that we talked about our worries, but now I say something about Rachel, and you get enraged. I mean, she's your daughter, too, but sometimes it seems like you don't care all that much. You hardly pick her up and play with her . . ."

"When have I been home — tell me."

"You were even busier when Charlotte was born, but you played with her all the time. You threw her in the air and rolled around with her and woke her from her naps. Don't you remember how I had to get over feeling jealous because you'd come home from work and be so busy with her, you'd forget to say hello to me? I can't remember a single time since Rachel's been born when you've picked her up without my asking."

"Get off me," he says, his voice rising.

"Well, it's true. Sometimes I feel as if she's my child alone, my blind baby."

He gets up and crosses the lobby. He has put on a few pounds since Rachel's birth, and he walks like a man with lead weights strapped onto his ankles. It is only when he is apart from me that my love for him wells up, and I can at last remember that he is hurting, too. I think of all the times he has told me that it is not his nature to worry, that he never thinks about her future, or imagines her a week, a month, a year from now, and yet how every morning after Rachel nurses he props himself up on an elbow and passes his hand across her face. He thinks I am asleep, but I see him study Rachel's impassive face. His hand goes across ten times, twenty. It is too early to be awake, but Paul will not give up: thirty times, forty, until the gray light of dawn becomes brighter.

"DO YOU HAVE FISH AT HOME?"

A boy in a wheelchair sits in front of the tank. His face is broken out, his body held upright by a cloth restraining device that has been tied around his torso. His hands are folded limply, his legs, like a doll's, crossed carelessly at the ankles. The therapist holds two cards in front of him: Yes. No.

"DO YOU HAVE FISH? WHICH IS IT, YES OR NO?"

Paul sits beside me again and slips his arm around my waist.

"BOBBY, DO YOU HAVE FISH?"

"I'm sorry," he says.

"*I'm* sorry," I tell him.

# ⚭ 7 ⚭

# We Dig

THE PHONE doesn't ring anymore. Our house has become so silent that I am reminded of the weeks after shiva, when the guests are gone, and the family has been left to stumble through their problems alone. We are stumbling in a calmer way than before, fewer mood swings, fewer quarrels, no more haunting sights of Charlotte watching our craziness silently, with wide frightened eyes.

It is not that we have suddenly grown, changed, come to terms, found comfort, rather that we are too weary to continue grieving so wildly. Our household has become more tranquil, and these tranquil moments enable me to compose myself, to pull back and keep my visions to myself. It hurts me to do this because it shatters my romantic notion of the two of us as soul mates, sharing everything. Nonetheless, it is the only way.

Sometimes Paul says of Rachel, "She'll never see," with such certainty that I am filled with terror. Sometimes he says, "She'll be just fine," and I can feel him demand, in his adamance, that I agree. I cannot coax these words from him or repeat them at a time when he is feeling the opposite. Nor does he give me a clue as to what he is feeling, whether inside is the despairing scientist who says that she cannot see because he has not seen evidence to the contrary, or the optimist who looks at the most hopeful picture and says, "She's beautiful, she'll be just fine."

Isn't there some axiom about a fine mind being one that can hold two opposing ideas at the same time? Paul is incapable of such things, though his mind is a fine one, indeed. He is up, he is down. It is a dyslexic's way, I think, for he is a man who cannot discuss the week's schedule while cooking a pot of oatmeal. One overrides the other. He says his thoughts are on either the quantity of oats that must be stirred into the boiling water, or the dates when he is working late.

I see my brain as a vast closet with shelves where I store memories, and hundreds of cubbies jammed full of work and household and personal things. Much of the time my conscious mind is such a clutter of messages — need milk, pay bills, get shoes, buy broccoli — that it has taken me many years to understand that his way is the result of physiology, not stubbornness. Even so, there are times when I am hurt by it, when I cannot *believe* that he is incapable of answering a simple question about whether he is working late on Thursday just because he's boiling eggs.

Once, in the midst of a quarrel, I stepped out of myself for an instant, and saw with great alarm how much he hated me. Later we were friends again, and I said, "Now I know why I find our fights so devastating. When you're angry you stop loving me."

"And you *love* me when we're arguing?"

"Beneath it all I do. I may hate you at the time, but my love doesn't totally vanish."

He cannot believe this. "You *loved* me when I hit Charlotte?"

"I did. It pained me to love you, it felt like my own tragedy that I did, but I did."

"Well, that's not the way it is for me."

"I know. And that's what I feel, this sudden loss of love."

He hates me, he loves me. She is blind, she will be fine.

## January 15

The report from Children's Specialized Hospital arrived today.

"Rachel, a well-nourished attractive baby of four months, was brought to the evaluation by her parents. She was cooperative and quiet during the testing except for a very brief episode of crying. She was very tolerant of handling."

According to the test items on the cognitive section of the Early Intervention Developmental Profile, Rachel was judged at the evaluation to perform at a three-month level. "She exhibited such adaptive behavior as bringing her hands to midline to finger a tactile auditory toy and trying to bring it to her mouth. . . . She does not shake a rattle. . . . Impression is that Rachel is a responsive, although quiet baby, whose cognitive performance upon testing was diminished by lack of vision and some fluctuating tone in the upper extremities."

The physical therapist wrote: "She is reportedly beginning side to side movements in prone . . . but reflexology and increased flexor tone seem to inhibit this action. In supine she is moving and kicking her legs alternately and assists in pulling up to sit. . . . When supported in standing she accepts weight and bounces slightly through alternating flexion/extension at hips and knees."

Her grasp reflex was still present, the occupational therapist noted. "It is stronger on the right, but she is able to release objects placed in her hand. Her hands came to midline during the screening only when facilitated and given scapular support. . . ." Slightly increased tone affected her upper extremity movements, but "this tightness is released with handling."

Rachel's linguistic skills were judged to be at the three-month level. "Vocalizations are limited in quantity and still tend to be random rather than in response to auditory stimuli," according to the speech therapist. "Laughter was not elicited or reported by parents." She also exhibited head and trunk asymmetry and an asymmetrical smile, which indicated "right-sided facial paresis. . . ."

Although these days I am addicted to all medical reports and study even the most obtuse of them, this one seems worth the effort I give to it, for when I read it the first time what strikes me is that every peep and grunt and wiggle Rachel makes is meaningful. She is passive and sleeps an inordinate amount, but to have assumed that she lay around doing nothing was a mistake. Look — she fingers toys and tries to put them into her mouth; she kicks her legs back and forth! She's only a month delayed cognitively, and less than that in some of the other areas, and this according to a standardized test that made no allowances for her blindness. Hadn't one of the therapists written that her "cognitive performance upon testing was diminished by lack of vision and some fluctuating tone in the upper extremities"?

*Fluctuating tone?*

During my next reading, I notice that in every section there is some mention of Rachel's tone. "Increased flexor tone" inhibited her rolling, "slightly increased tone" affected her upper extremity movements. Asymmetrical smile indicated "right-sided facial paresis. . . ."

I ask one of the therapists about these comments. "With blind kids it's hard to say just what these early tone problems mean," she says. "It could be neurological or it could be fixing, stiffening from tension."

Thursday is my infant stim day. I wait all week for the hour to arrive, the way earlier I waited for the social worker. The therapists who work in the building on the hill are my white knights now. They have the answers; they will show me what to do. In the morning I shower and dress with more care than usual, yet when the time comes that I must leave, something holds me back, and so I am always late and walk into the bright room armed with excuses that no one asks to hear: lost my keys, car wouldn't start, icy streets, no parking spaces, last-minute diaper change for Rachel. Hope lies here, but I am not ready to be part of this group of mothers and damaged babies.

Stuffed toys are lined up neatly along the window ledge, dishes are stacked in the sink of the play kitchen, dolls lie in cribs and cradles. Building toys are piled in boxes, puzzles in special slots. The slide has been set up; the sandbox is full.

The children lie on the kind of mats I remember from gym class, bright ones, in red and white. They have the same names as normal children — Steven, Tory, Alex, Katie, Lauren — and wear jogging suits and Yankee jackets, and tiny aerobics shoes, though two of them will never walk, and one will never run. While a scratchy recording of Pachelbel's *Canon* plays on an old record player, each therapist sits by a child. Terry blows soap bubbles for Steven; Joan sets out the colored cubes for Tory; Alex is bounced atop a waist-high ball. Faith makes a fuss over Tory's tiny shoes, and Mrs. Kaiser says, "Hello, *sweetheart,*" as she kneels in front of Rachel.

The mothers play with their babies and chat with each other. They have dreams and fears, I know they must, though when they talk it is of ordinary things — a sale at a store in town, the icy streets, their older kids. I am one of these mothers, grappling with the fact and repercussions of my daughter's condition, mourning for the lost dreams of a whole child. I wake up on time each morning, eat three square meals, get my daughter to school on time, go to meetings and movies, laugh at jokes, and yet I sit apart and wonder how these women get out of bed, blow-dry their hair, shop for shoes, talk so easily of mundane things. As if I were an outsider, I am awed and fascinated by their normality, and do not identify with it. Perhaps I study the others because I do not feel connected to the me that goes through the daily routines and hope their faces might help me find out who I have become.

The therapists are young and energetic and ask for nothing in return for the love they show these children. I understand that their job is to work with our babies, that they get paid for their efforts, and yet what they give seems far beyond mere competence. Mrs. Kaiser's "sweetheart" is not a stranger's idle "sweetheart." I can see in her tender care that Rachel *is* a sweetheart to her. It matters that Rachel is valued by others, that here, in this room, she is never judged by what she does or fails to do; it makes a difference to Alex's mother that her son is not greeted by unkind stares or questions, but is a baby, cuddled and loved by others.

A stranger looking in might see children play and nothing more — Steven swiping at soap bubbles, Tory transferring colored blocks from hand to hand; Alex held at the hips, laughing as he rides the big green exercise ball. It is purposeful play, however; play to elicit certain responses, or stifle others; play to stimulate.

Rachel starts the morning inside a bucket full of Styrofoam slugs. Next she is propped against a pillow in a laundry basket. Suspended in front of her is a paper tube, the kind used for gift wrap or aluminum foil, that has been covered with fabric of different textures, crinoline and velvet. Bells hang from it, a key dangles. When she reaches out she cannot help but touch this tube, and when she lets it go, she can find it again.

The theory behind Rachel's play was developed by Selma Fraiberg and her colleagues at the University of Michigan Medical School, who, in the mid-sixties, started a longitudinal study of children blind from birth. At the outset of their work, they noticed the high incidence of mental retardation and gross disturbances in early ego functioning among blind children who were otherwise intact and wondered why it was that twenty-five percent of blind children ("a conservative estimate") had "severe cognitive disabilities and/or emotional problems." In their article "An Educational Program for Blind Infants" they postulate that these ego disturbances and cognitive deficits had their origins in the first eighteen months of life, during which time most blind children lived in a void.

A normal baby spends much of the day just looking around. Babies study shafts of light and floating dust, the toys in their crib, their parents' faces, the neighbor's dog. Like the baby who watched us so intently in the restaurant, these children get pleasure and information from the visual world.

The sighted baby sees her mother and smiles at her; before long she learns that when she smiles she gets her mother's attention, because that smile makes her mother feel loved, and a loving mother is more apt to play with her baby. The sighted infant sees a toy and lifts his head and one day reaches out for it, mouths it, and discovers that it is hard and cool and will rattle if he shakes it.

But what of blind babies? They have no world of bright and wondrous things they strive to reach and so they do not easily learn about the world. They are passive and hard to rouse, and do not smile readily; they give so little back to their parents that they are difficult to love.

If Rachel were sighted, she would have moved her head from side to side as a newborn and propped herself up in order to look around. ("The sighted baby from the earliest weeks will find just looking at the world an absorbing, full-time occupation which will lead him on his way to struggle to keep his head upright and steady.") She would roll and reach out and creep and stand and walk, because she would see things that she wanted and strive to get them.

At the outset of her study, Fraiberg assumed that sound could be used as a lure, but this proved to be impossible. Sighted babies will not reach for what they hear but do not see — a music box hidden under a blanket, for instance — until late in the first year, and neither will blind ones.

Although blind children sit at approximately the same time as sighted ones, their crawling is delayed; they stand at around the same time, but do not walk. (It is not uncommon for blind babies to begin walking at the age of two.) Often they get locked into repetitive motions, like rocking. They rock because they are physiologically ready to move, but lack the visual incentives. The danger during this time, when Rachel has neither vision to stimulate her nor the locomotion that would enable her to acquire information about the world, is that she could live out her days in a sensory void.

In order to help the blind child during this early period, Fraiberg and her colleagues came up with the concept of the "interesting space," a limited area where toys and other appealing things might be found. Mrs. Kaiser puts Rachel at a play table that has a molded seat with a back support, and a tray that fits tightly. The toys that Rachel seems to like best — a rubber porcupine and a crocheted ball — are put on the table directly in front of her. We put Rachel's hands on the toys so that she will know where they are, though she would also find them if she accidentally rested her arms against the table.

"For too long during the first year the blind child lives in a world of accidental encounters with 'things,'" Fraiberg writes. "'Things' materialize out of nowhere, make chance encounters with his fingers and mouth and, upon loss of contact, disappear into nowhere." It is hoped that Rachel will grow to understand that the table is a place where things can be found, that she will begin to reach even before the toys have been set upon it; and that ultimately, she will learn that there are things elsewhere that are of interest, and that all she has to do is reach out to find them.

When the hour is up the therapists leave and a social worker comes in with a tray of coffee and cookies and encourages the mothers to stay. The first week I decline. The second week my curiosity overwhelms me and I join the others who cluster on the middle mat beside their babies.

What a varied group they are — young, middle-aged, chic, shabbily dressed, black, white — one from each stratum, as if someone gathered us in this room in order to prove that birth defects know no race or creed.

The talk is easy and low-energy, like the talk of mothers waiting for a PTA meeting to begin. Then suddenly in the midst of the chitchat, the conversation shifts, and it is health insurance, and which carriers are the best, the exorbitant cost of orthotic devices, a stroller on the market roomy enough to accommodate back and side supports, the grandparents' reaction to their children, the insensitivity of doctors, and they are no longer a group of suburban mothers, but a sorority of sufferers.

"He says nothing when we're in his office, not a single word. Then late that night he calls us up and tells us she'll be a vegetable, and we should start looking for a facility that will take her . . ."

"I told him the baby ain't breathing, and he says to get a vaporizer. A vaporizer! This baby's choking to death before my eyes, and the dude's telling me to go downtown and buy me a *vaporizer?*"

"So we start to tell the doctor about this article we had read, and he gets all bent out of shape and it's 'Who's got the medical degree, you or me?'"

As I listen I feel my heart quicken, and think at first that it is sympathy that overwhelms me. Then all at once I am back in the subbasement of Hospital City, receiving the news that Rachel's evoked response test is positive. The moment is so charged that I'd rather not think of it now. It comes back to me nonetheless: Paul weeping for the first time; his hot neck, his hair like silk, the gruff voice that says, "That doesn't mean she's going to see."

My need to talk is so much stronger than my resolve to be silent. I need to speak of this incident and all of the others, to tell these strangers the kinds of things that I was taught to keep to myself, because those who are closest to me cannot hear them. Paul cannot bear to think about Rachel. My mother aches too deeply when I am less than hopeful, because I am her child. My friends do not know what to say. I want to tell someone who can hear my worry, watch me cry, listen to my desperate jokes, someone who knows. This becomes the place, in this room with these women. It is here that someone can say, "She's a darling baby, what's wrong with her?"

We can ask what's wrong, and if it will get better. Will she see someday? Will he be able to make love when he's older? Will she ever grow up?

"She has something called optic nerve hypoplasia," I say.

*Hypo-* under; *-plasia* development, formation. Lashy eyes, soft skin, tiny nose, gherkin toes — she *is* darling, big and healthy, with a drum tummy, bracelets around her ankles and rings of fat around her thighs — perfect in every way except that her optic nerve did not develop properly.

"Did they tell you what happened?"

"An accident during development."

Caused by what?

"A virus, maybe." Or clams or the amnio.

Contracted how?

If there were reasons we could put this thing to rest. We could change our diets, move from the town where we live, have or not have other children; we could pass the word on to others at risk, take solace in our activism.

If there were more children, it would be easier to speculate, but this is an uncommon disorder. There is nothing in standard texts about optic nerve hypoplasia, and of the papers that Paul has begun to bring home, the samples are woefully small: ten children in one, seven in another, eight in a third, fifty-one in the largest study — and those fifty-one collected over an eleven-year period. And what of the conclusions? In one paper we learn that there is a known association of "some" cases of optic nerve hypoplasia with maternal diabetes and maternal ingestion of quinine. Seven patients had mothers who were on anticonvulsants.

In another study the authors found that children with optic nerve hypoplasia very often are the firstborn infants of very young mothers in mid- or late adolescence, ten percent of whom had drug and alcohol problems. Environmental factors that have a "very specific damaging effect on retinal ganglion cells, and frequently brain cells as well" are a possibility, say the authors of another study. Chromosomal abnormalities of trisomy 13–15 have been detected according to one researcher; chromosomal abnormalities of trisomy 18 have been spotted according to another. A genetic defect has been suggested, backed up by thirteen cases of familial occurrence recorded over a twenty-eight-year period between 1947 and 1975.

What can I make of this? I had an amniocentesis because obstetrically I was old. Before the actual procedure Paul and I sat before a genetic counselor and tried to unearth familial disorders, and all we could come up with were allergies and varicose veins. The amnio ruled out chromosomal abnormalities. I never smoked during pregnancy, drank only one glass of wine. Could that glass of Beaujolais have done the trick? I don't eat meat or overly processed foods, or use artificial sweeteners, or work with toxic chemicals — I did not own a word processor. There is no formaldehyde in our insulation, no asbestos in our walls, no radon in the soil beneath our house. I am not in my mid- or late adolescence. I am thirty-five years old, with plenty of problems at the moment, though drugs are not among them.

Paul digs, too. He will not corner a cardiologist at a party or make an appointment for a checkup because our internist is smart and may know something that we have not heard — both things that I have done. But he brings home a computer printout of abstracts from papers on optic nerve hypoplasia published in the last ten years. Digging is science, he says, as we cross out the ones that do not interest us, and circle those we want to read in full.

Although it's a depressing task, at least we are together when we pore over these papers, two detectives searching through these studies for a clue to her future, working side by side, the way we did in our happier past.

What grim reports they are. Many of the children have septo-optic dysplasia and associated endocrine problems. Growth retardation and dwarfism have been reported, and on the other hand, sexual precocity. There are children with motor problems, learning problems, liver problems, defects in various parts of their brain. Many are retarded, though not all; many have a seizure disorder, though not every one. What can we draw from these case studies? That Paul is right to be hopeful (Look at her, she's beautiful!) and I am right to worry.

Most people who hear about Rachel predict that she will be cured. All I have to do is recall my father-in-law describing the winters when he was a schoolboy, the chair beside him empty one day, the chair behind him empty, the child dead of measles, scarlet fever, whooping cough, diphtheria; or my mother talking about the fear that swept over parents the summers that polio was epidemic, and I understand the awe these people feel for modern medicine. Great strides *have* been made. Antibiotics and vaccinations have utterly changed our lives. And now we are years past the era of the Magic Bullet, living in a time when modern medicine has given us nifty diagnostic techniques, miraculous therapies, high-tech prosthetic devices, and yet . . .

Among Rachel's group at infant stim, there is Tory, developmentally delayed, "etiology unknown," Steven, cerebral palsy, "etiology unknown," Alex, spina bifida, "etiology unknown," Lauren, born twelve weeks prematurely, "cause of prematurity unknown," Rachel, optic nerve hypoplasia, "etiology unknown." These syndromes have been studied and characterized; what has happened to the brain and nerve impulses is often understood. When it comes to reasons and cures, there is little to offer.

Katie was a healthy child, bubbly and cheerful and precocious, a perfect child in every way. One Friday when she was seven months old, she woke with a high fever. Her mother thought at first it was the flu, but there was something odd about the way the baby cried, and so she took her to the pediatrician. It wasn't the flu, it was meningitis. Katie was in the hospital for a month, so sick she wasn't expected to make it. "But you're a tough cookie, aren't you?" her mother says.

The neurologist told the family that the disease had caused extensive brain damage, that Katie was blind and deaf as a result, a vegetable. "He was wrong. She turns her eyes when I come into the room. She watches where I go and fusses when I turn away."

Tory is a beautiful little girl with big hazel eyes, long straight lashes, and a headful of fine hair that stands straight up, as if electrified. She's a twin, with a sister who was a pound heavier at birth. When one twin weighs a few ounces less than the other, there isn't cause for concern. A weight difference that's as much as the one between Tory and her sister suggests placental insufficiency. Tory seemed fine to her parents. It was the doctor who started worrying because she didn't hold up her head when Erin did. "Comparing her to Erin isn't fair — she's been way ahead of schedule on everything. Erin sat up at five months. She's already *standing*."

Tory's mother is cheerful and denies what her doctor sees as her child's troubled future. Katie's mother is hopeful where there is no hope. "They told me that she was blind and deaf, and *look* —" as she holds her beautiful limp daughter across her lap, and feeds her through a tube. Alex's mother is young and unmarried and does not understand what happened to her baby, though her father, a preacher, has assured her that Alex is as he is because of her life of sin. "Why would God do that to Alex? He didn't have no life of sin. Why didn't he do it to me instead?" And I sit and worry that Rachel will never have any vision, that she might be retarded and have seizures.

We are all very different, and our reactions to our children's problems are different, and yet all of us dig through the same dirt, dig and dig, week after week. *Why?* What happened? What caused it?

Steven's mother had three easy pregnancies before her son was born, and three normal, healthy children. Her labor with Steven was uneventful until the very end, when she began to bleed. Why did she hemorrhage? Where was the doctor when it happened? She says she wants to go back and ask him why the nurses couldn't find him and if the bleeding caused her son's problems, but she's afraid to go because she liked him so much. Her husband says what's done is done. Why dig? Every week she tells us the story of her delivery.

Paul thinks it was the amniocentesis. He was there during the procedure and watched while the needle was inserted into my uterus and blood was withdrawn instead of fluid, and this three times before the amniotic fluid came up. He is convinced that a "bad amnio" caused Rachel's problems. One evening he shows me a drawing in a text that at first I think is a picture of a frog. We are looking down into the brain. There are the eyeballs, two bulging orbs, and at the back, the retina. The nerve fibers that leave the eyeball are the optic nerves, which in the illustration seem to cross in the middle of the brain. In reality, some of the nerve fibers in each optic nerve converge at a place called the optic chiasm, then separate and continue posteriorly as the optic tracts.

It is the optic chiasm, where optic nerve fibers cross, that interests Paul. What if during the amnio, this area were damaged? Couldn't it have been possible when the needle was inserted so many times? And if it wasn't damage caused by the needle itself, couldn't a virus have been introduced? Development of the optic nerve begins at about the fifth week, and optic nerve hypoplasia can be acquired at any time before the eye is fully developed. He tries out this theory on several physicians, and hears that it is ridiculous, impossible, remote, at best. He casts it aside, but he is too hungry for answers to stop digging.

Perhaps it was air or water. Such basic things that never troubled our parents. Air and water. Childhood leukemia in Woburn, Massachusetts, and in Rutherford, New Jersey; birth defects in Love Canal, New York, in Times Beach, Missouri. The news is full of such stories.

No, says the social worker who leads the mother's group. There were not an unusual number of children born with problems in the winter of 1983. There was some concern when three children were born at the same hospital with spina bifida until it was seen how far apart the children lived . . . Yes, we do see more children with congenital problems, because so many more survive than in the past. Downstairs there were children born weighing two thousand grams, children that never would have lived, and now stood a substantial risk of having neurological problems, cardiovascular problems, visual defects, learning impairments . . .

*Maybe you did something to cause her problems.* I ran while I was pregnant (proud and vain, it serves you right). I ran with the encouragement of running magazines and my obstetrician's consent, though not very much, not ten miles a day, but perhaps two, not seven minutes a mile, but twelve, never incurring oxygen debt. I had run while pregnant with Charlotte, too, and others have run, and no defects to the child have been reported. There was nothing in the literature apart from an increased sense of well-being for the mother. Even so . . .

*Were you sick?* We rented a house in the country for three days around New Year's. The friends who joined us knew that Paul and I did not eat meat, and planned a dinner of sushi and raw shellfish for New Year's Eve. Although we had given up raw seafood (such cautious souls) we did not have the heart, once the seafood had been bought, to turn it down. We were polite and ate. When we returned home, Paul had what he thought was a stomach virus, and I spent one crampy afternoon, a month or so into my pregnancy, hovering close to the toilet. Could that have been it? Or could it have been the leftover tomato herring that I vomited after eating? Or the ammonia I used when I stripped the floor one afternoon, that filled the room with fumes that were so vile that I had to leave? Was it an accident caused by politeness, or one caused by muddled thinking? You were pregnant, what were you doing cleaning the floor with ammonia? Or was it simply a virus, some bug, benign to mothers and devastating to the fetus, like German measles?

It is not only my private obsession with answers that makes me dig, it is an obligation I feel as a parent, for I have been raised to believe that it is a mother's job to fight till death for her child's survival, and my way of fighting is to learn all there is to know. I am afraid that if I meekly accept the fact that nothing can be done I might deprive her of . . . something.

Under these circumstances, the skepticism I prided myself on suddenly seems unhealthy, and I find myself listening to things that before Rachel's birth I would have argued, and a month ago would have filled me with rage, and which now sound reasonable. Megavitamins. Why not? "Green magma," in her juice, because this high-priced grassy stuff is said to turn weaklings into superheroes. You never know. I still say, "It's a static condition, nothing can be done." I still tell believers in medical science that the optic nerve is in the brain and that brain transplants are not on the horizon, because I know that both of these things are true. I also know that more than anything I want to be proven wrong.

Joyce calls late one night. She is a friend and therapist, a smart, sensitive woman whose medical ideas go from mainstream to outer fringe.

She tells me about a workshop she took with a healer, a very gifted woman who worked with burn victims and had some real success with cell development and regeneration where conventional medicine failed. "I don't know what she could do for Rachel — if anything — but I thought I'd tell you about her because she lives in California, in Glendale, and I have a ticket to L.A. that has to be used by the end of the month. I can't use it myself, so if you want to take Rachel to see her, I'd like to give it to you."

A healer? A hot-handed charlatan who'll use words like "energy" and "white light" and charge exorbitant fees and give me false hope? What is there to heal in Rachel? She is not sick, she feels no pain. What is done is done. And yet . . .

"What's her name?" I ask.

Joyce gives me the woman's name and the address of the "healing center." She tells me that people often wait for months in order to see the healer, and that what I must do is immediately write a letter explaining Rachel's condition and including her medical reports. Then I should follow up with a phone call.

I hang up and stand by the telephone. I see myself bundling up Rachel in her fleecy suit and packing a small bag for the two of us, and it seems so pathetic, flying her across the country in search of miracle cures. Rachel's condition is untreatable and unchangeable and our job is to love her the way she is. Nerves do not regenerate — it's as simple as that. And yet . . . What's to lose? The ticket is free, friends could put us up. We'd only be gone a day or two.

Paul says, "Who was that?"

"Joyce."

"What did she want?"

Can I tell him how badly I want to go? He will tell me I am ridiculous and be right.

Or will he? Hadn't I heard him on the phone with a churchgoing friend, my long-lapsed-Catholic husband, who insists on listing his religion as "Irish," saying, "Light a candle for her." Didn't he swallow a garlic oil capsule when he had a cold the week before, take a nap, and wake up announcing that he was cured? Scientist, yes, who calls my lay speculations "anecdotal," but trumpets the curative effects of garlic to whomever he meets.

Like a child with an awful confession, I begin to cry before the words are out. "Joyce has a ticket. I know it sounds crazy, but it won't cost that much and she won't be hurt in any way, and maybe . . . you never know."

His face is blank, his expression utterly unfathomable. I remember how I had stood across from him in the cavernous lobby outside the ophthalmologist's office, and how there had been nothing in his eyes that I could interpret, absolutely nothing after all our years of closeness.

"If you want to go, then go," he says at last.

Now I am the woman in the garden apartment across from my parents' home, dragging her retarded daughter from doctor to doctor.

I write the healer a long letter and include copies of the letters from Hines and Klibansky, just as Joyce has suggested. The healer has an odd name I have never heard before. I picture her dark and gypsylike with long thick hair, a flowing skirt, and black all-knowing eyes.

Five days later, I call the center and ask to speak to the healer with the odd name. She gets on the phone. The connection is so crackly I feel as if I am speaking to someone orbiting high above the earth.

I tell her who I am and then ask, "Did you get my letter?"

"Which was that, dear?" she asks in a soft voice.

"The baby with the . . . visual problems?"

"Ah, the little girl, yes. Hmmm . . . You live in New York, don't you?"

"New Jersey."

"Yes, so far away. It's a pity to bring her all the way here when I really don't know that I can do anything to help her."

"My fare is paid one way. I have friends who'll put us up. It's really no problem." I am practically begging.

"There's a wonderful man in Baltimore. That's near where you live, isn't it? If you like, I could give you his name. But to take the little baby all the way to California . . ."

When I hang up, I realize how surprised I am by how kind and ethical this woman was, when my image had been of a charlatan and exploiter. And even so, I was ready to go.

Paul is sitting at his desk when I tell him I'm not going, stacks of paper beneath his elbows, jars of garlic oil capsules on the shelf above.

"Goddamn Joyce," he says. "A healer. She wants to send you to a healer. And at a time like this, when you're so vulnerable to that crap."

"I wanted to go."

I think of the garlic oil capsules, new elixir, magic pill, the fact that neither of us is consistent after all. He believes in the scientific method, and was cured with garlic oil; swears he never thinks about Rachel, and wakes at dawn to pass his hands across her face. I am the rational one, steady skeptic, waiting for lightning bolts, heavenly words, a magic cure.

# ❦ 8 ❧

# We Lift Our Heads

*February 2*

TONIGHT WE ARE NOT GRIEVING or fighting or digging. We are together in my office, the warmest room on this cold night. Someone gave Paul a computer printer that works only intermittently, and he has taken off various panels to inspect its parts. I am sitting nearby reading, keeping him company because he asked. It is so quiet that I can hear his soft, regular breathing. I put my book down and watch him take off the metal assemblage that guides the paper, and then the carriage, his concentration unbroken, and I realize that we've been at peace for a while now, that we have begun at last to have small quiet moments that were lost to us these last few weeks.

I still vacillate wildly between hope and fear, cry when I hear my mother's voice, lose whole afternoons testing Rachel, suffer from Merckus Interruptus. The images still come upon me without warning, the smallest things plunging me into a despair so intense I cannot breathe — a pretty teenager, a sleep from which she cannot be roused. When I see her beside another child her age, her head bowed, her hands in fists, I feel as if my heart will break. And yet when she smiles, when I see her squeeze a toy, mouthing every inch of its surface — such normal baby things! — I am filled with hope and happiness.

It is only now when I have begun to lift my head that I can see what an exclusive emotion grief is. In the throes of it there is no room for anyone else. *But you did so well! You went to parties, laughed at bad jokes, sent birthday cards to friends!* Not that I had room for them really, or patience for their head colds and heartaches, all of which would end . . . while my daughter would still be blind.

In the throes of it, I abandoned Charlotte. I fed and dressed her, colored pictures at her side, built Lego beds and houses with little windows, but I depended upon her to take care of herself, and she saw that

I was hurting and did, with little fuss. She brushed her own teeth, poured her own juice, got into her nightgown, fetched Rachel's diapers, picked up the phone. Please, I said, and she did it. I need your help, and she helped me.

I remember the day that Paul brought her to visit me in the hospital, how she had worn her knit dress with the satin hearts across the front and new buckle shoes, her hair and bangs long and thick and silky like her dad's. When she saw me standing in the doorway of the sunroom, she sat and swung her legs until Paul said, "Go on now." We stepped toward each other, strangers all of a sudden — her mother with a brand-new baby, my baby all grown up. I knelt and put my arms around her and held her long, tight little-girl body. "I have a lap now," I said. Then I began to cry. She was so big, so fully formed compared to Rachel.

Since the diagnosis, this bigness has been all that I have allowed myself to see.

On Saturday Paul has to go to the labs to feed his neuroblastoma cells, so I make plans to take Charlotte to the library.

I help her dress and send her downstairs. In the time it takes me to get Rachel ready, she puts three dolls inside the open stroller, two blankets, a corrugated packing insert, a bib from a lobster restaurant in Maine, her new lunchbox filled with bracelets and pearls, pencil stubs, and scraps of fabric. She'd still be my baby if Rachel had not been born.

As we walk to the library she asks about snowflakes and groundhogs and Mr. Lincoln. Why is Mr. Lincoln on all the pennies? Why did he study by candlelight? How come we celebrate his birthday when he's *dead?* What kind of a party do you have when someone's *dead?*

Her enthusiasm reminds me that holidays are more than times when sales are held, and wakens long-forgotten stories from within me, log cabins, cherry trees, Queen Isabella.

"People celebrate a dead person's birthday as a way of remembering him," I say. "You could invite your friends over on Lincoln's birthday and talk about the good things he did."

This explanation has no appeal to her. "What holiday is next?" she asks.

"Daddy's birthday. His fiftieth."

She clutches the stroller handle and says, "That's *old,*" with an edge of disgust in her voice.

I can remember when forty seemed old to me, when of all that was mysterious about Paul when we first met, his age was the most forbidding. Forty! How could I be in love with a man who was forty! He swore he rarely thought about his age, though he referred to himself as a forty-year-old man, instead of simply saying, "I," and his conversation was laced with discourses on the finite number of times a cell can divide, and man's inability to comprehend the nothingness beyond death. He spoke of having children as "passing on your DNA." Turning forty was nothing, but he kept a camera mounted on a tripod so that each morning he could take a picture of himself against the bare wall in order to record his deterioration. Now he was turning fifty.

"Fifty's not *so* old," I say.

She wants to have a party for him, with blue streamers, helium balloons, an ice cream cake. As she talks, the idea grows in my mind and I add more adult things, wine and kisses, old friends, toasts to his future happiness.

I don't think Charlotte can count to fifty, and yet she ruminates on his approaching age, and on the way home from the library says, "That's old," a second time.

This time it really hits me. Fifty. I am married to a man who will be fifty years old. "The big five-oh," says Paul, who swears that approaching the half-century mark is hardly worth his notice.

It is not his age itself that upsets me, though I have always regretted the years that I have missed. What bothers me is that fifty is such a dangerous age for men, a time when they drop dead shoveling snow or playing tennis. Never sick a day in his life, and then the day after his fiftieth birthday, he's mowing the lawn, and boom . . .

He says he does not want to have a birthday party, and I believe him, just as I believed him when he said that turning forty meant nothing. "You've got enough on your hands without throwing a party," he says. And so it's back to the four of us, an ice cream cake and helium balloons, or so I think with some disappointment.

Monday he calls from work and says, "Guess who I spoke to today?" Just as I am taking in the news that he has phoned a friend he has not seen in twelve years, he gives me the name of a second and third friend he has reached. He does not want a party, but the next day he hands me a list of twenty-five friends (times two, if you count spouses or dates) that he has a sudden yen to see. By midweek the list has grown by another ten names because he can't invite Tom and not George to this party that we are not having, and if George comes, it would be rude to leave out Hank. And so on until eighty people are on this list.

"I thought you didn't want a party?" I ask, hopefully now, for I am getting cold feet.

"I didn't."

"And now?"

"Do I have to be consistent?"

"You bet."

"Okay. I don't really want a party, but I'm a good guy, so I'll let you throw one for me."

It is crazy to have a party at a time like this, to add so many new worries to the ones I already have. At the same time, it feels like a sign that joy will creep back into our lives, not for a moment here or there, but for long stretches, and that one day we will find it hard to remember that we grieved for so long.

When the party gets closer, the preparations begin to fill my days — good wine, rental urns, basil in the winter. I fear failure and suffer from recurring dreams in which guests arrive a night early, while I am in my running clothes, and Paul shows them around like a lord in his manor. If asked I would swear that I would never attempt another party this size, not as long as I was sane, but on the night the yes list hits seventy, Paul creeps downstairs and comes upon me singing in the kitchen.

He sits on the step stool and listens to me fret. Seventy people. We can't fit seventy people in this house. We'll have to call them up and persuade them to come in shifts, the cousins at five, the oldest friends at seven, the newer ones at nine, and so on.

He puts his arms around me and says, "You're happy, aren't you? You won't admit it, but you were down here just singing away. I know why you're happy, too."

"Why?"

"Because you have something new to worry about."

If this is worry, it is a different kind indeed. It is motivating worry that it wakes me, transports me, fills the cubbies in my brain, relieves me of the very real, tormenting worries I have about Rachel. I never enjoyed worrying before, or at least never thought of it as pleasurable in any way, though now I must confess it has its rewards.

It is hospital policy that all children in the infant stim program be examined and evaluated by the hospital's pediatric physiatrist (an M.D. who specializes in rehabilitation), and so four days before Paul's party, I take Rachel downstairs to see Dr. Goldstein. Downstairs is the hospital part of the hospital, the in-patient therapy rooms and beds, the pool and cafeteria. Wheeled through these halls are children in the last stages of degenerative diseases, and once-normal adolescents who've suffered head injuries. Downstairs you see children who are malformed, who suffer from genetic disorders and birth defects. Life is at its cruelest down here. Everything that can go wrong has.

Dr. Goldstein meets us in a small room that has an examining table against one wall and, across from it, a play area consisting of a mat, a mirror, and a box of toys. He is young and casually dressed — no white jacket, no medical paraphernalia in his pockets. He sits on a stool with casters, scoots to the examining table to pick up a clipboard, and then scoots our way, hunching low to greet Rachel, whom I hold in my lap, with a long, friendly, "Hel-loooooo."

No smile, no laugh, nothing.

"I had to wake her from her nap," I say, which is both true and beside the point.

He asks the same questions as every other physician who sees her — pregnancy, delivery, parental observations, except that he is genial and relaxed, and I do not feel the pressure to get it out in exactly the right order, in thirty seconds or else.

The history takes a minute or two, and then he hunches low and calls, "Rachel! How are yoo-oooo?"

And I say, "She's fine, a little tired, maybe."

"Uh-huh. Does she smile?"

"A *lot*. When she was little we had to stroke her cheek, but now she smiles without any tactile stimulation. Don't you, baby?" I hold her high above me. "Smile, sweetie."

She floats up there, loose lips, fisted hands. Smile, goddamn it.

Nothing.

"Well, she does." Then, seeing *him* smile, I add: "Really."

"A lot of mothers say their kids do better at home . . . Tell me, does she alert when she hears your voice?"

"Yes."

"Why don't you get her undressed . . ."

I peel off her clothes and lie her on the examining table. Dr. Goldstein pulls her to a sitting position, lifts her arms, taps her knees, tickles the soles of her feet — all so playfully that I think, gee, this guy really likes babies, look what a good time he's having with her. He pulls out a tape and measures her from head to toe, then wraps the tape around her chest. "This —" he says, as the tape winds around her head — "is the most important thing the pediatrician does."

I am reminded of the seriousness of this play. Is her brain growing properly?

"Is her head the right size?"

"Yep," he says. "She looks good."

I ask if he knows anything about optic nerve hypoplasia. I know it's foolish to expect him to have answers when Klibansky and Hines have not, but that has never stopped me.

"Have you had a blood test yet?" he says when I am through.

"For what?"

"You ought to have your antibody levels checked to see if you had a virus. She's what — four months old? It's still possible to determine whether you had a virus when you were pregnant."

Virus. Hadn't Klibansky mentioned virus among his list of possible causes? Why hadn't he suggested a blood test?

Dr. Goldstein walks us to the door. "Get the baby checked out, too," he says. "Urine and blood. Make an appointment with Mrs. Barrett before you leave."

I go about my chores that afternoon, and absorbed with fennel and shallots, and cheese enough for seventy, I think little of it. The word itself lies dormant in my brain until I am home and the groceries are unpacked. Then I take my trusty *Merck* off the shelf and leaf through the thin pages, skimming entries that I have read dozens of times these last two months. The habit of digging is firmly entrenched. I dig the way others crack their knuckles or bite their nails, and it is futile, for it gives no vent to my anxiety, soothes me in no way. But there I go, like a dog in a flower bed.

This time I find a bone.

*Cytomegalovirus,* CMV — a ubiquitous virus infection "occurring congenitally, postnatally, or at any age, and ranging in severity from a silent infection without consequences, through disease manifested by fever, hepatitis, and (in neonates) severe brain damage. . . . The extent of the pathologic process is highly variable in congenital infection. . . . Over 90% of infected newborns have no clinical evidence of the disease, but among those with symptoms at birth, problems that show up include microcephaly, intellectual impairment, neuromuscular disorders, hearing loss, chorioretinitis or optic atrophy, and dental problems. Central nervous system involvement also appears in about 10% of those children who are totally normal at birth. . . ."

Optic, optic nerve. Optic atrophy, optic nerve hypoplasia. Were these terms sometimes interchanged? Was this the virus that both Klibansky and Goldstein referred to, this ubiquitous asymptomatic bug that did no harm to ninety percent of the babies whose mothers harbored it but could cause profound damage to the other ten percent?

The manual said that intellectual impairment showed up in sixty percent of the infants with symptoms at birth.

"I felt compelled to remind the parents of the significant association of intellectual deficiency . . . with optic nerve hypoplasia . . ."

The next entry stops me as well. *Toxoplasmosis* — "a small, banana-shaped parasite . . . transmitted by ingestion of raw or poorly cooked meat containing tissue cysts, or by indirect or direct exposure to oocysts shed in cat feces. . . ."

My mind is spinning — we don't eat meat or have a cat, but Charlotte's caregiver had a house full of them, and who knew where a four-year-old's hands go, and anyhow, "infectivity of the oocyst is preserved for several months, and certain invertebrate vectors such as flies and cockroaches have been implicated in their transmission.

At birth about seventy percent of the newborns are asymptomatic. Ten percent are born with ocular involvement such as retinochoroiditis, optic nerve atrophy, blindness.

Optic nerve atrophy, optic nerve hypoplasia. Are *these* the same?

"The prognosis of congenital toxoplasmosis is poor. Most symptomatic newborns develop severe neurologic and ocular sequelae. . . . Even infants with inapparent infection at birth have a risk of developing in later years a wide range of intellectual deficits and retinochoroiditis, which may lead to blindness. . . ."

I read this paragraph over and over again. "Ten percent born with ocular involvement. . . . The prognosis . . . is poor . . . risk of developing . . . a wide range of intellectual deficits . . ." and I can't figure out why no one told us about this. Then I recall Dr. Hines telling us that the optic nerve hypoplasia appeared alone, and that she would be fine in other ways, and Klibansky mentioning the other associated problems only after I questioned him.

I run upstairs and find the stack of journal reprints in Rachel's file. Cytomegalovirus is mentioned in the top one. "One child had a significantly high titre for cytomegalovirus, including a high level of specific IgM. . . ."

I dial Paul's number at work.

"A virus?" he says when I tell him what I have found. "Then that means we can't have any more children."

"He didn't say anything about other children."

"Who the hell is this guy, anyhow? Klibansky didn't say anything about cytomegalovirus."

"I *know,* and I think it was incredibly irresponsible, but I don't know why you're angry with me."

"You called me in the middle of an experiment."

He hangs up before I can say another word.

I stand holding the phone. It is as if we are at the start of all this mess, my rib cage battered by the pounding of my heart, my whole body aching.

Charlotte hovers close, waving a picture that she has drawn, then a while later bringing me a doll that she has dressed. All I can say is, "That's nice," in an absent way. I scramble an egg for her, butter a piece of toast, and then stand in the kitchen, turning the pages of the newspaper.

When Paul arrives, he is so quiet that Charlotte, attuned to the smallest sounds of his homecoming, does not look up from her plate until he puts his keys on the mantel. I know he will come into the kitchen next, so I edge into the far end of the room and turn away, as if my hidden face will make me invisible to him.

He stands by me silently, waiting for me to turn and speak. I am supposed to be the one who is good with words, whose job it is to break the silence after we have quarreled. Tonight my mind is empty.

He puts a hand on my shoulder and nudges me until I turn.

"I can't let myself cry," he says. "I feel like I'll lose a part of myself when I do. Can you understand that?"

I don't until he puts his arms around me. Then everything inside me breaks, and I am inside out from weeping. "We were doing so well, I thought it would be over. I really did."

"It will never be over," he says.

The next morning, I drive Charlotte to nursery school, and continue on to the hospital. The door to the examination room is partially closed, and the screams of the child with Dr. Goldstein echo throughout the corridor. The screams penetrate my skin and vibrate within my body. After a few minutes the door opens, and a wet-faced boy encased in a rigid cast from waist to toes is wheeled out. He's smiling. I'm still vibrating.

Dr. Goldstein scoots from the examination table to the door when he sees me coming. I tell him what I found in the *Merck Manual* and wait for him to say that I am wrong to be upset.

He listens without comment and then asks, "When are you having the blood tests done?"

"Tomorrow."

"Let's wait until the results are in before we start drawing conclusions. Babies with CMV or toxoplasmosis usually have microcephaly and enlarged livers, and Rachel looked good. But we can't say much else until we hear about the tests."

### February 25

Seventy-two people show up to celebrate Paul's birthday. The food is ready and I am dressed in time. The birthday boy stands at the door and waits to be hugged seventy-two times. Most of the evening I spend in the kitchen, though several times I work my way among the cousins, high-school friends, college friends, work friends, car-pool friends, sailing friends, former girlfriends, and listen to them reacquaint with one another. Wherever I am I hear Paul's wild laugh as he greets his friends, and later as he tells his joke. "In my department, there are two men named Ross, two men from Taiwan, two men who are bald, and two fathers of blind children . . ."

There is so much happening that I feel disoriented, which is no change from these last few months, when I rarely feel as if I have a hold on things. Even so I am pleased to see all these people in my house, to hear Paul's laughter come in volleys.

By midnight it is all over. I pour myself a glass of wine and sit on the step stool. Paul brings his calculator into the kitchen and divides the minutes that people spent here (240) by the number of guests (72). He figures out that if he divided his time equally among our guests, he had 3.33 minutes to spend with each one.

"But it was good, wasn't it," he says. "People really enjoyed themselves."

He looks at the gifts he got, a copy of *The Old Man and the Sea,* a homeowner's repair manual, a T-shirt that says, "Fifty Is Nifty," and he says, "You're not going to leave me now that I'm fifty, are you?"

There was a time when I craved absolutes — always, never, forever — when I could not imagine a minute apart from him. But when he asks if I will leave him, he is asking me to look into the future, and I realize that I can no longer make these assumptions.

"I don't know. Can you say you'll never leave me? Most of the time you don't even like being married to me."

"It's not you. These days I haven't liked anything."

He tries on the T-shirt, a gaudy thing with huge sparkly letters, so awful it makes me laugh. "I feel like the world's passing me by," he says. "I feel old."

"No one would believe you're fifty."

"Not old that way. Do you remember how I always read the boat ads on Sunday to see what kind of boat we could get? 'Thirty-five-foot double-ender, six sails, inboard, auto-pilot, Loran.' I'd think about the trips we'd take and how I'd teach Char to sail. I don't do that anymore."

"And the deck?"

"I don't build the deck either. I don't sing in the shower, I don't dream."

I think of these last weeks, how he gets into bed beside me, turning his back before I can touch him, how seldom it is that we make love. Sometimes I feel as if I have become used to it, that because I am descended from a line of tough old peasants, I can take whatever is handed to me and get on with the fundamentals. Still, there are times when the knowledge of all that we have lost creeps back and wounds me terribly.

He stands before me in the sparkly T-shirt, and I know that despite all of our disappointments, I still love him deeply.

"You know what's hardest for me? All the forbidden topics. I'm always telling myself what not to say. Don't talk about Rachel, don't tell him what the doctor said, don't talk about your fears. Because if I do, we'll have an argument, and I just can't keep fighting. I've gotten good at keeping things to myself, have you noticed? What scares me is that I'm afraid I'll get too good."

He reaches out and takes my hand. "Tell me."

"I wanted to feel that no matter what happened at least we had each other."

"But we do."

"*Sometimes*," I say.

"Sometimes," he agrees.


The results of the blood tests come back early in March, and they are negative.

So. "If she doesn't have a virus, then what?" I ask Dr. Goldstein.

"It could be a degenerative disease, but there's nothing you can do about any of those, so forget it; there's no use going on a wild-goose chase."

*What disease, give me a name, how will I know, when will it happen?*

"We'll watch her motor development. We'll watch her hearing. She could be a year old, or two, or six before anything shows up."

Five days later Paul and I drive to New York, where Rachel is scheduled for an EEG and a follow-up with Dr. Klibansky. It is our first time in Hospital City since the initial tests in December, and as soon as the beige buildings appear in the skyline, memories of these appointments rush back, each of them as clear and sharp as glass.

The EEG is first, followed by an examination, much like Dr. Goldstein's. Dr. Klibansky measures Rachel crosswise, lengthwise, around the head, tickles and taps her, holds her by the hands until she stands on her boxy little feet, then asks if she can sit. Paul pulls her upright, spreads her legs, arranging them, as if she were a posable doll, in just the right position. She sits for a half a minute, then slowly begins to lean and sway. Dr. Klibansky says, "I'd like it if she were sitting by now," and starts into his office.

When we are together I tell him about my recent findings and ask why he never suggested that the blood tests be done.

"For what purpose?" he says.

"You mentioned virus as a possible cause, didn't you?"

"I said *virus,* not cytomegalovirus. Optic nerve hypoplasia and optic nerve atrophy are completely different things. If you want to read about optic nerve hypoplasia, read about it, but to come in here talking about cytomegalovirus and toxoplasmosis is a waste of time."

"I was digging," I say, rather embarrassed. "I was looking for causes."

"I already told you that the pathogenesis of optic nerve hypoplasia isn't completely understood. If it was known what caused the hypoplasia, I would have said so."

He gets up, a not so subtle hint for us to do the same. Paul slides Rachel into the baby carrier and follows me to the elevator. Rachel has grown since her last visit. Then, only the top of her head showed when she rested across Paul's chest. Now her head and neck are free, and her hands peep out of the special slots on either side so that it looks as if she is embracing her dad. Her hair sticks up in gummy tufts, and in neat rows across her scalp are red X's the technician drew on her head for the EEG. I feel foolish for having made such a stupid mistake and for digging so much when I have been repeatedly told that I will not find an answer. And yet I know that if she were someone else's child instead of my own, my relentless quest for answers would be regarded as noble, and that it is because she is mine that I am seen as nothing more than a neurotic mother. I will not give up, I think. Never!

I have not even finished the thought when I know that it is untrue. I am too weary to go on at this pace, too eager to divert my thoughts from Rachel to the others in my life.

# ❦ 9 ❦

# A Slow Awakening

*March*

RACHEL DOES NOT WAKEN SUDDENLY, like Sleeping Beauty kissed by the prince; she rouses slowly and quietly from her dormancy, and Paul and I, absorbed by the chaos of everyday life, do not fully notice the change at first. To all but the most perceptive she is the same. She is still heartbreakingly passive.

If she were a normal baby of six months, she would most likely roll from stomach to back, push up onto all fours, rock with her limbs extended, and possibly creep. She would reach and grasp, transfer things from hand to hand, splash and kick in the tub. She would laugh, babble, tease, and play games. She would protest if abandoned for a moment. She does not roll over or move, and whether this is because of her blindness alone, or a sign of other problems, is still unknown. She sits, which in itself is hopeful, since she has begun to sit within the normal range; however, if left alone, she will sit and sit — for an eternity, it seems, head bowed, hands in fists, never complaining. The change is that she has become sensitive to our movements and listens with her head cocked to our comings and goings. When one of us nears she calls out; when we touch her or put a toy on the tray of her walker, she shrieks, her whole body wiggling with pleasure. She has also learned to reach for an object after we brush her hand with it, thus satisfying the first goal in the plan to get her mobile.

Paul comes home from work and looks for her. He approaches slowly, whispering as he draws close, and when she brightens and cries out in anticipation, he swoops down and lifts her high into the air, calling, "Babykins!" I watch him play with Rachel, and I am filled with awe. Look at the way he holds her close, kissing her nose and belly and toes, the way he bounces her, bathes with her, sits her on the couch, surrounded by a wall of pillows, so that she will keep him company while he reads. Their bond was so slow to form that I despaired of him ever experiencing the pure, joyous love he felt for Charlotte, but look at how he arranges her in the high chair every evening, moving her chair close to his so that the soles of her feet rest against his leg while they eat. He loves her! He really loves her. And his love for her brightens the whole house and fills me with hope for all of us.

All this is hard on Charlotte. Another babykins, one who is easy to lift, and can be tossed into the air, whereas she is too heavy to hold at arm's length. Even so, I notice that, like Paul, she is more interested in playing with Rachel, and that her play is no longer the possessive kind meant only to keep the rest of us from getting near. Now she talks and sings to Rachel and in the morning climbs into the crib beside her. She proudly tells her friends that Rae-Rae is blind, though she has no sense that anything is wrong with her, only that she is called this particular thing. Rae-Rae is her baby sister, hers to dress in scarves and hats, to wheel in the street, to call a special name. And when I dare to refer to her as Rachel: "Her *name* is Rae-Rae."

When I see Paul or Charlotte play with Rachel I realize how completely her blindness has cut her off. I had read the literature and knew this was a danger, yet I never believed that she would be deprived, not by us, not in *our* house. Isn't that what has happened, though?

For the six months that we have been struggling with the idea of Rachel's disability, we have had in our household a sleepy, silent, uncomplaining baby who grew but hardly changed, who rarely smiled, never laughed, showed no interest in her family. Although her long naps made me feel frantic, I came to depend upon them, for when she slept I had time to work, or time for Paul and Charlotte, or time simply not to think of her blindness.

I loved her because she was mine, and took pleasure in her soft, sweet babyness. How often did I play with her? When I think of all the simple games that amuse parents and babies for hours — funny faces, peek-a-boo, bouncy-bouncy, gotcha nose, splish-splash in the tub — I realize that there are a million ways to make a sighted child laugh, and no way to delight our little daughter.

I never played with Rachel, I worked with her, using the techniques I learned in infant stim. Charlotte and I unwound paper towels and wrapping paper, decorated the cardboard rolls beneath, and strung them across the head and foot of her crib, and catty-corner across the playpen

I set up in my office. We held her at the waist and bounced her on top of the exercise ball I borrowed from the hospital, the way the physical therapist showed me. Rachel always rode up there, head bowed, fists clenched, utterly silent. "Does she like it?" Charlotte would ask hopefully. Did she? "She isn't crying," I would say.

Now Rachel cocks her head when we are nearby and calls out to us. She gives a little shriek when we draw close, and wiggles all over. Paul comes home, tiptoes into the solarium, lifts her high, kisses her forehead, calls "Babykins!" A little shriek was all that it took to form the bond between them, a little cry that tells him she loves him and needs him and knows who he is.

There is something so charming about the way Rachel sits with her head cocked — our little bird, listening for her daddy's approach — that I do not stop to question it until I pick up a roll of photographs I have taken of her, the first since the diagnosis. In each one she sits with her head angled in exactly the same way. I can recall what I did the day I took the pictures, how I posed her at the end of the room, then backed up with my camera and called her name so that she would lift her bowed head. And she did each time, tilting it in the same funny way.

*Why?* I ask myself when I lay out these photographs. If she were totally blind, why would she look up when I called her name? Blind babies do not turn toward sound — hadn't I read that many times? Isn't that what we have been trying to teach her in infant stim, to turn and reach out for what she hears but does not see? Is it possible that she cocks her head because she is trying to see and not because she is listening intently?

Seeing has an entirely new meaning to me these days. It is not faces and pictures and landscapes, but vague forms, light and shadow. This is what I allow myself to hope for, cautiously, for it would be so easy to be deluded by my own yearning, and by the sentiments of family and friends, who, since the very start, have insisted that Rachel can see.

Their observations are due mainly to the nystagmus itself, for her eyes roam (not as jerkily as in the past), slowly in one direction and more rapidly back, not unlike a sighted person tracking an object. I know this is why my friends say, "She *sees*," and yet each time I hear those words, I feel a surge of hope, for I want to let go of all my skepticism and believe. At the same time, I keep searching for the truth so that in time I will learn to accept it.

The truth has been that Rachel is blind, and so what I have wanted since the diagnosis was to begin to think of her as blind and to use the word not to shock myself into believing it, but in order to accept her condition. The irony is that just as this has begun to happen, I find myself studying her sudden attentiveness and suspecting that she can see.

The next time Sharon tests Rachel with her penlight, she records in her notes that Rachel "seemed to attend" to the light. These three words fill me with such nervous hope that the house is too small to contain me.

It is a miserable gray day, and the streets are clotted with blackened snow. I bundle up my kids and take them to the park. Mud and slush have collected beneath the swings and where the end of the seesaw rests. Charlotte has the park to herself, sits on each wet swing, slides down the big and little slides. The park is gorgeous in all its grayness, the slush, the spindly-looking trees. Once again I see what hopelessness does; it has dimmed my vision, blinding me to all that gave me pleasure in the past. These simple words — "seemed to attend" — have enabled me to see again.

I do not keep my happiness inside me where it will only be muted by time. I tell Hinda and my mother. I write letters to people who sent baby gifts, because now I can say that she was born blind, but she has begun to blossom, that our expectations are great. "Today the social worker from the Commission for the Blind agreed that she seems to attend to light."

When Paul comes home, I repeat the experiment. He watches for a moment, then angrily dismisses Sharon's words. It could have been noise that caused her response, an air current, her nystagmus. It could have been random. He does not want to hear about these "tests" that I conduct or listen to the well-meaning blather of friends. Rachel cannot see; she cannot see a thing.

He will not call her blind. Not for three more months, he says, because Dr. Hines had told us that the visual system continued to develop until a child was nine months old.

Her blindness terrifies him more than it does me. I have accepted it, and when I engage in magical thinking, I hope for it — blindness over intellectual impairment, blindness so that she will be spared in other ways, please, please, please. He shares the horror of blindness that most people feel.

As soon as Mrs. Kaiser sits beside us, in infant stim, I say: "I think Rachel has some light perception."

After the words are out I wonder if I am crazy for being so sure. I imagine her telling me to stop being foolish and accustom myself to the way that Rachel is. "Paul says it's just the nystagmus, but I could swear that when I flash a light in front of her, she follows it. The social worker thought so, too."

Mrs. Kaiser finds her penlight and directs the beam across Rachel's face. Rachel's eyes move, at times in the direction of the beam, and just as often not. "Are you *bored?*" she says to Rachel. "Are you sitting there thinking, 'Lady, get that light out of my eyes?' *Are* you? Let's put this old light away, and play with something *interesting* for a change."

Mrs. Kaiser shakes bells in front of Rachel and then to the side, and we wait for her to reach out for them, because the next step, now that she responds to a tactile cue, is to respond to an auditory one; that is, to reach out for something she hears *without* a tactile cue. She won't become mobile until she can do this.

The bells jingle. My daughter sits, pretty face blank; hands fisted, head cocked at an odd angle. Maybe I am wrong after all and have let my desire for her to see trick me into believing that she does. I am saddened to see her this way, and feel her failure in the pit of my stomach.

Across the mat, Alex lies on his back, swiping at a ball suspended from the ceiling; Tory watches a therapist blow soap bubbles and cries fat tears. Steven is supposed to pick up two blocks, but turns to touch the bubbles, and having little trunk control, flops onto Katie, who has bows in her pigtails today, lavender to match her jeans. Todd's mother rushes in, her son still encased in his snowsuit, and says, "Todd can sit up!" The applause for her two-year-old son fills the room.

Rachel cocks her head and listens to the clapping, then listens to bells that are jingling inches away. Mrs. Kaiser begins to laugh. "Look at the way she *attends*," she says. "She's so sensitive to sound."

She strokes Rachel's cheek, and gets a smile and a body-wiggling chortle. "She's made *such* strides," she says to me.

I sit very still, and the joy that washes over me is dizzying. I believe, I believe — and it is so sweet. Maybe she will be blind, but blind people can have full lives, I know it in my heart, just as I know that I will be able to show her the world.

I can feel the therapists' optimism when they work with Rachel. Though I have never detected a moment's impatience among any of them, never seen a single one give up on any child, now their hope is palpable. They are attuned to the smallest changes in her development, the tiniest improvements. How well she sits, and just when she should! How nicely this seems to fit the profile of a visually impaired child, whose movement is delayed, though not the neurological development itself. She always held her head up well, and now she sits well, and if she is still passive — isn't that to be expected of a child who has no visual lures? And if her head is always bowed — what reason would she have to lift it high? And if her hands are always fisted at her sides — didn't Selma Fraiberg talk about the irony of the expression that the blind person's hands are his eyes, when blind children have "blind" hands unless they're taught to use them? Isn't that what we're working on now when we teach her how to reach out?

Faith works with Rachel next. She bends her leg, and helps her to roll over, something Rachel cannot do alone. Pachelbel's *Canon* plays on the stereo; Tory wails. Loudest of all are the volleys of applause for the wondrous accomplishments achieved this afternoon. Tory reaches, Steven sits, Alex bangs blocks together, Rachel squeezes a duck. The sun shines through the row of windows, dappling the dolls that line the sill. The big bear droops at the shoulders like a weary man. This room is not part of the world outside. It is a separate place, governed by its own rules, a place where the love we have for our children is not tarnished by the opinion of others, where their progress is not seen as pathetic. We celebrate the victory of a two-year-old boy who sits unsupported for the first time; he is laureate of the day, and we congratulate both him and his mother, who tries to shrug it off, but then admits, "He *is* coming along."

The magic does not last long. The therapists leave. The children get cranky. The social worker comes with coffee and cookies. We talk about yard sales, and furniture refinishing, medical expenses, insensitive physicians, and then we dig and dig until we end up deep inside a hole in the middle of the everyday world.

*April 2*

Linda calls to tell me that a woman at one of the movie studios is interested in a script the two of us wrote a couple of years ago.

How do I feel when I get the news? Like a fossil, buried a few eons ago, and this mysterious woman is the archeologist who has just dug me up.

"Well, dust yourself off, she wants to meet with us on Thursday," Linda says.

Although I obsess about what to wear (as if the ultimate choice of earrings or shoes will determine the fate of the script) the real issue is, who will take care of Rachel?

It is mother's work, taking care of a handicapped child: This much has not changed in modern times. All of the women in the mothers' group (the *mothers'* group, as if fathers do not exist) have spoken of the difficulty of finding someone to care for their children for as little as an hour. Who is there to care for Katie so that her parents, who have not had a vacation since she got sick two and a half years ago, can go away? Who will mind Steven? "My mother-in-law was great with the other two, but I ask her to look after Stevie so I can go to the doctor's, and she gets so panic-stricken, I cancel out," Steven's mother told us one Thursday. "It's 'I don't know what to do with him, I don't know what to feed him, what do I do if he cries?' I mean, what can I say? He doesn't climb or crawl, he's got the constitution of a horse. It's not even like he can get into any mischief."

Who will take care of Rachel?

Paul says he'll take a vacation day, but that only masks a larger problem. Who will take care of Rachel when she is too old to play at my side? Who will take care of her if something happens to me?

By the time Charlotte was six months old, I had hired a woman to look after her for five hours a day. This caregiver was loving and attentive and I trusted her. I also knew that Charlotte would make her needs known; if she was hungry, she would cry for food, if she wanted attention, she would demand it. Rachel is so quiet. The one time I left her with a baby-sitter, I returned to find my daughter rocking in a windup swing. "Such a *good* baby," Beryl had said, and I knew that she had been left to rock all day, a good baby, no trouble at all.

"So she'll lose a day," Paul says when I tell him why I don't want to ask Beryl again.

I imagine her falling down a dark black hole, tumbling into the void.

"One day won't kill her," he says.

There is no time to find someone else, so on the day of the meeting, I edge into the baby-sitter's house with Rachel in my arms.

Beryl takes her from me, cradles her closely, and makes little lovey sounds. "Are you a good girl, are you, are you?"

I open my mouth to say something. I want to believe that one day won't kill her, yet I cannot help seeing it as a kind of death. "Please don't put her in the swing," I say at last. "Don't let her sleep all day."

I feel as if I will never be able to shake my worries, that the only thing left in my mind is concern for this child. I stumble onto the train, find a seat, stare out the grimy windows, gloomy, gloomy all the way into New York.

Then suddenly I am inside the Russian Tea Room, shaking hands and introducing myself, drinking fizzy water, talking with great ease about characters I had forgotten existed and situations invented long ago. Two fine hours pass this way, during which time a dormant part of me comes alive. I am no longer the mother of a blind child and nothing else. I am a writer, my thoughts of home so distant that when, toward the end of the lunch, the woman asks if either of us have children, it is Linda who points to me and says, "*She* does."

"How old?"

"Four and six months."

"A *baby!*" says the woman.

I am a writer even then, as I smile and hide my secret (she's blind, you know), because I know that no one sees that I am wounded, that I have somehow pulled off this disguise.

March is going out like a lion this year, and when I leave the restaurant, a powerful tail wind carries me down Fifty-seventh Street. I shiver and hunch into my coat. The world looks brighter than it has for many months.

The sidewalks are jammed with a lunch-hour crowd; women in chic dresses and sneakers, Japanese tourists, Senegalese street vendors. The sight of other people reminds me how cut off I have been these last few months, how divorced from the goings-on in nation and town, the small hurts and disappointments of others, from my own pleasures and aspirations. All the ups and downs, the good days and bad days, have centered around Rachel. She will be blind, she will see. Her intellect will be normal, she will be slow.

No wonder I am so vulnerable to the opinions of spouse, therapists, and friends, and the style of doctors' prognoses; no wonder I take so seriously quacks, obscure reprints, newspaper articles. Rachel's well-being has been my whole life. I want to be part of the world again. I want to find someone to care for Rachel so that I can breathe.

I stop in front of the Doubleday bookstore on Fifty-sixth Street and peer into the window, where four and a half years ago, while waiting for a bus, I saw my book for the first time. I remember how vivid it was when compared to the others, how easy to spot from outside the store, how it stood out the way my own child does among a crowd of children. I went inside the store that afternoon in order to hold my book, and while bus after bus went by, I studied the cover and jacket and typeface with such interest that a woman beside me picked up the copy beneath and tried to figure out what I found so mesmerizing. I stood beside her and thought, I'm the writer, I really am!

I am that writer as I continue down Fifth Avenue, trench coat flapping in the wind, and there will be more stories, I know there will; I can feel from just this one afternoon how much I have opened up. I am that writer until I pass St. Patrick's Cathedral and see the black man whose eyes are covered with a milky film, and the sign he wears around his neck. *I am blind please help me god bless you.*

Two more meetings in New York; two more walks (detouring down Madison Avenue to avoid the beggar), two more afternoons when I leave my daughter at Beryl's, where she will sleep away the day, because no matter how often I explain, Beryl cannot bear waking a baby who naps so peacefully.

What is it that buoys me then? All the obvious things, the possibility of earning money, which we need, work for someone else, with a deadline that I will be forced to meet no matter what. Then there are the reasons that are harder to explain: getting dressed to catch a train, talking to strangers. When I walk into a room with people who do not know me, I cast off my history like an old overcoat. When I am on a street crowded with anonymous bypassers, the world feels so bright and new that when I think about Rachel, it is with optimism. She reaches out, feels my arm and wrist watch, alerts to our voices! She has awakened at last.

Even Paul enjoys the reports I bring of meetings and afternoons away from home, and when I fret over leaving Rachel (for I have lost the knack of leaving my children), he says, "Don't you remember our deal? I support you, then you support me?" I hear him telling people on the phone, "Next year I'll retire."

I put an ad in the newspaper. "Loving caregiver needed for eight-month-old girl with special needs." The next week the phone rings as much as it did the week after the diagnosis.

I get calls from a woman who wants to take care of a baby because she's stuck at home anyway, from a pregnant woman who wants experience with a child before she has her own, from a recent widow whose children told her she might be less depressed if she had a baby around. I get a call from a twelve-year-old who wants a dollar an hour and from the sister of a brain-damaged boy who asks for four times the hourly wage that I can afford to pay. The young woman with the best qualifications — near completion of a degree in communicative disorders — sits in the solarium with us and tells us all about her course work, and never once approaches the baby who sits at her feet.

In the midst of all this, Paul's niece calls to ask if she can stay with us. She has quit her job making false teeth and arrives from California (via Florida) with several suitcases, a hundred pounds of dental plaster, and vague plans to stay at our house, go to Upstate New York, or drive back home. In the meantime, she agrees to look after Rachel.

I have so curiously little to say about my own child that it only takes a minute to go over all of her likes and dislikes and daily habits. She isn't really interested in toys, her diet of solids is limited. A bath seems like a nice idea, though it is a sad sight indeed to see the way she sits hunched and fisted in the tub. Only one thing is important. "Don't let her sleep too long."

For the first time since her birth, I climb the stairs to my office alone, free of worry that Rachel will sleep too long or wake up too soon. The room is mine, my thoughts are my own. I pick up my manuscript and open it to the chapter I have been staring at for seven months. It is absolutely quiet.

Too quiet. I stand at the door and listen. Is she talking to Rachel? Is she playing with her? Could she be reading a book while Rachel sits and sits? No, she's good, she loves kids, she's done this before . . . I lock my office door to muffle whatever is going on downstairs, silence or sound, and will myself to work.

After a week she decides to leave. I can't blame her. The smooth, eventless days that I cherish make dull company for a girl in her twenties. I work every day until three, finish up, get the kids, do household chores, eat, bathe, and tuck them into bed, and try to hurry into bed myself. Heaven for me is in the sack early with Paul and a good book, and because the evenings have gone this way, I am suffused with a sense of well-being. Life works, I think, though when I see my life reflected through her eyes, I realize with a bitter shock how far I am from twenty-five.

*May*

No more meetings, no word at all about the script. I've been unable to bring myself to call Linda and hear her confirm the bad news.

"Do you know how often these things fall through?" I tell Paul, trying not to speak of my disappointment.

"Of course I do," he says. "But you got something out of it, didn't you? It was good experience."

A little voice inside my head taunts me several times a day. *Hey, stupido, did you actually believe in cosmic justice? Were you dumb enough to think that just because you've had rough times, a success would come and balance it out?* (Well . . . sort of.)

I remember going through a phase where I believed in this kind of justice. Like this, as I roamed through bad streets late at night: My sister died young, therefore, I won't. But grief is not divvied up like a pie, one slice for each person. In the mothers' group last week I found out that all of us have been hit at least twice. My older sister was murdered and my daughter was born blind. Steven's mother has a son with cerebral palsy and a husband who had cancer; Katie's mother has an autoimmune disease, a dying mother, a severely brain-damaged daughter. Todd's father was badly wounded in Vietnam.

The world sees one tragedy as sad. Stack them up like this and we become the target of nervous laughter. We're so unlucky it's ridiculous. Maybe we deserve it.

Our days of optimism about Rachel are broken by a call from Dr. Klibansky with the results of the EEG. It was abnormal, with low-amplitude spikes in the left occipital region. He apologizes for his delay in calling, and says he is "confounded and frustrated" by the meaning, and cannot predict whether this suggests that she will have a problem with seizures. "Sometimes this kind of spiking shows up with cortical blindness. . . . We'll just have to wait and see." He sounds upset rather than hostile.

What does the spiking mean? That she has a seizure disorder that is subclinical, or that the lesion begins at a higher level than the optic nerve, in the visual cortex itself? "There's no reason to believe that the damage is confined to the optic nerve," Klibansky says.

She is brain-damaged if this is true, intellectually impaired, retarded. When I think about the changes that encouraged me a month ago they now seem so pitiful. It's true she wiggles when she hears us and calls out when we're near, but she doesn't do much else. Nine months old, and she cannot creep or crawl or pull herself up; her hands stay fisted by her sides. She cannot even roll.

After I hang up the phone, I sit at my desk, mind flooded with stories about parents who devoted themselves to making whole children the world saw as hopeless. An autistic boy, unable to relate to those around him, now totally normal. A hopelessly spastic girl who walks without crutches. Where have I been? Worrying about the fate of my script. My ambition embarrasses me. It seems inappropriate and selfish to want for myself at a time like this. If only I were as persistent as those parents, as selfless as Mother Theresa, as patient as Mrs. Kaiser. If only I had taken Rachel to the healer, tried alternative therapies, given her mega-doses of vitamins, worked with her for long, steady hours, truly wanted nothing except her progress.

Paul thinks these thoughts are ridiculous self-flagellation. "She's only nine months old," he says. "There's not much you can do with her."

Who knows if that's true. I never heard the end of the story about the woman from Queens who dragged her retarded child from doctor to doctor. Maybe she found the right one.

Of all her delays, the fact that Rachel does not roll obsesses me most. It is the one thing I cannot explain away, for normal babies roll from stomach to back at about four months and blind ones not much later, and here she is, nine months old and showing no inclination at all. Each week at infant stim her physical therapist arranges her legs to start her on a roll. Rachel, sweet and uncomplaining, accepts this helping hand, but makes no attempt to get herself over. And I am questioning, questioning everyone. Why doesn't she roll?

A mobility instructor from the Commission comes to visit us one Friday. His job is to help blind and visually impaired people travel as independently as possible. Until recently this kind of training did not begin until the blind person was in high school. Current wisdom stresses starting soon after birth.

"Even when the baby's still in her crib, she should have a sense of where she is in relation to the environment," he tells me. "That's Mommy coming in, that must be the door. If Mommy stops talking, does she still exist in other places?

"A child has to bump into something to learn that it exists. She has to explore the tables and chairs to understand over, under, around. Try not to be too overprotective."

"I wish I had the chance," I say. "Rachel doesn't move at all. She can't even roll from her stomach to her back."

He looks up at me, then quickly averts his eyes. "It's odd for her to sit so well and not be able to roll."

Yes, he is telling me. Yes, you're right to be concerned.

I wake the next morning and recall the way he met my eyes and quickly looked away. *Yes. Yes, you're right. She should be rolling over by now.* And when I see Rachel sitting on the floor, I see a pretty, cheerful baby who will sit forever if we let her. In the busyness of the day, his look fades, and during quiet moments it is back again. When I get into bed at night, his words echo in my mind.

Rachel cries out in her sleep as she does most nights. It is a peculiar cry — sharp and mournful — and ends so quickly that by the time I get up to check her, she is asleep again. This time when I adjust her blankets, I think, she knows what will happen in the future. Somehow she understands.

Charlotte awakens with the crows the next morning. She jumps into my bed and tugs on me until I am up, too. As soon as my eyes open, she slips a bulging envelope into my palm.

Inside is a card, folded numerous times. "I love you Jan," it says. "Happy birthday Jan."

"I knew it was J-A-N-E, but I didn't feel like putting the *E*," she says. "I was in too much of a rush."

The gifts are just as great — a seashell and a small ceramic dog from her own collection wrapped inside a wad of taped tissues.

After breakfast, we gather in the solarium. Paul and I divide up the Sunday paper and Charlotte sorts through a box of dress-up clothes and starts the morning in a black velvet cloche, sequined gown, and leopard platform shoes. Outside, a chorus of birds nibble at the mulberries, and at my feet Rachel rolls from tummy to back, and then, as if she knows what a doubter I am, and how easy it is for me to think that it's an illusion, she rolls again and again and again.

# ❦ 10 ❦

## He Believes

THE WEATHER GETS HOT all of a sudden, and Paul and I come down with a bad case of Maine fever. I find myself thinking about the smell of pine needles, the cool water, so clear you can see the seaweed waving beneath the surface, the hermit and horseshoe crabs, the small island where the herons rest, the larger one, where cormorants line up in neat rows, the berry bushes along the dirt road, the little house we bought the year after we were married, far from the world of work and stress. Late at night, when I think that he has been fast asleep for an hour, Paul starts to talk in the darkness about getting the mast repaired so we can sail this summer and putting in footings for a deck. Last year, he forfeited vacation days, something he swears he'll never do again. "I'm taking every day that's due me, every goddamn day."

The next afternoon, a Saturday, he builds a scale model of our cottage and the land that slopes down to the bay, and plans a deck that overlooks the water, with notched corners to accommodate the tall pines that neither of us wants to chop down. Charlotte sits beside him and cuts tiny chairs and couches out of paper that she folds and tapes until they'll stand, and figures that she bends to fit upon this play furniture, which she sets inside the model house. It is the first time I have seen Paul do anything recreational since Rachel's birth, and it touches me.

Charlotte catches Maine fever, too.

"There are gulls, Mommy," she tells me that night.

"There are mosquitoes."

"You can catch tiny, tiny, *tiny,* little fish —" holding her thumb and finger a fraction of an inch apart.

You can catch encephalitis, I think.

"Oh Mommy, the bay is so *blootiful,* don't you just want to go?"

In fact, I do, for we have always been happy in Maine. It is a yearning that cannot be easily satisfied, however. Paul has cells to feed and commitments to a colleague; he's in the middle of an experiment and then, when the experiment has been completed, it is his turn to use the NMR machine, and he cannot possibly leave.

By the time the month ends, I am the one with excuses. Money has come through for Linda and me to rewrite the script for Linda to direct.

*June 20*

Linda moves in for a week. She brings her clothes and books upstairs to my office, and tucks her special foods in a corner of the cabinet and inside the fridge. A girl named Lourie, who answered my newspaper ad, takes care of Rachel so that Linda and I can work without interruption from nine until three, when Charlotte comes home. It is not easy for Linda to be here. She is a single person, and the confusion that's an expected part of my life upsets her — the noise, the end of the day irritation of tired and hungry children, the burst of chores that begins when Charlotte returns. Tend to kids, cook, clean up, bathe them, tuck them into bed, and then upstairs to work with Linda again. When I see the pitying way she looks at me — Jane-donkey tied to the post — and the way she watches Paul, her eyes telling me what I already know — he should do more — I remember my own horror of family life from the distant past when I was single. *No way, not me . . .* Sometimes I see myself through her eyes, a hapless beast of burden, though more often I realize that someone else's chaos is like someone else's hard luck: unbearable only in the mind of the outsider.

One of the curiosities in our house is that my third-floor office shares the same heating duct as the second-floor bathroom, so that whatever goes on downstairs in the bathroom rings clearly at my desk. What I hear while I work is Lourie's voice as she bathes Rachel, her deep laughter, her cheer and energy. When I go downstairs, I see them in the solarium, Rachel with her back to Lourie's chest, her hand in Lourie's, while Lourie has her stroke a toy. "Soft, Rae-Rae, feel how soft?" I see them sitting by the fireplace so that Rachel can feel the bricks; or on the lawn beside our house, Rachel in a bonnet and shirt, her bottom bare so that the grass is next to her skin. Sometimes when I finish work they are just returning from the supermarket where Lourie took Rachel to smell flowers; or sitting on the steps, a young woman with fair skin and long spiral curls and pretty milkmaid looks, brushing rose petals against the cheek of a beautiful baby.

Lourie bathes Rachel every day so that she will get comfortable in the water; she lets her "experience" her food so that she will learn to feed herself. She understands that in order for Rachel to learn about her cup she must explore its shape and weight and texture, its cupness. Messes are nothing to her. She gives Rachel a spoon each day, guides her hand toward the dish, and makes no complaint if the cereal leaves splotches on her shirt or if the spoon is flung and splatters the wall behind her.

The day that Linda and I finish our revisions, I go to make tea and find myself watching Lourie feed Rachel. She scatters pieces of banana across the high-chair tray, and says: "Banana, Rae-Rae." Rachel sweeps her hand across the tray, works a piece of banana into her palm, then shoves her hand across her face. Her mouth moves like a vacuum cleaner, sucking it in. It is the way she sits when she does this, her head cocked, that stops me. She is not *listening* to those slices of banana. I watch her cock her head as she captures each piece this way, palm across the tray, hand to mouth, and what I think is: She does this too well for a child who has no vision.

When Lourie leaves, I sit beside Rachel in the solarium. I know that she does not see, yet I kneel in front of her so that my face is near hers. The late afternoon sun leaves stripes upon her blanket. I stay quite still, and wait for recognition. She seems not to perceive my presence at all; not the warmth and smell of me, the sound of my breathing, my sigh of disappointment. I sit her up, and she stays just the way I have arranged her, head lowered, never stirring. The plants on the table above her have turned to the light, their stems twisting up and slanting toward the window, the broad begonia leaves like cups to catch the sun. Rachel pats the carpet, her dimpled hand in sunlight. She clenches and unclenches it in a strange spasmodic way. I slide her a few inches from the light and wait, and she leans forward and reaches out, as if sunlight can be caught and mouthed. I move her again, and again she reaches for the brightness.

Paul comes home early. He is too weary to absorb anything new, so I turn my cheek for a kiss, cool and aloof, and go back into the kitchen. The knot in my stomach is the news that I carry. He lifts Rachel high into the air, calling, "Babykins!" and hearing his voice, Charlotte races down the stairs and jumps into his arms. I do not interrupt their play, not even for a second.

Linda joins us for dinner. Paul asks her the kinds of technical questions about the film that intrigue him — what filters and lenses will be used when the film is shot, the cost of processing and making prints. He asks her about night shooting and opticals — questions that would interest me if I were not waiting for the perfect time. Charlotte tries to divert his attention by sitting in his lap, playing with his shirt buttons, asking aimless questions. When nothing works for long, she leaves.

As soon as she is upstairs, I say: "I want you to watch something."

He sees the flashlight and says, "Haven't we been through this?"

"You know me well enough to know how cautious I am. You know I've avoided false hope. Can't you believe me when I tell you she can track a beam of light? I've tested her several times, and she's consistently done it. Can't you at least be happy?"

I know that she will not convince him. I know even as the spot of light shines upon her high-chair tray that she will abide by the First Law of Baby and not perform on request. I know it, and yet I have no other way to make him believe me.

"Lourie saw it, too. She put pieces of banana on the high-chair tray, and Rachel got each one."

"What's so remarkable about that?"

"Give her a second, Paul," says Linda.

I move the flashlight so that the spot travels across the tray. Rachel sits with her head bowed.

"Try it with the banana," Linda says.

"Oh, for Christ sake."

Paul grabs his plate. I hear the dishwasher open, the rack of plates clatter out, his footsteps as he climbs upstairs.

He goes to sleep at ten. An hour later, I come to bed and find him rigid and turned away. When we were new to each other, I could not spend a night turned away from him. If he would not respond to words, I switched on lights, tugged on blankets, provoked fights — anything to unbend this human wall. We have been married for eight years, and the hurt I feel is not as sharp. I can live without you, I think.

At dawn I wake. Rachel lies on her back between us. I watch Paul pass his hand across her face, thirty times, forty. Then I fall back to sleep.

\*　　\*　　\*

*June 30*

A weekend in Maine (at last!). On the way we pull into a restaurant off the road, a dim, defeated-looking place with turquoise booths, stained carpeting, and unhealthy-looking waitresses. Paul takes Charlotte to the men's room; I set Rachel in a high chair and go off to get her some kidney beans from the salad bar. The vegetables are so pale they look as if they have been grown underground. I scoop a few canned beans from the murky liquid and bring them to Rachel, who sits with her head bowed and her hands drawn in, like a threatened animal retreating into its shell.

"Food, baby," I say, as I put a few in front of her. I don't think she understands me, but I talk anyhow. "Beans, baby, here."

I stroke her beneath the chin, and she turns her head to the side. Her eyes jitter. A fist unclenches. She moves her arm, then lowers her hand onto a bean. The actions are slow and jerky, as if the arm is a mechanical one worked by an inexperienced operator. When I see Paul leave the rest room, my heart begins to pound. Rachel's palm closes around a bean. Paul says: "Excuse me!" and a waitress ambles over and drops menus onto the paper placemats in front of us. He asks for coffee and milk, "cow's milk," he says, so that she will know that he means milk, and not cream or an edible oil product. He turns the cup right side up, and Charlotte says, "Cow's milk — moo," and I remember Paul saying, "Mommy's got the bovines," on that August night before Rachel was born.

Rachel lifts her arm and drops her hand clumsily onto another bean and then another. I scatter a few more beans in front of her. The tray is brown, and the beans are only a shade darker. She cocks her head, and her fist unclenches. I do not want to start anything, not now, but he leans toward me as if waiting for a word, and so I say: "I know what you're going to tell me — it's the breeze, it's the noise the bean makes when I put it down, it's the shadow of my hand, it's random."

I enclose a bean in each palm, then hold my fists on the table in front of her. A bean drops from one. As soon as I pull away, Rachel's hand descends clumsily upon it.

"She sees," he whispers.

He edges close and tries the trick himself. Rachel cocks her head and finds the bean. "Goddamn it, she *sees*."

The waitress returns to fill Paul's cup, and I straighten to greet her, like a guilty person caught in the act. I do not see Paul reach for me, only his elbow as it knocks into his cup. "She sees," he says, and the coffee colors the tablecloth a deep brown.

The waitress mops up the stain with a towel, and sets a clean paper placemat before him. She asks if we know what we want. I am not with her, though. I am back a few months, on the day of Rachel's CT scan, when Paul threw his arms around me and wept. Though I sit upright, I can feel his hot neck; his arms crushing my ribs, the surge of love and hope I had felt for the two of us. *Goddamn it, she sees.*

The waitress squints her eyes and gives me a long, hard look.

"Cow's milk," Charlotte tells her. "Cow's milk, moooooo."

# ❧ PART III ❧

# ❦ 11 ❦

# Maine Fever

*July*

SHE SEES KIDNEY BEANS on her high-chair tray, peas, chunks of cheese, brightly colored toys. We suspend a string in front of her, place a penny on the brown carpet, or a pea on her high-chair tray, and she cocks her head to catch the image, then reaches tentatively to snare it. The way she angles her head in order to see an object makes us think that the vision she has is not in the fovea, and therefore is not clear. Other things suggest this, too. She is unresponsive to faces. Mirrors do not interest her, nor do dolls, or soap bubbles, or stuffed toys with big eyes. Paul has explained that there are not enough receptor cells in the periphery of the eye for her to have much visual acuity, and that the most she can have are vague, blurry images, and yet she has changed so much it is as if this little bit of sight has enabled her to join the world.

She wakes in the morning and calls, "Ooo!" from the nursery, and Paul stirs in bed and calls, "Ooo!" in response. If he is drowsy, and slow to get her, she calls, "Nun nun nun," until he rises and crosses the hall. "Nun nun nun," he says in return. While I struggle for a little extra sleep, I hear my two birds call to each other, "Ooo!" from the hall where she sits, "Ooo!" from the bathroom where he shaves, "Ooo!" as he lifts her high and lets her explore his face, grabbing his nose and lips tenaciously. He lets her play with his glasses, mouthing the lenses and earpieces as they go downstairs to get breakfast ready. "Ooo!" she calls on the stairs; "Ooo!" he calls back.

She has been lifted from the dark, inward state where she has been trapped, and if she is still passive, now she reaches, and calls out, "Ooo!" to tell us that she is alive. She wiggles with delight when we lift her, yanks hair, squeezes noses, lips, ears, as if she must dig into our flesh to make us real. Paul and I both have little crescent-shaped scratches all over our faces, mementos of her progress, some of them quite painful.

She's a real baby, we whisper to each other. And when she whines we say, "She's complaining!" in awe.

The straight dark hair she was born with (and never lost) has turned light and curly, and when we go places with her, this is what people see: a baby with curls. If the sight of a baby transforms normally reserved people, curls turn them into gushers and cooers. Such hair! Look at that hair! I didn't know that you could be born with hair like that — soft curls that you can put your finger through. Angel's hair.

I don't know what it is, but strangers appear from the shadows to comment on her hair; her hair commands so much attention that no one says a thing about her eyes, which still drift to the side and to center again, except perhaps: "Oh, she's *sleepy*, the little darling." I feel no urge to spill our secret when I hear these compliments (she's blind, you know). I enjoy them, and hurt when I hear them (she is beautiful, and she will never know it), and I am grateful for them, for now I know mothers of babies not so perfect to the public eye, and the level of idiocy and insensitivity out there is staggering. A stranger approaches the mother of a boy with spina bifida, a radiant, almond-eyed child, and says, "It's a good thing there are abortions now." A stranger sees Katie slumped in her stroller and reprimands her mother. "She's a big girl, make her *walk*," when Katie is so damaged she cannot even hold up her head. What possesses a grandmotherly type, so sweet-looking in her flowered dress, to walk over to the mother of a handicapped child and say, "What on earth is *wrong* with her?"

When strangers stop to admire our curly-haired baby, Paul holds her high to demonstrate her accomplishments. "Where are Daddy's glasses?" he says, and Rachel pulls them off. He shows this trick to friends and cousins, to waiters and salesgirls. He says, "She's going to be fine," and I incorporate his voice, and will myself to let go of my fears of all the complications that could befall her. I try to disregard the abnormal EEG, which confounded her neurologist, and try to let go of the images of the other babies her age, so different it is as though they are a different species.

Believing brings me more anguish than relief. I want her to be whole so badly that it is easier to doubt than to face the risk of letting myself dream great dreams for her and then find out that I was wrong. Nonetheless, I try on this optimist's pose, allowing myself to become the mother of a child who had a rough start, but will make it after all, and in this guise I collect and repeat the stories that months ago drove me wild: blind musicians, programmers, mathematicians; babies diagnosed as retarded, now mainstreamed in the public schools. I allow myself to imagine what she might become — visually impaired (for that is what we call her now) and otherwise intact. And when it is time for her to be reevaluated at the hospital, I show off her tricks to Dr. Goldstein, who coos at her, and bobbles her on his knee, and while I am dressing her tells me in a cheerful voice that she is at a solid six-month level, and: "Have you had her hearing checked?"

She is ten months old, and I have not worried about her hearing for months. I sink deep that day. I go home, bang things in front of her face, stamp my feet, call her name from just outside the room, and feel as if I will never be able to pull myself out of the pit of despair. I hear Paul on the telephone telling someone how well she is doing, and when he gets off, I am practically hysterical. "What's so wonderful? She's at a six-month level, and he's concerned about her hearing." The next night, we hear music from her room and tiptoe in to find her pulling the handle of her musical bird and listening to the tune. Paul puts his arms around me. "She's going to surprise us, just wait."

"I hope so," I say, but my chest aches so much I can hardly breathe.

We talk constantly about going back up to Maine, but the days pass, the sun gets fiercer, the tar softens at the edge of the road, and here we are, working so hard there is barely enough time to ask ourselves why. Paul says he must redo certain experiments, *must* for they are the core of his thesis, and he promised to be done with the experimental work long before now, *must* because there are pressures on him to shift his focus to other areas of research, *must* on weekends and evenings because the NMR machine is shared by many investigators, all of whom scramble for machine time, and since his dissertation is personal work, after all, the only available hours are the most unattractive ones.

When we see each other we talk of domestic issues — who will do what when — bicker about inconsequential things, apologize, and bicker again. We make up and Paul says, "Let's just chuck it all, and leave for Maine tomorrow." Maine is where we want to be; Maine will restore us, and bring us back together. I ask him when he thinks we can go, and he cannot give me a date. "And anyway, you said you wouldn't go until you finished your book."

He wakes up in the middle of the night, and cannot get back to sleep (whereas I sleep soundly, grinding and clenching my teeth with such ferocity that my jaws ache when I rise). He has spent so many early mornings in front of the TV that on one of them he clips the extension cord with a wire cutter, as if this might break his bad habit. Now when he wakens he plots data, or sits at the computer until the children begin to stir. At work, he drinks coffee to keep himself going, ten or twelve cups, sometimes. Although the coffee keeps him awake, it gives him such a buzz that it is hard for him to concentrate.

These cycles of insomnia and fatigue repeat themselves several times, until at last he gets sick and sleeps for two or three days solid. When he rouses from his illness, he is full of good cheer, and comes to me with a calendar so that we can choose the day when we might leave for Maine. He opens it to July, studies the squares, and slowly makes X's across each one. Next week's no good because his cells need to be fed and no one will do it if he leaves. The week after that he has to run experiments with a colleague. The following week he has time on the machine.

I close the calendar, and he looks up at me, eyes filled with regret. "At least I'll get my book done," I tell him.

Although he is a man of science, with both feet planted firmly in the twentieth century, he is a believer in magic, too, and when I tell him the following morning that I want to enroll Charlotte in a two-week session of day camp at the Y, he says that it's a bad idea to tie ourselves down. "What if we can make it out of here next week?" He is so persuasive that when I close my eyes I feel the car as it crawls slowly down the winding dirt road. The bay sparkles behind the cottage and the wind is cool. I open my eyes when he leaves for work and look at the black X's that fill the squares on our calendar. Later that day, I register Charlotte for session one at Camp Runamok.

The Y is only four blocks away, so in the morning I put Rachel in the stroller and walk Charlotte to camp. She wears a gym bag across her shoulder, in it her lunch, swimsuit, towel, several small dolls, crayon stubs, greeting cards, the fat pencil and wooden apple with her name across it that she received at a ceremony for children entering kindergarten in the fall. The bag knocks against her knees as she walks, and every few steps when she stops to adjust it, she shows me holly leaves and marigolds that have come up. She kneels in a flower bed, sinks her face into a daylily, and says, *"Mommy. Aren't they blootiful."*

Whenever we walk, we are friends; away from the house, there are no scolds or suggestions. We walk and the world is grand, the flowers, her sneakers, pigeon feathers, pebbles, fallen leaves, all are blootiful. I will myself to absorb these moments, to etch them into my brain — her voice, her hand in mine, the world as she sees it.

The grass on the side of the Y has been flattened by the children who wait for the buses that take them away. Most of them climb onto the big yellow bus, but some travel in the van parked behind it, which Charlotte says is for the "special" children. Sometimes she will mention a camper, and then say, "Oh, he's on the van," without any judgment at all.

I pass the van on my way home, and the campers inside, most of them fully grown, wave at me. I wave back and think of Charlotte getting into the crib with Rachel, dressing her in bonnets, kissing her soft flesh, calling her "honey," boasting about her. My sister. Did you bring my sister? Mollie wants to meet my sister. *Please let her be on the yellow bus,* I think. It becomes my daily prayer.

When I return, Lourie is sitting on the front doorstep, with a cigarette and a can of Diet Pepsi. She takes Rachel from the stroller and holds her close. They are so beautiful together, Rachel with her flushed cheeks and fair curls; Lourie with flawless ivory skin and long dark hair that falls in thick spirals. I go upstairs to my office, and sometimes hours go by when I do not think of them at all, and other times, I find myself listening to their laughter and wishing that I could join them.

"I'd love to have a baby like Rachel," Lourie says one afternoon.

"No, you wouldn't."

"Why not?"

"Because she's blind and may be retarded."

"But she's so beautiful."

"Yes," I say. "And when she's older?"

"Everyone loves her. Wherever she goes people are attracted to her."

"People love pretty babies."

We have this discussion many times. Her point of view seems romantic at first, divorced from reality, and I find myself thinking: She's not your daughter, you don't know what it's like. It is only after I know

Lourie better that I understand that her way is not to judge those around her by their intelligence or worldly success. It is warmth and kindness and honesty that mean the most to her. She sees a place for everyone; she sees fullness in the most limited lives.

We grow wearier as the days pass, Paul with his cells, me with my words. We don't visit friends, sleep in, eat out, take in a movie, because these things would take us away from work. If asked in July what irks me most I would go on at length about how grossly unfair it is that Paul gets to work more hours than I do. *He* can work a full day, choose to skip dinner, put in hours in the evening and on weekends, whereas I have household chores, children who need tending, feeding, and bathing no matter what else is on my mind. And it matters now because I must get this book finished so that I can go up to Maine, *must* because of all the lost months when I could not shift my mind from Rachel's problems to the imaginary world on paper, *must* because of all the deadlines made and broken, extensions begged, new deadlines missed, because I have nothing to show, *must* because when I am not working I must confront the fact that we have made many sacrifices so that I could write, and that I have failed despite them all. That is what I aim to reverse now that I can work at last, for now there is no child beside my desk to disturb me with her sleep or wakefulness. Now that I am myself again, I want to make up for lost time and finish this manuscript, and five hours a day, five days a week is not enough time.

I confront Paul with this obvious inequity, demand and get one weekend day for myself, a sixth day on which I can lock myself upstairs. This seems grand and free and truly equal until I hear Charlotte ask Paul one Saturday morning whose day it is, his or Mommy's, and I see, reflected in her words, how twisted our lives have become, how empty of all the small pleasures that make life sweet.

It is so rare that we go out even for a walk that one day when we decide to go downtown for a bagel, the manager of the restaurant rushes over when we come in and asks us where we've been.

"Working," Paul says.

"Working," she says. "And that means you don't eat?"

"We eat," he says. "We have no choice."

We carry our trays to a table that Charlotte has chosen beside a mirrored wall, set out our food and flatware, and then look up and catch ourselves unaware in the mirror. How drawn and worn out I look; and he has hollows beneath his big sad eyes. Paul kisses my cheek so that I will see that he still loves me, and says, "We've got to get out of here before it kills us. We've got to get up to Maine."

In the meantime, Charlotte begins another two-week session of Camp Runamok. She is the youngest and smallest camper, and after a month among older campers and counselors has developed a flirtatious walk, and has come to recognize boys as troublesome and mysterious creatures. "*Boys,*" she says, with a weary sigh. "I try to be friends with them, but I just can't do it."

She comes home singing the same songs that I learned in camp, and at night while I wash sand from her crevices, and soap up her smooth brown body, she sings: "Jake and Jennie sitting in a tree, k-y-s-s-m-n-g . . ." with a perfect teasing singsong, and no knowledge of what she has tried to spell. I sing with her:

> First comes love
> Then comes marriage
> Then comes a baby in a baby carriage.

Vacations have become the biggest topic of conversation at the mothers' group. Katie's mother, Gina, has a trip scheduled, too, the first since Katie got sick. The hospital has agreed to take care of Katie, and the social worker promised Gina that she would visit Katie every day. Gina would be all set to leave, "if only my mother would die." Her mother is in the final stages of cancer, and her death is imminent, though no one can predict exactly when it will occur. "It's a terrible thing to say, but when the phone rings, I always hope it's her doctor telling us the end has come. I'm just afraid that she'll die the day before we're set to leave for England, and Larry and I will have to cancel our trip. All I want is my vacation. I can't help it, that's all I want."

Every week we ask how her mother is, and every week she says, "All I want is my vacation."

By the time July draws to an end, I have begun to echo Gina's words. We are tired and irritable and all I want is my vacation.

Once, when he says, "Let's just leave tomorrow," I take him seriously and carry all the houseplants into the yard and start to pack the children's clothes. It is already August and the weather is such that we sleep nude and move in slow motion and live on seltzer and yogurt and cucumbers. Gloves are needed before touching the car's steering wheel, and on my infrequent forays outside, I notice a new crop of bumper stickers that have on them a picture of a mosquito and beneath it, "NJ State Bird."

Paul returns from work and finds me folding the children's clothes and piling them into a huge plastic bag. He listens to me yammer on about gas and tires and the old man who sells blueberries and corn three miles from the cottage, and he says nothing, but the calendar is on his lap, and when he gets to August he starts drawing ominous X's across the second two weeks in the month. Something about an NMR meeting in New York, one he simply cannot miss.

I grab the corner of the plastic bag and upend it so that little shirts and shorts fly above our heads. "Forget it," I tell him. "Let's just forget about going."

I can't forget. Maine is life, love, joy; Maine will save us. To forget it means that we have given up. And so we set a date to leave, and proclaim that day — August 23 — unbreakable, unswitchable, rain or shine, hell or high water.

"Don't get sick," I tell Charlotte when I pick her up from camp five days before we are due to leave. "I'll kill you if you get sick —" when she sneezes. I check her tongue and throat, scrutinize the spots on her legs, chase her around the living room with an open palm to press against her forehead, and pin her to the floor, thinking: All I want is my vacation.

Two days before we are set to leave, I am sitting upstairs in my office, running off chapters of my book on Paul's temperamental printer, when there is a knock on my door.

Lourie stands just outside the room with Rachel perched against her hip. She has never climbed these stairs before, not once in all these weeks. Right away I know that something's wrong.

Rachel's cheeks are flushed, and her curls are slick with sweat. Lourie says, "I think she just had a seizure."

"Describe it."

"We were sitting and playing when she just all of a sudden jerked forward. The same thing happened last week, but I thought maybe she was tired and lost control, and it seemed stupid to alarm you. Only this time she'd just woken up from her nap, and it happened twice. I'm sorry."

"Can you show me what she did?"

I take Rachel from her arms. Lourie sits cross-legged upon the floor and jerks forward at the waist, arms extended. Right away I know what Lourie has seen. I have seen it myself; I have felt it at dawn while Rachel nursed — a sudden flexion, a loss of control.

When she leaves I slide the *Merck Manual* from my shelf, and find what I am looking for.

"Infantile spasms are characterized by sudden flexion of the arms, forward flexion of the trunk, and extension of the legs. The attacks last only a few seconds but may be repeated many times a day. They are restricted to the first 3 yr of life, often to be replaced by other forms of attacks. Brain damage is usually evident."

Brain damage is usually evident.

Something stubborn rises within me to push this knowledge away. Paul and I must go — we must do it, or there will be nothing left of us.

I spend the next hours packing for our trip, clothes for rain and heat and spells of cold. I make my trips to the attic and basement and silently plunder the children's drawers, and the stubbornness grows like yeasty dough. I have confronted every awful possibility, spent months in search of the truth. Now it is before me, too hot and bright to face.

Paul wants to call Dr. Klibansky.

"Why? To hear bad news? What have any of them done except give us bad news? Nothing. We're going away," I say, and the force of my assertion stops him from disagreeing.

It is a mantra now that floods my weary brain — we have to leave, we have to leave.

The next day I take the train into New York and divest myself of a weighty manuscript that is complete from beginning to end but which I know, once it is out of my hands, shows all the signs of my weariness. Then I continue downtown to meet with Linda. She tells me that there's more work to do on the script, a day or two at most, and asks me to delay my trip. My head as it swings is heavy on my shoulders. "No," I say.

"One day? Can't you just postpone it for a day?"

She argues, proposes alternate plans, reminds me that the pressure comes not from her but above. My need to leave is so intense that it blocks out my ability to judge. I am out of my mind with fatigue. I cannot stay behind a single day longer.

When I return home from New York, Paul and I finish packing. We jam everything into boxes and bags that we pack in the car, then dine, like children, on a dozen ears of corn, and climb the stairs to bed. Paul whispers sweet words I have forgotten he knows. He wraps his arms around me, brings me close, and says, "Ah, I've missed you."

He is nervous and uncertain. Perhaps he can feel my own fear, for although I want him with me, I know that pain and pleasure twist like vines within me, that if I allow him to touch me too deeply, the stubbornness will die. I must separate myself from him, and draw inward and apart.

He sleeps with his arms clasped around me. I feel myself tumbling down a deep well, lower and lower, until I am dizzy and lose my resistance. I know what Lourie has seen. I know in the deep recesses, where the stubbornness has failed to penetrate. I think of all the times that Rachel has cried out in her sleep, the times she stiffened suddenly while nursing, and I understand that those were seizures, too.

Rachel wakens at dawn. Paul carries her into bed and sets her beside me. She wags her head in search of my breast, and captures the nipple between her strong gums. Her rhythmic tweaking relaxes me, and I fall into a light sleep.

This time when her body stiffens, I waken fully and break free. Her face is waxen, eyes rolled back so that only the whites show. She is dead, she is dead. Something breaks within me and I cry out to Paul: "That's it. She's having one now."

I jump out of bed and stand alone weeping. Paul slides over and takes Rachel in his arms. He strokes her brow and murmurs, "Ah, sweet baby, Daddy's here," while I stand across the room, my face in my hands.

Such a long time passes before she whimpers and comes to life. A minute, two . . .

"She's okay," he says.

I uncover my face and see Charlotte standing in the doorway holding a blanket and her doll.

"I'm sorry," I say. What I want to say is that my crying was a dream, that nothing in real life has changed. "I'm sorry" is all that I can manage.

Paul says: "Come next to me, Char. You, too, Mommy."

He tries to draw us close, to press the four of us into one human sandwich. Only I resist: Mommy the onion, acrid and hard.

"We're going," I tell them.

## August 23

In the old days I read to Paul whenever we drove to Maine. I could read fairly steadily until around New Haven, when my voice got hoarse. As soon as he saw me put the bookmark between the pages he slowed down and veered right, cutting in front of oil trucks and Winnebagos, and let the car idle on the shoulder. "I'm tired," I would say, and he always answered, "I'm tired, too." "I can't go on," I would say, and he would shut off the engine, and throw back his head and wait until I opened the book. This game got more refined our first few years together. He rolled up the windows on even the hottest days in order to cut down on noise and save my voice. He bought me a reading lamp that plugged into the cigarette lighter. We read a lot of books this way.

Charlotte does not like it when I read to Paul. She cries, experiences acute boredom, and tugs at her seat belt, so we drive in silence in two-hour shifts, stopping only for gas, or to use the rest rooms. We eat sandwiches and fruit in the car. After a while Charlotte and I trade camp songs. She sings, "Jake and Jennie sitting in a tree, k-y-s-s-s-r-g," and I sing "The Good Ship Titanic." Later in the trip, Paul sings, "Cigareets and whiskey, and wild, wild women —" and Rachel stirs for the first time in six hours.

I am unusually nervous behind the wheel. The highways curve without warning; trucks edge up on my tail or trap me in a center lane, two in collusion. We could die on the road, all four of us wiped out in an instant.

Paul sees me tense and says, "He knows you're there, don't worry," and I realize that he still sees the world as a place where logic prevails. For me, randomness rules. The driver could be drunk or distracted, his brakes might fail; he could be a daredevil, or suicidal. Poor idiots, I hear people say. First their daughter is born blind, and then they die in a car crash.

The children are both asleep when we reach Brunswick, our two little

fish, damp of flesh, mouths gaping. The car smells from overripe bananas and apple juice. Paul opens the window to let in the cool air and
speeds up the long hill into town. It is there, it is still there, the post
office, the churches, the college, the long straight road that leads out to
the islands.

Our house stands intact among the trees. We leave our sleeping children in the car and walk through the damp grass. The sun is low and
the bay glistens. Paul puts his arm across my shoulder and the two of
us listen to the water lapping against a boat.

"Should we call Klibansky tomorrow?" I ask.

It is our first mention of Rachel.

"Monday," he says. "She'll be all right until then."

The ceiling and walls of the cottage are knotty pine, and the knots
often appear in pairs, like eyes. A year ago I taught Charlotte to look
for these animal eyes so that she would not wake up and be frightened
by them. And now, on her first morning, she creeps into bed with us,
holds her arm straight up and names them for us, a raccoon, a Cheshire
cat, a bear. As soon as I am fully awake, I remember the seizures.

I heat water for tea, and set out bread and leftover cheese. The cottage
is nestled among evergreens, and the air is scented with pine. Paul puts
Rachel in a walker that had been Charlotte's, and we sit by the window
and eat and plan the day. The edginess that colored our conversations at
home has already left our voices. He calls me "sweetness," a name I
have not heard in months, and when I get up to clean the table, he
pulls me close to kiss me before I leave.

The tide is low, and the bay is as glassy as a lake. A heron stands
motionless on a mussel-covered ledge.

Charlotte nibbles a little cheese and begs to be let outside. At home
she cannot walk in the street alone or visit a friend by herself. Here we
say, "Don't go down to the water," and listen to the screen door slam.

She crouches in the pine needles near the house, collecting pine cones,
and tufts of dark green moss, and white stones veined with mica.

"She's beautiful," Paul says.

Beautiful and innocent. She does not know about wrinkles, money,
sickness, death. She is never depressed.

Rachel whimpers, and I turn from the window. Her arms fly and she
jerks forward. Paul lifts her from the walker, and holds her against his

chest. Neither his love nor the strength of his arms can stop what is happening to her. Her body convulses again. He kisses the top of her head, and walks with her, up and back until the spasms stop.

After breakfast we carry the canoe from beneath the house and brush the caked mud and webs from the hull. When we are ready to go, we call to Charlotte. She runs over carrying a handful of pine cones which she displays for us one by one: rotten, smashed, misshapen. They are her treasures, each of them beautiful to her. She does not see these bruised pine cones as inferior to those that are firm and straight and whole.

We put an orange life vest over Charlotte's neck and tie the ribbons around her waist and chest. The smallest of the vests is still so large for Rachel that it pushes up her chin. She cries when I carry her down to the water, and again when I sit her between my legs in the canoe.

The wind rocks the boat, and Paul paddles hard and sprays us. Charlotte laughs and Rachel cries. I imagine letting her fall into the cold water — how much easier life would be for everyone. I can feel her soft, fat body slide into the bay. I know what she would look like because I saw her that way the morning before last, her skin waxen, her eyes rolled back. I have seen her die already. I imagine her floating facedown in the water, and the funeral, like my sister's, on a sunny day. I imagine packing the toys in the room that we painted and papered for her, taking down the sampler with the cross-stitch figures four times the size of the ones on Charlotte's sampler, because my mother insisted that one day she would see. I imagine this and she whimpers because I am holding her too tightly.

We stop at one of the green islands in the bay, and take our plastic cups in search of blueberries. Osprey nests are perched on the high, bare branches of trees, and the male birds circle above our heads, squawking harshly as we walk by. The berries are tiny and very sweet. We pick and pick, and return to the canoe with full stomachs and empty cups.

Charlotte walks heel-toe along the granite ledge that slopes down into the sea. I slip off Rachel's clothes and sit her where the water is shallowest. When she feels the cold water against her skin she takes a deep intake of air, and her arms rise, the way they do when a spasm overtakes her. This time, her arms go down slowly, hands palm down to pat the sea. The whole thing happens so slowly it is like watching a time-lapse film; she sits with head bowed and fists clenched, opens a hand, tentatively hits the surface of the water, then, feeling the droplets, she hits harder the next time. "She's splashing!" Charlotte cries. "Mommy, look, she's splashing!" Rachel lifts her chin and all of a sudden begins to beat the water. She screeches like a gull, the water in choppy waves around her. Laughing, splashing, her face wet. Paul stands beside me to watch her. He says nothing, but I know what he thinks, because I am thinking the same thing, too. Just like a baby, like any baby. Just like a normal one.

On Monday morning, I call Dr. Klibansky. He is on vacation, and it is an associate, Dr. Gutman, who gets back to us an hour later. I tell him that Rachel has optic nerve hypoplasia, and that low-amplitude spiking in the occipital region showed up on her last EEG. I describe what Lourie saw, and then the seizure she had in bed on Saturday morning, and how she looked as if she had died. He is silent for a moment, and what I hear is the gurgle of an idling outboard motor on the bay.

Then he says: "Get her in to see me."

"Today?"

Paul walks in, holding Rachel on a hip.

The outboard gives a surge, and the boat takes off.

"I'm asking because we're in Maine right now."

"How long were you intending to stay?"

"Another week."

"Watch her. If she has another episode, call me immediately. If not you could wait. But don't put it off once you get home."

I do not know this man, and so I cannot imagine what is in his eyes just now.

"There's an airport an hour from here. I could catch a plane this morning and get her to you by late afternoon. Please tell me if I should do this."

Again there is a pause. "See how she does — but call me right away if she has another episode."

Several times a day Rachel has spasms. It is upsetting to watch because they rack her little body and make her cry, but they do not alarm me. These are the little, hiccoughy ones — like those that Lourie saw; they seem trivial compared to the seizure she had in bed on Saturday morning. Even so, it is no longer one spasm every few days, but a series

of them, so that just as she has stopped whimpering from the first, a
second, and third — a sixth and seventh — come upon her.

When Paul is around, he sets his stopwatch, and times each spasm,
and the total elapsed time of each occurrence. He uses the same kind of
bound book that he used to time my contractions when I was carrying
Charlotte and when he asks me to keep a record of the spasms she has
when he is not around, I do not take him seriously. Lists, graphs, flow
charts — he has always been fond of these things. These are not "epi-
sodes," and so I do not want to time them. They are mild spasms that
come over her when she is sleeping or nursing or has just woken up,
and when they happen I hold her hard against me, and when they stop,
I go on to other things.

We get visitors on our fourth day in Maine, an Israeli couple whom
we met in childbirth class when I was pregnant with Rachel. Hannah is
an Iraqi Jew, a small, intense woman, with black hair and eyes; her
husband, Uri, is blond and genial. (A Dane and a Pakistani, we had
decided, seeing them across the room a year before.) Paul and I have so
little time up here that we had not planned on inviting guests, but Uri
has just been diagnosed as having advanced lymphoma, and his chances
of survival are slim.

What a grim group we are when the facts are tallied up: Paul and I
with our blind baby, who suffers from infantile spasms ("brain damage
is usually evident"); Uri with cancer in his bone marrow, gut, and lymph
system, taking a last trip before his chemotherapy begins. And yet the
days are filled with warmth and quiet pleasure from the very start, when
Hannah enclosed my daughters in her arms and held them in a great,
warm embrace, and Uri dropped his bags, took a deep breath, and said,
"Ah, splendid!" then turned and walked down to the bay. I followed
behind and saw that his face was suffused with bliss.

He and Hannah take turns lying on the Yucatan hammock and paddling out toward the islands. The sun is brilliant day after day. We
shop for groceries and drive out to Mackerel Cove to see the sun set.
We stay up late to talk — not of life and death, but of trivial things —
our favorite mysteries, our theories on getting children to sleep through
the night, the trips we took when we were single. I am always aware of
Uri's cancer, just as I am always aware of Rachel's problems. His neck
is swollen; the light hair that springs from his head in wild curls will
soon fall out. My daughter jerks forward at the waist and whimpers

several times a day. But the sky is blue, the bay sparkles with pinpoints of light, and the beauty around us is stronger than our fear.

They eat lobster for the first time, following step by step the instructions on their placemats. Uri tells us that there is a street in Jerusalem named after his father and Hannah talks about their courtship at the university four years ago. The next day Uri and I swim. We are far out in the bay when he stops to tread water. His face, bobbing above the sea, has that wonderful, blissful look upon it. "Now *this* is the life," he says.

Once, while Hannah and I are walking through the woods looking for mushrooms that neither of us will have the courage to eat, she tells me she has read about Uri's cancer. "He's going to die, I know it," she whispers, and her dark eyes flood with tears. Once, I look from their little boy, four days older than Rachel, who runs, climbs, jumps from beds and tables, his arms spread wide like wings, calling, "*Abba! Eema!*" to our daughter who sits and sits, and I know with awful certainty that my last dream has died.

After Uri and Hannah leave, I phone Linda and tell her that I am ready to work. She makes arrangements to fly up and the following afternoon I drive to Portland to get her. We meander home, stopping for bread and produce at the farmers' market.

Paul is pacing back and forth with Rachel in his arms when we return to the cottage. "She had ten this time," he says. "It's been going on for six minutes. We better call Gutman again."

Dr. Gutman returns our call at nine that night. I describe the cluster of spasms we have seen, "little ones, like hiccoughs," and wait for his reassurance. *You worried for nothing, she'll be perfectly fine.* After all this time, all the grim letters and examinations, I am still expecting someone to laugh and tease me for being a worrier.

"Those seizures are considered a neurological emergency. They tend to snowball, and when they do, they're extremely difficult to control. I want you to get her in here."

"Okay."

"Without delay. I'll get a room for her at the hospital, and we'll start treatment right away."

"How long will she be there?"

"A week or two — it depends upon you."

On me? I imagine her in a steel cage, crying at dawn and no one there to hold her. I don't know what I mean to her, if anything, but there is no way I can abandon her now.

"Can I stay with her?" I ask.

"You'll have to."

He treats me to a cheerful description of the pediatric unit, in a different, "more humane place" than Hospital City. "You'll love it there," he says. "It's like a hotel." His words cannot camouflage the ominous pauses between them, and all at once, I need to know everything. I ask about the seizures and what they say about her future.

"In a child her age, seizures are usually a sign of brain damage."

"What kind of damage? I won't hold you to anything, I just need to know."

"Kids with infantile spasms are often retarded. Not always, but often — very often. There's a whole spectrum, from those who've never shown any problems before the spasms, to the ones who are already delayed in several areas. How old is your daughter?"

"Almost a year."

"Does she walk?"

"No."

"Crawl?"

"No."

"Pull herself to stand?"

"No."

"What can I say? The kids who go into seizures with problems stand a good chance of having further problems."

"What kind of problems?" I ask.

"Ah, well . . . a whole range of psychomotor problems show up."

Details come next. Where to meet him and when. I jot down room numbers and times on the paper that Paul has thrust before me, but my thoughts have already shifted to Charlotte. She starts kindergarten next week and she doesn't have shoes. All summer we have talked about this happy day, the four of us walking together, Charlotte in the middle with the wooden apple around her neck, the brand-new dress and shoes we have yet to buy. A very special day that will forever be tainted by sadness.

When I hang up, I say to Paul: "Charlotte doesn't have shoes."

"Was it Gutman? What did he say?"

"The little ones are seizures, too. We have to get her into the hospital before they snowball. She might be in for a week or two, and . . . Charlotte starts school in ten days and I haven't gotten her any shoes."

"Did he say how much damage the seizures cause?"

"I don't know what to do," I say.

"Answer my question — do the seizures cause damage?"

"Yes. I don't know. I don't remember what he said."

"We should have gotten her in there right away."

"But I asked Gutman if we should come home."

"And he said what?"

"That it was okay to wait. That we should watch her and wait and then when we got back . . ."

"He said to call him if she had another episode, weren't those his words?"

"Yeah, okay, those were his words, and we're getting her in, aren't we?"

"But she's been having seizures all along. Didn't you tell me you thought she'd been having these seizures at night for a long time? We should have taken her in immediately."

"It's my fault, I understand. It's my fault. What do you want from me?"

"I didn't say it was your fault. I said it was a mistake coming up here."

"Can we just not fight? It's as awful for me as it is for you." I keep my eyes on him and wait for a response. "Can we at least be friends?"

"Start packing," he says, and I feel as if I am being cast out.

I hurry through the small rooms and out to the clothesline, where we have left our bathing suits and towels. I pass the pine cones and rocks that Charlotte lined up outside the door, and I think of her starting school while I am gone, without a decent pair of shoes. I think of the days I spent here and see, not something miraculous in my forgetting, but something dangerous and crazy. I ignored what was happening to Rachel. I was tired, and did not allow myself to understand the implications, and now the seizures have snowballed. I cannot believe what I have done.

Once again there are calls I have to make to Paul's parents and mine, his so they might drive up from Florida two weeks earlier than planned, mine to take care of Charlotte until they arrive. It is as bad as a year ago, when I called to say that she was blind. She is no longer completely blind, but she is most surely brain-damaged.

I dial my parents first, and when I hear my mother's voice, I start to cry. I sit on the bed that Paul built with logs that drifted ashore, set high enough so that we would see the bay when we awoke, and I cry until I am so sore I feel as if I have been beaten. Although what I need to say is fairly simple, when at last I can speak, all that comes out is, "Charlotte doesn't have any *shoes.*"

Charlotte knows nothing, and feels everything in her small body. She is nervous and edgy, and the moment we get into the car insists that I sing. Folk songs, Beatle songs, Bible songs, show tunes, nonsense tunes, and all the while my mind is on the ragged little sneakers on her feet, and how the day will not be special if she wears them. Song after song while Paul drives in silence and Rachel sleeps.

We arrive late at my parents' house and leave with Rachel early the next morning. For a while I try making conversation in the car until I realize that Paul cannot take in anything I say. Now that we have been thrust into hard times, he has grown distant again and orbits alone, completely apart from me. I cannot touch him. I cannot try to remind him of the love that he felt two days before because he can no longer reach those memories.

When we get to the hospital, I wait in admissions and he takes Rachel for her EEG. The whole process of sorting through papers and signing them takes over a half hour, and by the time I meet Paul, Rachel has already been wired up.

He sits in a rocking chair with Rachel in his arms and rocks her gently, crooning until she falls asleep. What reserves of tenderness he has for her. Less is there for Charlotte, who wants more than his arms around her when she is needy of attention; less still for me, though in truth it is his warmth that I desire most, his arms, someone to lull me into peace.

Rachel's brain waves are scratched onto paper, yards of it that spill onto the floor. She sleeps soundly until they strobe her. Then she jerks in Paul's arms.

He stays to meet Dr. Gutman, and after that, to see me to my room. As soon as he puts Rachel into the metal cage, he says good-bye. He turns and walks away, no kiss, nothing to sustain me.

"Wait!" I call after him. He looks at his watch and then his feet, and it is like being back in the cavernous lobby after the diagnosis. All I know is that the bad news has been a wall between us, that I keep pounding my fists against the wall, while he wants only to turn away, that after almost a year of living like this, we have not learned a thing.

"What?"

"Will you make sure Charlotte has shoes?"

His head bobs. "I'm going to get stuck in rush-hour traffic."

"A kiss?" My voice is small and pathetic.

He kisses my cheek and leaves and I think: You are a big girl now. You are alone.

# ❦ 12 ❦

# Giving Baby the Needle

*September*

THERE IS NOT MUCH TO DO, and so for most of each day I walk up and down the bright corridors of the hospital — orange on the surgical floor, yellow in cardiac care, green in the neonatal unit. Rachel, in pajamas with the hospital name stamped across the back, rides on my hip, her head against my chest. Everywhere we go we are stopped — by nurses, and guests, and patients in paper slippers. An orderly who is wheeling a toothless man into the elevator sticks his foot between the closing doors and pats Rachel's head. "Isn't she the dolly?"

"It dates me to say so, but she's a little Shirley Temple," says a middle-aged woman in a silk kimono. Her elaborate wig is worn too far forward. "What's she in for?"

"I'm learning to give her shots."

The woman whistles in order to get Rachel's attention, then comes closer and clicks her tongue. After all these months I still don't know how to explain why my baby keeps her head against my shoulder, her eyes cast down. "She's shy," I say this time.

"She'll be fine, God bless her."

"She won't," I say.

"Don't be crazy, she's beautiful; she'll be better in no time flat."

The woman has problems of her own — she has lost her hair; her teeth are not real. She wants to be reassured that beauty means goodness and health, and that this baby has nothing more serious than a nasty cold. All I need to do is nod and agree to give her this pleasure, but I cannot do this, for I cannot allow myself to believe, not for a second. "Thank you," I say. It's the best I can do.

Home these days is pediatrics, where the walls are cobalt blue, a white stripe runs the length of the corridors, and glittery stars are suspended from the ceiling. I am halfway to my room when I think of a boyfriend of years back, who, in the midst of his Frank Stella–psychedelic period, painted our apartment like this — bold stripes across the walls, constellations above our bed. It is strange to think of him now, to remember a life that is so distant from my present one that it feels like someone else's story. It is not just those East Village days, either; the whole world has receded: fresh air, Chinese food, Charlotte's body, the sound of my own laughter.

My roommate is six weeks old and weighs five pounds. During the day she is attended by an ancient nanny from Ireland, a shriveled little spinster in a short white uniform who has cared for 304 children, and refers to this one as "my baby," so that I have to sneak a glance at the chart to find out that the baby has a name — Constance Tyron Hewitt. Mrs. Hewitt, the biological mother, is a nervous blonde with a pinched face and flat buttocks, who appears unannounced once a day, sets down her shopping bag, says, "Hello, dear, how's the little one?" to me, and before I can respond turns away and has a fit about the bruises on the baby's arm, her elevated temperature, the draft in the room, the pediatrician's tardiness. A great deal of scurrying ensues, with nurses, residents, and pediatricians dashing in and out. Mrs. Hewitt, exhausted, collapses in Nanny's rocker, complains to me about Nanny and the hospital, makes a few phone calls to relay the same complaints, and leaves. Nanny reclaims her chair, rocks her baby, croons: "Ah, ya poor thing, with such a mean old mother," and when the child is asleep, says, "The mother doesn't love her, no-o-o, not a single bit. It's me who cares."

But when the baby wakes at night, which she does several times, I am the only one around. Reluctant to touch her — she is tinier than either of my own at birth, and her arm is taped to an IV — I run bleary-eyed into the corridor and call: "The baby's up! Someone help the baby!"

On my third night, when I ran into the hall to shout: "The baby's up!" a dark-haired nurse who had outgrown her uniform said: "Parents are not permitted to wear nightgowns."

"What about pajamas?"

"Parents are not permitted to wear nightclothes."

I had not been sleeping well, and my eyeballs throbbed. The baby's cry began to rattle. "What do I sleep in?"

"Street clothes."

"Street clothes? You mean to tell me you ask the mothers who've been here for weeks to sleep in their clothes? I mean, my God, make me feel at home, why don't you."

"This is not your home," she said, snapping her eyes shut. "This is a hospital, and there are adolescent boys on the floor. Ambulatory adolescent boys."

In truth, the floor was rather empty, for it was Labor Day weekend, and no surgeries had been scheduled. "Show me one goddamn ambulatory adolescent boy. One. Come on, one, goddamn it."

I was screaming, the baby was screaming. The nurse said, "Hospital rules," as she whipped past me.

I have come a long way since then, and have learned pragmatism. I sleep in my nightgown, but I no longer go into the corridor, and instead call, "Someone help the baby!" from my doorway. I do not make a fuss about the indignity of parents being asked to use public toilets, but quietly make my way into the patients' bathroom, bypassing the tiny, low-to-the-ground toilets for the single grown-up bowl. I do not rave about the surcharge for a parent's plate of hospital food, instead ordering heavily for Rachel, and dividing it between the two of us. This is what I am doing when Dr. Gutman comes in.

Yogurt and juice for her, a grilled cheese sandwich for me. The cheese is glossy orange; a lacy black design covers the bread. The whole thing is quite beautiful, and looks as if it has been urethaned for posterity. Dr. Gutman greets Nanny and says, "Hello, pretty baby," as he brushes his finger against Rachel's cheek. He is young and tan, and wears photogray glasses, which are still dark, a pink polo shirt, and running shoes. I am reminded that it is a Saturday.

"Fake food," I say, showing him the glossy sandwich.

"You look tired."

"She cries all night," I whisper, gesturing with my chin at the other crib. "No one comes for her."

He puts his hand on my shoulder and squeezes, two short and one long, and I worry that he is sending me a signal that I cannot decipher.

"I'd like to see you out of here. You've got a husband who wants to see you and a little girl who misses you."

"I know," I say, though they, too, belong in someone else's life.

"Have you started yet?"

I pull the IV board out of my pocket and show him the holes that I
have punctured through the plastic.

"Fine," he says. "Terrific —" as he tosses the board into the trash.
"Now try it on her so you can go home."

He cups his hand around Rachel's foot. He does not say, "No baby
this pretty can have such problems," the way the others do, but calls to
her softly, as if to wake her from a deep sleep. Look up, I think. Smile
for him. Her head stays bowed. "She hasn't slept well," I say, knowing
before the words are out how ridiculous I am to speak them.

Other mothers pace through the blue corridors, some with their babies in hospital carriages; the ones whose children are bedridden meander alone. Everyone ends up in the lounge to smoke cigarettes and talk.
The walls are scuffed; the couch cushions are stained. On one wall is a
bulletin board covered with photographs of former patients. "Danny —
Mayor of peeds!" it says below a picture of a chubby boy. And across a
formal portrait of a little girl in braids: "Trudy — I'm home now."
Sitting on the couch is an Indian woman with a red caste mark in the
middle of her smooth forehead, whose son rides his IV pole around the
lounge as if it were a scooter, and a stylishly dressed Hasidic woman,
whose husband drops by each day with cooking utensils and food. Sandra, a cheerful young mother from Coney Island, is describing her
neighborhood to a German woman when I walk in. She speaks with a
Brooklyn accent, so pure it thrills me, of white sand beaches, a bleached
boardwalk, the stretch of ocean, the wheeling gulls, and it sounds so
fabulous that I ache to slip away and take a subway to this seaside
paradise. The German woman listens, nods, says, "*Ja,*" and dabs at her
eyes.

I step closer to avoid being rammed by the boy on the IV pole, and
Sandra says, "Oooh, here's the doll baby I was telling you about. Can I
hold her?"

Everyone likes to hold Rachel. She is soft and placid and uncomplaining. Also she is the only one on the floor not attached to tubes or poles
or locked in a plastic tent.

"What I wouldn't give for curls like that."

Sandra is small and snub-nosed and wears her hair flipped up at the
ends, exactly the way I wore mine in my high-school graduation picture.
She has circumvented hospital rules by wearing a flowered housedress,

night and day. She kisses Rachel on the cheek with a big "M-wwwah," and says, "So what did your doctor say? Did he give you a date yet?"

We are all inmates, and this issue of release is the most compelling and painful topic.

"I can go as soon as I learn to give her the shots."

"You'll get used to it, believe me. I had an uncle was a diabetic, and I know for a fact at first it's hard and then you get to thinking how it's making her better, and it isn't so hard anymore." She holds Rachel at arm's length, and says, "You tell her, honey. Say, 'Gimme those shots, Mama. Make me all-lll better.' "

"She'll never get better."

"Look at her," she says to the German woman. "Take one look and tell me this baby will not be just fine."

"*Ja*," says the German woman, tears running down the sides of her face.

"Look at those men with their artificial hearts — a year ago, two, I would have told you a man would go gallivanting around with an artificial heart in his chest, you would have locked me away. Hey, look at Ryan."

Her baby lies in his carriage with tubes up his nostrils. His breathing sounds like the rattling of stones. Once I would not have been able to look at a baby like Ryan, but now that I divide my world into those who will get better and those who will not, I look at him and see the future in his face.

The substance I am supposed to be injecting into Rachel's legs is called ACTH — adrenocorticotropic hormone. It will not cure her, though it is supposed to stop the seizures for now. Although no one can tell me exactly how or why this occurs, the physicians are not entirely ignorant. Dr. Gutman has given me a list of probable side effects — lethargy, irritability, gassiness. She will become moon-faced and round-bellied. The *Physicians' Desk Reference,* which I have gotten from a kind nurse called Miss Theo, has filled in the rest: possible damage to the muscles, the nervous system, the heart, kidneys, lungs, the reproductive and sensory organs. Psychic derangements may appear, ranging from euphoria to "frank psychosis." The drug can impair wound healing, mask infections, bring on hirsutism, suppress growth, cause glaucoma with possible damage to the optic nerve. Its use is suggested only when the disorder is intractable to more conventional therapies. There are so many prohibitions and cautions that it seems to me that the manufacturer does not believe that the drug should be used at all. Nevertheless, it is the drug of choice because it works in mysterious ways, and more effectively than those that are less devastating.

At first I was opposed to starting her on the harshest drug, but the seizures have worsened since her admittance, and now, half a dozen times a day I race over to the nurses' station so that a pediatric resident can see a child having infantile spasms. Now it seems I have no choice.

No one is sitting at the nurses' station, but singing emanates from the room behind the desk. Inside, four nurses surround a skinny guy in blue scrubs. Miss Theo perches on the resident's lap.

"Ummmmm," I say, a human buzzer.

"Come in!" Miss Theo swings an arm around the guy to steady herself.

"I want to give my daughter her shot."

"Wonderful! I'll see you in, like, twenty minutes?"

Nineteen minutes later I am in my room. Nanny is sitting in the rocking chair, or rather, in the right quadrant of the seat, like a child grown prematurely old. "*She* was here; never asked about the baby, not a word; no-o-o-o; it's the dog she talks about; that's all she cares for, that dirty creature. No-o-o-o," she whispers to the baby, so tiny in her hollowed lap. "Poor wee thing, your mama doesn't love ya."

Miss Theo bustles in, thighs rubbing, a nylon swish swish. The sound brings me straight back to grade school, when girdles and taffeta slips and straight skirts were de rigueur.

"Okay, Mommy, I'll do it this time, you watch closely," she says.

"I've been watching, and I'm ready to do it myself so I can go home."

All lies, though I know enough to repeat what is correct to say.

"Watch carefully, listen to what I have to say, and tomorrow morning, Mommy gets to do it herself."

"You aren't here in the morning," I say.

"Sherry will let you."

Sherry is the nurse who believes that ambulatory adolescent boys might be worked up by the sight of my nightgown.

"Go to it."

"Now. What I have here is prepackaged from the pharmacy, but the first thing Mommy will have to do when she gets home is swab the vial, okay? Then look at the syringe and find the right mark. Now. Everybody has their own way of holding a needle, but I like to hold it like this, like a cigarette."

Constance Tyron Hewitt's biological mother walks in. Nanny wrinkles her nose like a child smelling something bad, and says: "Good *evening*, Mrs. Hewitt —" her way of castigating her employer for the late arrival. The baby changes hands. Nanny puts on her coat.

"Now. While the gel is dripping into the syringe, Mommy is flicking it with her finger like this to break the bubbles. Fill it a tad above the mark, because you've got to get that air out, and that's a must 'cause the last thing Mommy wants to do is inject air into the baby, right?"

"WHY IS THIS BANDAGE OFF? MARGARET! GET THE RESIDENT IMMEDIATELY, THERE'S PUS ON HER ARM. NURSE!"

". . . push the plunger in until you get a . . . drop . . . of . . . ah . . . here we go . . ."

Miss Theo's friend gallops in to examine Constance Tyron Hewitt. His voice is soft, and calming words come easily. It's a scab that Mrs. Hewitt sees; a nothing. The baby will go home on schedule without even a scar. Miss Theo lowers the side of the steel crib, unsnaps Rachel's hospital pajamas, and draws one of her legs through. Her leg is short and chunky, with a ring of fat around the upper thigh. Miss Theo kisses her.

"You don't want to end up giving the shot in the same leg all the time, you have to alternate. Some moms tie a ribbon around the ankle of the leg that they've used so that the next time they know to use another."

The resident leaves. Mrs. Hewitt pulls Nanny's chair to the phone. "Here goes. Swab, pinch the muscle, and when the needle goes in draw back the plunger a tad to make sure you're not in a vein."

Miss Theo holds Rachel's arms above her head and pins her left leg with a forearm. The drug is a gel and it takes time for it to drip. I watch my child be hurt and do nothing. Rachel stiffens and turns red, but she does not cry until the needle is out. Miss Theo puts a Band-Aid over the wound, and Rachel begins to wail. The nurse has to say, "Pick her up, Mommy," before I lean over and hold her to me. She is slow to comfort. It is as if she no longer trusts me.

\*     \*     \*

Midnight? Two A.M.? Four?

"The baby is crying," I call from the doorway. "Someone get the baby."

Sherry flips on the lights and eyes my nightgown. The glare of the light and her disapproval waken me fully. I have just figured out my error when she says: "So why don't you pick her up, she's your baby."

"She never cries in the middle of the night."

"So she had a nightmare. So pick her up."

Rachel does not stop crying. I sit in Nanny's chair to nurse her, and she bites down on my breast and pulls away. I rock her, walk with her, sing. The light comes up, and her cry becomes a moan, a soft primitive mmmm that cannot be soothed.

"Why?" I ask Gutman when he sees us that day.

It is a question I have asked hundreds of times over the past year, one that is as primitive and meaningless as Rachel's moan. I cannot stop myself.

"Why is she like this?"

It embarrasses me to be a textbook case, to ask the same question as every other grieving parent, to go through the appropriate stages in exactly the order in which they are listed in books — denial, anger, bargaining, depression. I have worked so hard to live a life of clarity, and here I am, my *why* a moan, my voice shaking like an adolescent's. How could this have happened? How could she look so perfect, with her long-lashed eyes, her tiny nose, and rose-colored lips and nails — and yet be so damaged?

Gutman looks over the list of symptoms I have copied and says, "I'm glad you read that stuff. I ask all my parents to be informed. I tell them — read the literature, learn what the side effects are, and then take it with a carton of salt. A carton. Everything even remotely possible is listed there — everything."

"So what's happening? She has problems, but she's never been like this."

"Some babies vegetate during treatment; some scream from sunup to sundown."

"Why are we putting her through all of this? What difference does it make?"

"Babies on this regime fare better than those who have no treatment. It's as simple as that."

His shirt has the flat smooth finish of pure cotton that has been washed and pressed at a Chinese laundry.

"Better, worse, what kind of life will she have? Why do we bother?"

"Don't bury her," he says wearily.

"You were the one who told me what her future would be — I didn't make it up."

He takes off his glasses and massages the bridge of his nose.

"You have a baby," I say.

"I have a baby — what can I tell you? I have a baby, and he's strong and healthy, and I worry about him just the way you worry about yours. No one is spared."

Paul arrives a short time later with a bag of fresh fruit, and a small stuffed bear in overalls, which he places in a corner of the crib. Rachel has just fallen asleep. He looks at her for a long time, then adjusts her arms, one of which is tucked awkwardly beneath her. He takes the fruit from the bag and places it on the window shelf — flame grapes, a melon, a green apple, a pear — next to the fruit he brought the evening before. A few feet away, Nanny rocks her little baby, singing a lullaby filled with curses.

Paul and I are so awkward together that it's hard to remember that once we had so much to say to each other. He used to call me every day from work, and on the nights that he worked late, I always woke when he came home and kept him company while he ate. Before the diagnosis good news was never really good until I shared it with him, and even the worst news was softened by his loving response. Now we sit in silence most of the time, as if our minds have emptied of all the little twists and turns connected with work or people we know.

"My parents will be up tomorrow," he says at last. "Your mother got Charlotte shoes in town, sneakers, actually. Pink was what she picked out. Twenty-seven dollars for them. I couldn't believe it. Twenty-seven dollars."

"Did anyone call?"

"Hinda called twice when we were gone. She wants you to call back."

"That's all?"

"That's all."

"Hinda was the only person who called the whole time we were gone?"

"There were three hang-ups," he says.

"You know what that stuff will do, don't you?"

"What stuff?"

He does not understand what I mean the way he once did. Everything has to be spelled out. "The medication they're shooting into her."

"It'll help her."

"You really believe that?"

"Yes," he says. "Yes, I do."

"She's in pain," I say. "All last night and all today she cried and moaned. Already she's puffing up."

Her beautiful face will be distended. Beauty is all she has, and now that will be taken, too.

"Maybe the thing to do is switch," says Paul, handing me a ticket. I have to read the print twice before I understand that it is from a parking garage. "You go home tonight, and I'll stay here. The place is a mess, but you'll get a decent night's sleep, and you'll get to see Charlotte. Tomorrow you can visit a friend."

"What friend?"

"Do you want to or not?"

"I can't. I have to learn to give her the shots, or I'll be here forever."

"Okay," he says, as he tucks the ticket into his pocket.

As soon as he leaves, Nanny says, "What a handsome man."

"Yes," I say.

"And nice!"

"Yes," I say again.

"Mr. Hewitt is like that, the father, yes. He never loses his temper, never for a second, not like her."

"Yes," I say, as I flee from the room.

Rachel sleeps fitfully, as I do, crying off and on throughout the night. By morning her face is puffy, and her eyes are red. Nothing comforts her; not my voice, or my body beside hers, or the sound of my voice. I try to hold her on my hip to walk her, and she pushes at me, and moans; mmm with each step I take, mmm when I stop. We walk down orange halls and green ones. I am searching for someone. I am looking for a person to tell me that nothing could be wrong with a baby this beautiful.

Charlotte joins Paul the next time he visits. She is not allowed upstairs, so I take the elevator down. She sits on a molded blue chair in the waiting area, dressed in the same outfit she wore when Rachel was first born, the aqua dress with satin hearts across her chest. New pink sneakers are on her feet. Her hair is glossy, bangs in her eyes. She is very busy swinging her legs together, then one at a time.

I whisper her name and she turns and runs to me. Most often she is too restless to stay trapped in a parent's arms, but today she gives me a hug that is so tight I can feel her arms quiver. Her hair is clean and smells fruity; her small, ragged nails have been polished red.

"Where's Rae-Rae?" she asks.

"Upstairs. I like your new sneakers."

"*Mommy* —" she breathes.

I wait and wait, and when nothing follows I say, "What, darlin'?"

"When Rachel grows up, will she be able to drive?"

"No."

"Does that happen to all blind people?"

"Yes."

"Awwwww," she says. "You're *kidding!*"


The mechanics are not difficult. I swab the rubber stopper, attach the needle to the syringe, and insert it into the upended vial. As the medication drips, I flick the syringe to break the air bubbles. Then I push the plunger until a drop of fluid rises to the needle point, bright as a diamond.

Miss Theo lowers the side of the crib and pats Rachel's head. "Mommy's here, lovebug," she says.

Mommy's here to hurt you.

My hand is trembling. The nurse unzips Rachel's hospital pajamas and draws a leg through. Her thigh is already mottled with bruises and needle marks. Now I understand the stories of parents who pull their children out of hospital beds or take them away in the midst of treatments. I put my hand over her leg, and the nurse pulls it away, saying, "Swab her first, Mommy."

I work at the foil packed, trying unsuccessfully to tear off an edge, until the nurse takes it from me. Inside is an alcohol swab. Rachel's body stiffens when I touch her with it. Her feet move in circles. She knows I am going to hurt her. Her brain is damaged, there are connections that have not formed, things she might never perceive or understand, but this one she knows: Alcohol means pain. Her mother hurts her. Her chest heaves. She begins to cry.

My hand is so weak that the needle trembles in my fingers. The nurse holds Rachel's knee straight and pins her arms above her head. "You can do it, Mommy; come on now; come on."

I find an unmarked spot and touch the needle to her leg. Her skin offers such resistance that for a moment I feel as if the needle will never break through. I push hard, and when it pierces her skin, I feel her grow rigid. "Mommy is helping," croons the nurse. "Yes she is, she's helping her baby." I push the plunger and the gel seeps slowly into her muscle. The nurse cheers me on. I am in the kitchen, still in my terry robe, a mug of coffee at my elbow. Rachel hurries past; she is rushing by me, ready to play. I catch her sleeve before she leaves me. Once we were afraid, I say. Once we were afraid that you would never grow up.

# ❦ 13 ❦

## Some Babies Cry

I AM STUFFING FRUIT into my suitcase early the next morning when Miss Theo arrives. Rachel is moaning in her crib. Nanny rocks in her chair, reading the September issue of *Town & Country* that Mrs. Hewitt left for me. Miss Theo sets the vial and hypodermic on the night table, checks her watch, and asks when *he* is due, with the kind of reverence Charlotte showed for Him at four.

"Any minute," I say. "Unless he hit traffic."

Paul bounds in just then, smiling, cheerful. Miss Theo dimples. Nanny snaps her magazine shut and holds out her hand as if she expects that he will kiss it. She has the freckled skin of a former redhead and green eyes that glitter in his presence. She is so comfortable with men that I realize that once, 304 babies ago, she was pretty. Ah, what children do to a woman.

"All ready, Mr. Glynn?" Miss Theo asks.

I have graduated and can be trusted to give Rachel her shots at home. Now it is Paul's turn. If he passes, we can leave the hospital together in time to walk Charlotte to her first day of class.

"This shouldn't be hard," he says. "I do rats all the time. A shot of Nembutal, which knocks them out. For good. Did my wife tell you I was a surgeon? I operate on rats, too, and I must say my technique is really quite elegant. I can open them up without a drop of blood. The only problem is I can't put them back together again . . ."

He's nervous and cannot stop talking. It's true that he operates on rats. What's also true is that he turns greenish when anyone says "blood," "needle," or "hypodermic." He covers his ears and leaves the room if I discuss something as trivial as a flu shot, and once, when *I* had blood drawn for a routine test, *he* came close to passing out. Now he stands chatting amiably with Miss Theo as if she might forget why he is here.

I touch his shoulder and call his name in order to rouse him. Nanny looks up. Miss Theo turns and makes me feel like an ill-spirited wretch interrupting my charming husband's discourse on surgical technique. He *is* charming, too. It annoys me that his public self is so untouched by all our troubles.

Miss Theo lowers the side of the crib and unsnaps Rachel's hospital pajamas. Paul says, "Here we go, Babykins," and swabs her leg. He does not hesitate after that. He takes the syringe from Miss Theo, squeezes Rachel's flesh, jabs her, checks to make sure that he hasn't drawn blood, then turns his head away. For just an instant, as he presses the plunger, his face contorts with anguish. Then he sweeps her into his arms and walks across the length of the room humming to her until she quiets.

When it is time to go, Paul carries Rachel, and I drag my suitcase down the blue halls. My comrades are in the lounge, smoking cigarettes and waiting. Sandra sees my bag, says, "Ooh, lucky stiff," and kisses me. The German woman waves with the tips of her fingers and mouths, "*Auf Wiedersehen.*"

It is not entirely pleasant, this prospect of entering the free world. Like a convict, I am hungry for freedom, but I fear it as well. Out there, my movements will not be so prescribed. I will be lost in the world of the whole, the world of those who cannot possibly understand.

Of course there is traffic. Fifteen minutes before school starts, we pull up to the curb, behind Paul's parents' car.

Home. My couch and chairs, my pictures on the walls. My rugs and tables, my great-grandfather's portrait on the wall, my refrigerator, and tacked across its side a chart that Paul drew up in my absence that lists the day and the amount of ACTH Rachel is to get. The dose decreases slightly every second day, until, at the end of November, she will be through. Already the first week is scratched out with big X's.

Paul yodels, and Charlotte runs in through the back door and tackles me, arms around my knees, nearly bringing me down. Her dress is new and matches her sneakers, and her hair has been brushed smooth and shiny. Paul's parents follow behind. My mother-in-law approaches Paul with her arms extended, and he gives her Rachel. I want to say something, to thank them for driving all the way here for what will not be much of a vacation, but I just stand dumbly. My mother-in-law is confused by my expression and says, "I gave Charlotte a cheese sandwich and a glass of orange juice. And some prunes. I've never heard of a child eating prunes, but that's what she wanted."

"Prunes are fine," I say.

Paul takes one of Charlotte's hands, and I take the other, and we walk her up Elm Street to her school. In this, we are just like the other parents we see; the stay-at-home mothers in casual clothes, and the men in jackets and ties. Charlotte skips, bounds over cracks, and pirouettes; the flat red apple that says "Charlotte Glynn" in perfectly formed letters bounces against her chest.

Charlotte's school looks much like the one that I had attended at her age, a red brick building built in the thirties with a disconcertingly modern wing to accommodate the children of the postwar baby boom. Signs have been hung on the wall with each teacher's name and section, and children have already begun to form lines beside them. A mother nudges a little boy with a new haircut toward his classmates, and he goes forward at first, then stalls, and screams, "No no no!" He breaks free of his mother's grasp, throws his apple in the trees, and runs, elbows pumping.

Our kindergartener gets rid of us before we can slobber all over her and stands with her classmates. She is a head shorter than the others around her, which surprises us because we have never thought of her as small. She looks very confident in this new situation, much surer than I would have been at her age.

Paul and I join a group of parents who stand in a grove of trees, waiting with their infants and toddlers for the kindergarteners to file inside. Everyone's gregarious, stunned that their babies are starting school. Paul makes a fuss over a pair of twins, seated face-to-face in a stroller, and I say, to no one in particular, "This school looks *exactly* like my old elementary school," and find out that the couple beside me attended the same school the same years that I did.

A woman I knew from Charlotte's swim class, whom I have not seen since both of us were pregnant, asks what I had. "A girl," I say, and she says, "Oh, me too, we'll have to get our babies together." Her husband takes her picture, and Paul takes mine. We finish a roll, reload in the shade and shoot some more, and when Charlotte follows her teacher into the building, we stand for a moment longer.

"Should I take a picture of you two?" says the woman from swim class. "Give us a smile there, come on. A big one for the birdie . . ."

In the pictures, Paul's arm is wrapped around my waist, and I lean against his shoulder. Both of us smile wanly. There is no sign of the misery we felt, no sense that we were stunned and exhausted. If any-thing, we look a little queasy. Paul studies the pictures and says, "It's hard to look pretty when you're constipated."

On the same roll are a series in which his parents sit in the yard on white wire chairs, my father-in-law asleep with his head thrown back, my mother-in-law facing the camera, her deep-set blue eyes filled with helplessness. Rachel lies rigidly across her lap, hands in tight fists, toes extended. Her face is swollen; her mouth is in a straight, tight line. I have seen pictures of babies crying, and photos in glossy magazines of hungry, destitute children, who stare listlessly at the camera. This is different, the grim expression on her face, and what the camera could not record — the sound that was emitted from between those clenched lips, the unearthly mmmmmmm that went on and on, flooding our ears, penetrating through skin and bone, filling the house with her pain.

This is what we live with now, a cry that cannot be soothed. Habit or biology itself makes us try to calm her, though we know there is little we can do to help. We rock and feed her and try in vain to interest her in songs or toys or motion. We try to distract ourselves with food and conversation, but the cry is always in the background, always with us, so that nothing can settle for long in our minds except her needs.

Once in a while she quiets, and whoever is with her will summon up the exact moment when she stopped crying and exclaim, "She likes when I press her feet!" or "She likes Vivaldi!" or "She likes having her back tickled." Then the quiet spell ends and we try desperately to get it back with what becomes, as the days pass, a long list of worthless cures: press her feet, play Vivaldi, tickle her back, hold her upside down, sing "Hush, Little Baby." One evening she quiets while I am telling Paul what to pick up at the store, and the next day, after she has failed to respond to having her feet pressed, Vivaldi played, her back tickled, etc., we try repeating the shopping list.

We are doing just this, chanting, "Cream cheese! Skim milk! Rye bread! Napkins!" when Hannah, our Israeli friend, comes over with a blueberry cake.

Paul explains our bizarre behavior, which is not really necessary be-cause every evening for the past year Hannah has taken her son for a long car ride in order to get him to sleep, and she understands a parent's desperation. Although we reject as impractical her suggestion that we take Rachel out for a ride, **Paul** is very enthusiastic about her offer to lend us a baby swing that worked for her son when he was newborn.

An infant swing to lull her, when all these months we have worked so hard to keep her alert . . .

"I can't bear the thought of her sleeping all day," I tell Paul when Hannah leaves.

"You want her to cry all day instead?"

The thought of her rocking and rocking is so awful. "You haven't read all the papers I have, all the stuff about the psychological problems babies develop when they're deprived of stimulation."

"That's a healthy child. Rachel is sick. She can't *learn* anything when she's this miserable. Our job should be to make her comfortable and nothing more. She'll catch up when the treatment is over."

"You believe that?"

"Of course I believe it."

"Then pick up the swing on your way home from work."

I say this only to end the discussion. What I think is, We will not set up the swing. Never. I will work with her. I will spend all day at her side until I can figure out how to make her comfortable enough so that she might join us again. I know I can do it. I know I can.

She cries when I hold her, when I rock her, sing to her, pat her, leave her. Her ceaseless moaning is such exquisite torture that I break down before noon.

Paul comes home from work, sets the swing in the living room, and jams Rachel into the seat made for infants. It is awful seeing her hunched into the tiny seat, head bowed, fists clenched. He winds it up, and we gather around and watch. She straightens momentarily when the swing begins to move, then struggles feebly to free herself.

There is no escaping the moan, even at night, for she wakes, crying and wanting to nurse, like an infant, at two-hour intervals. I feed her so many times each day and night that my breasts are like those of a new mother, tender, and engorged with milk. She bites down on me, not the way an infant bites, to experiment, to soothe the tingling gums, but in misery. She does not smile or laugh or respond to our voices and gestures. She cannot reach out, and when we try to comfort her, she pushes us away. The only connection we have is when I nurse her, though she bites me so often that even this is filled with pain.

"Tell her 'No!'" says my mother. "Slap her if she does it."

A useless suggestion, for she is no longer of this earth.

On Saturday we take a ride down to the shore to visit a childhood friend of Paul's. What are we thinking when we make these plans — that the moaning comes from the house itself and can be left behind when we close the front door? Do we really think that it is all over? We pack diapers, wipes, and snacks for the car, needles, syringes, and gel. Then we get into the car and head for the Garden State Parkway.

Rachel struggles in the car seat. She cries and moans steadily. The car is far smaller than the house, and each of us is tightly belted and powerless. It is torture to listen helplessly to her agony, and no one survives torture unchanged. My father-in-law becomes a sergeant, my husband an erratic driver, my older daughter absorbs her sister's discomfort and suffers herself. My mother-in-law is speechless, and I have murder in my heart.

The sergeant issues frantic orders to signal, slow down, pull over; the little girl moans along with her sister, *hafta, hafta, hafta* . . . All this buzzing distracts the driver, who squirms and slaps at his face, as if the words were flies. And the sergeant says: "Ahhhh, don't you think you ought to have both hands on the wheel?"

My thighs stick to the plastic car seat, and when I lift them one at a time, I feel as if I am being flayed. Who is it that I want to kill? Perhaps it should be Paul, who imperils us all with his driving. Or Charlotte, whose steady chant of *hafta, hafta, hafta* makes her a likely candidate. I consider the victim, all along knowing that murders of passion are not committed by weary people — passion implies energy, zeal, fire, none of which burn inside me today. I also know that Charlotte does not need to pee; she is bored and irritated by Rachel's moaning, and this is her way of showing it, no more obnoxious than her father's aggressive lane-changing. I know it, though I cannot chance a sobbing, humiliated child, and when her haftas become high-pitched and pained, I say, "Stop the car."

Paul goes from seventy to zero in a few seconds, and hurls us onto the shoulder of the road.

"Out," I say.

Charlotte searches for her sneakers, and puts them on, laboriously crossing the Velcro straps so that they fasten, not horizontally, but in perfect *X*'s, the way the big girls did it in summer camp. She squeezes in front of her moaning sister and gingerly steps into the road. Confronted by the pitted asphalt, the weedy slope that ends in oily water, she says, "I don't hafta anymore."

"Oh, yes you do." For once, my voice is enough, a simple statement uttered softly, once.

"*Okay,*" she says, with Paul's inflection, exactly.

She steps out of her underpants, white bikinis decorated with paw prints and a grinning Garfield the cat, and squats and pees. She watches the arc her urine makes and the descent as it soaks her sneakers. I hand her a tissue and she squats and wipes and tries to hand the tissue back to me. I tuck my hands behind my back. "Just put it down. Go on."

"You *said* not to litter."

"Down," I say.

"But I'm not supposed to —"

"*Down!*" and my molars clench.

She sets the tissue on the ground, and as I drag her back into the car, she keeps her head turned and eyes it sadly. The car pulls off, and she leans against the window and watches the litter I made her drop get smaller and smaller.

Ah, how easy it is to yell at a child. Take pity on her, I tell myself. Remember that she is shaken up, too, and has no words to express what she feels. Go easy on her. This seems simple until the haftas start again. This time it's hunger — and all the snacks that I have packed are gone. *Hafta, hafta* for so long I can feel my fist in her face, her small, square teeth loosened by my punch.

Both my daughters are crying by the time we arrive. I sling Rachel over a shoulder and follow the others into our friends' house. The woman has not seen Rachel in a long time and makes all of the appropriate comments about how adorable she is. The man says: "She needs Weight Watchers."

I put her on the carpet, and she sits with her head lolling against a shoulder and cries. I press her feet, hum Vivaldi, tickle her back, recite "Cream cheese! Rye bread!" all to no avail. I pick her up, and she bites my shoulder and struggles to get free.

The visit centers around her distress. She is hot, she is tired, she is hungry, she wants to nurse. Everyone has a reason; all of the reasons are wrong. At last, my mother-in-law takes her from my arms and carries her outside. I listen to the gravel crunch beneath her feet and the shaky lullaby she sings, and I remember her telling me a year ago what a thrill it was to hold Paul's babies.

Paul's friend invites us onto his new boat. My mother-in-law insists that I leave the baby with her and join the others. She says, *"Go.* You're his guest —" in a stern voice that doesn't quite mask her kindness.

We put on life vests and stand in the bow while he motors from the canal. The boat slaps against the waves. As soon as we're in open water, the sails go up. The main rustles as it's raised, and with a thwack of the canvas catches the wind. Charlotte and I watch Paul tie off the sheet. The wind blows his white hair into his face, and he laughs the wild unrestrained laugh I have not heard in months. He reaches an arm out for Charlotte, and she scampers onto the cabin roof, as surefooted as he, and stands beside him, her face turned up to the sun.

"Next year," Paul says when I join them. "Next year I'll teach her how to sail."

It's all perfect, the sun, the pinpricks of spray upon my skin, the sound of his laughter. Perfect, absolutely perfect, a moment that seems plucked from a happier time. And yet I want to go back, I miss Rachel so badly. I don't think she knows me, and even if I'm wrong, my presence does not soothe her. It's just that it feels so unfinished, my walking out, as if we have quarreled and separated with bad words between us. We are miles apart and there is no way for me to show my love. The gulls circle above our heads and cry, and the buoys moan sadly. I want to go back and hold her in my arms.

And then my wish comes true, and I am on land and racing into the front of the house, where I find her crying in her grandmother's arms. My mother-in-law says, "She's *so* uncomfortable," and gives her to me.

We take turns patting her, tickling her, holding her upside down. Everyone has methods, everyone knows reasons, nothing works.

We will not go out, then. We will not subject others to her distress. But my parents call and ask if they can visit, and it seems unkind to turn them down.

My mother and father walk into the house laden with shopping bags, and in their own enthusiasm to show us the gifts within, and their very real tolerance for chaos and noise, neither seems to notice the moaning child in my arms or the one that writhes upon the floor, collecting dust balls in her hair. They greet my in-laws, drop the bags, and wait for us to plunder the loot.

The gifts are a funny assortment of things that have been bought, made, grown, or found: a handmade sweater for Charlotte, a straw fan from a wedding they attended, three jars of gourmet mustard, plastic produce bags to use for dirty diapers, a turnip, several Jersey beefsteak tomatoes wrapped in newspaper, a pair of shoes that I left at their house several years ago and do not really want, a flame starter, a kitchen timer, a wooden-handled cleaver that my father holds up machete-style. And more and more until my arm muscles quiver from the dead weight of my sick child.

Paul leaves when the show is over, my father steps outside, and I am left with bags and crumpled paper, one writhing child, one moaning one. I set Rachel on the rug and am stacking the presents on the table, when I see my mother's eyes flit from moaning Rachel to Charlotte the mop. "Feed your children," she tells me.

I head into the kitchen and peer into the refrigerator. It is lunchtime, isn't it? And I have invited my parents for a meal? I toss a piece of cheese upon the counter and start to unwrap it when I hear my mother call, "She's crying, do something." I drop the cheese, take Rachel in my arms, jam her into the swing, and hurry back into the kitchen to do what? Sing Vivaldi? Change a diaper? Where's Paul? The cheese cues me. *Lunch.* I recall that our parents like coffee and run water in the kettle, and my mother appears again, her voice shrill with what sounds like anger. "She's slipped in the seat, *help* her."

I adjust Rachel, give the swing a push, then return to the kitchen to find the water cascading over the sides of the kettle and the sink half filled. Rachel's cries grow louder. I take her from the swing and race upstairs carrying her across my shoulder.

Paul is lying on his back in bed, arms crossed over his head. I search his face, trying to find a glimmer of the man I loved in Maine, but I see nothing of him.

"Here," I say, as I put Rachel on his chest. *Take this* is what I imply.

At lunch the grandfathers exchange hardship stories. Who was poorer? Whose shoes had more holes? One father slid cardboard inside his shoes, the other used newspaper. Who experienced worse prejudice, the Jew in New York, or the Irish Catholic in Boston? One father recalls the signs that said "Irish need not apply." The other tells of employment quotas against the Jews. One saved coal, the other did menial work for twelve cents an hour. One got beaten up by Italians, the other by Germans.

Rachel pushes her plate off the high-chair tray. My mother says, "She doesn't like what you gave her."

"She doesn't like anything."

While I am cleaning up the floor, Paul lifts her from the high chair and attempts to hold her on his lap. In a soft voice he tries to entice her to eat a piece of bread. Charlotte takes a bite of her sandwich and watches, her eyes stormy. She turns back to the table, and opens her mouth so that we can see what she has been chewing.

"Cut it out," Paul says.

She feels the tension in the room and it panics her. She is not in control. If it were me, thirty years ago, my mother would have said, "She's looking for trouble." Trouble is not what Charlotte seeks, however. It is relief, love, laughter, *something*. She sticks out her tongue, and shows us cheese and dough.

Paul rises, and his chair clatters backward. In one fluid movement, he dumps Rachel in the high chair and grabs Charlotte by her shirt. My father's coffee sloshes into the saucer; a knife clatters onto the floor. Paul stands above Charlotte, a giant clutching her shirt in his white fist. She looks up and her eyes are huge with fright. Paul lifts her from her seat and when the fabric splits, he catches her upper arm and drags her up the stairs. I hear her feet bump against the steps; I hear him hurl her onto the bed, the slammed door, the crying that begins only after he has started down. My mother's sigh brings me back, and I am aware once again of Rachel's ceaseless moaning.

"Feed her something," she says.

From the doorway, Paul says, "I'm going out."

The door slams. The car starts. He has abandoned me. He has said, I cannot take it, and left, just like that. I cannot take it either, but I have no choice. Now there is no question whom I would like to kill.

My father goes outside. My mother-in-law carries her plate to the kitchen. My mother scrutinizes my face and, when I return her glance, says, "She was looking for trouble."

At night we go upstairs together, Rachel in her daddy's arms. How romantic it looks, the two of us climbing the steps, side by side. Paul flicks on the overhead in our room and the light sparkles against a crystal bowl filled with syringes. Also on the night table are cotton balls, a mug full of needles, and a bottle of alcohol, whose odor pervades the room and makes it smell like a doctor's office.

Paul passes Rachel to me while he assembles the paraphernalia. I unsnap her suit, and she arches her back and struggles to be free. It is hard to believe that two weeks ago she smiled and reached out for us. Now all signs of humanness are gone except this: As soon as we place her on the bed, she stiffens and whimpers, her feet rotate.

This is the only thing we do together. He gets the air from the syringe, swabs her leg, and holds it at the knee. I jab the needle into her flesh as quickly as possible. I do not feel the awful resistance of the skin as I once did, nor do I think of it as Rachel that I stick. It is not my child, it is a patch of unmarked skin that I seek, muscle instead of vein. It is a job that I must do properly, though I do not allow myself to consider why.

I want to pick her up when it is over, but I am afraid that she will form an equation, Mommy = pain, that will never leave her. In the second that I hesitate, Paul scoops her up and holds her against his chest, and the blood from where I pricked her soaks into his shirt. He paces the room, a hand across the back of her head, while I stand with empty arms.

Then he sits and sings, "Hush, Little Baby." The tune changes into something else, the words fade away. I envy the strength he has to meet her agony head-on. I know that it takes every atom of his tenderness, and yet when I listen to his soft, off-key song, it reminds me of who he is, and makes me ache for something for myself.

"You've hardly spoken to me since I've been home," I say.

He does not answer until I ask him a second time, and then he says, "There's nothing to say."

"Nothing?"

He rocks Rachel and continues humming his atonal tune.

"Nothing?" I am as desperate as Charlotte, when she showed us a mouthful of masticated food.

"That's right."

"I thought we were going to pull through this together. Isn't that what you told me? That we'd hold on to each other?"

"If I said it, I was wrong."

"*Why?*"

"Because it isn't possible."

"But that's what we always did before she was born. We always turned to each other when we were upset. Always."

"This is *different*. It's different, and I don't want to talk about it; I just want to be left alone, can you understand?"

I should by now, but I don't. "I'll leave you alone," I say.

# ❦ 14 ❦

# One of Us Tries to Run

THE SCRIPT that Linda and I rewrote in early summer is in pre-production, and orders have come from above asking that we make it funnier and sexier and snappier, to be tailors who sew buttons onto the end of each scene, surgeons who cut twenty pages *immediately,* for a crew has been hired and awaits these changes, and their plans depend upon the changes that we make.

I find myself working outside the house for the first time in years, waking at six, worrying about clothes and clean hair, vying with Paul for the shower, mirror, and sink. What a difference it is working for and with people. Not only must I be presentable, which at home I frequently am not; I also need to be alive and alert, to produce no matter what my mood. Though I have always prided myself on being disciplined, there is no escaping the fact that my own writing has been a victim of my preoccupations. I cannot *afford* to be distracted, not that it has been a problem, for I find that when I leave the house, I leave everyone within it far behind.

I have come to think of the life that I have begun to live as a man's life. Women work, of course. I see them on the buses and trains, hunched over small mirrors, putting on eye shadow or blush, eating yogurt with flimsy plastic spoons; I see them carrying bags of bread or vegetables, ankle socks over panty hose, running shoes swift against the pavement as they gallop down the incline to catch the homeward train because there are children they miss, suppers to prepare, too much life at home in far too little time.

The men walk; they chitchat, they read company reports and use their hard-sided attaché cases as lap desks. They do not rush or fret when missing trains. Work is work, and home is home, and these areas do not mix. Men may diaper babies these days, but they do not take them to work. They do not buy groceries at lunchtime.

I search for my children before I leave the house, kiss them fervently, and say farewell to Paul as if it might be our last good-bye. I close the door, and scoop up the newspaper, and by the time I slide it from its plastic bag, my family is gone. No matter how long my workday, I never think of them until it is over.

If, on a break, Linda asks after them, I cannot summon them in all of their heartbreaking detail, and so I relay whatever news seems appropriate in a cool, detached way. Rachel is miserable; Charlotte likes school. She says that I am courageous to work like this, which shames me. What is courageous about my ability to run from the unhappiness in my house and leave my family behind, to run even if they call to me? Leaving is a relief.

The production office where I find shelter is a cluttered T-shaped room with a view of several porno houses outside. It has the look of a place set up in haste, rented desks and gooseneck lamps; boxes of office supplies, open, but not unpacked; movie posters tacked onto the wall with pushpins; Polaroid snapshots hung with tape. One day I study these photos, and it looks as if the colors have already faded from them. Then I glance around the office and see that the people clowning for the photographer are all around me, talking on telephones, typing on rented machines, running the copier, perched on desks and tables — all wearing clothes in fashionably drab colors: khaki, olive, black, pants cropped midcalf, black pointy-toed shoes, shirts that slide off one shoulder, revealing an undershirt beneath, in a dark, mildewy color. They are all young and unencumbered, without spouses or children or babies who cry night and day.

Often, in the midst of our work, Linda is called away to meet with a songwriter or study snapshots taken by location scouts, and I find myself listening to the conversation around me. There is so much laughter in it, so much ordinary good cheer, that I ache for my own lost past, for the time when my life held promise, when no doors were closed, no die cast, and all my dreams were possibilities. During these quiet moments, I imagine shucking off my present life and taking on something new. Why not? People do it all the time. Why should I feel compelled to stay with Paul? We have lost our history, our desire for each other, our laughter, our dreams; we are nothing more to each other than the parents of a moaning child. Why not leave it all behind? What is noble about holding on to such unhappiness?

The work goes on from morning until late at night. The powers that be praise each draft that we complete and find new things for us to change. I am tired, bored, grateful to be here, amazed that my brain works after all, that just like a man I can neatly separate home from work.

As soon as I leave the building, it is all over. Something within me says "home," and I find myself running to get there. Broadway glitters with neon. The street corners are three-deep with theatergoers clutching rolled Playbills and saluting for taxis. I run down Eighth Avenue, past dreary sex shops and all-night delis and men too blitzed to leer, though habit makes them try, because I am a mother again, and my mind is flooded with images of my children. As I run I think of the soft flesh of Rachel's legs, so mottled with bruises and pinpricks that I must search for an unmarred place to damage, and how in the mornings, when it is still dark, Charlotte climbs into bed and throws an arm around me so that I wake, feeling her glossy hair against my cheek. How docile and uncomplaining she has grown since I have started this job. She sees that Paul and I are fragile and has taken it upon herself to make it up to us. I know that she is struggling to be twice as good, that she will fail because it is impossible, and that she will think of the failure as her own.

I have time before my bus is due to dash into a Greek bakery to buy a piece of baklava for Paul and then into an all-night drugstore, where I find a coloring book and a frog-shaped eraser for Charlotte, and barrettes to clip into Rachel's beautiful curls, for every morning no matter how rushed I am, I pick out her clothes and fix her hair.

I think of Katie when I fuss over Rachel's hair. Once I did not understand how a mother could buy pretty clothes for a child like this, tie hair ribbons, polish nails. Now I do. Reciprocity means nothing to us. We love and cannot help it. Like mother rats we suckle our young because it is our way. Rachel nurses, and in her misery she bites me. I push her away, but when she roots and nuzzles, I take her back because she is mine.

An hour later, I am in town, listening to my footsteps as I hurry down the dark street toward home. The traffic light blinks yellow and a single car speeds by, its windows rolled down, Bruce Springsteen filling the air with his raspy voice for just a moment before he's gone. Only the ice cream store is open. Three boys stand on the sidewalk outside, all dressed in wrinkled shirts, button-fly jeans, and heavy boots, worn unlaced. All of a sudden I want to see Paul very badly — the Paul I married, with his wide eyes and wild laugh, the awe he had for simple things, his healing touch.

I remember sitting with him in a coffee shop on the Lower East Side not long after we had met, making flow charts on napkins and plotting our career decisions in order to see what the future might bring. What promise those days held; what a sense I had at twenty-five that through sheer will alone, we could carve out a wonderful life.

It was around this time that I read *Pentimento* and came upon a section about Dashiell Hammett, in which Lillian Hellman wrote about the good years and the bad years, and because my feelings about both Hellman and Hammett were so romanticized, and because I knew about Hammett's drinking and ill health, and about the red-baiting of the fifties and their subsequent financial woes, I believed that they had had bad years, and was haunted by the thought — whole years that were bad, hundreds and hundreds of days — though I could not comprehend how anyone could remain at a job or in a relationship that made them unhappy.

These are bad times, and we have made things worse by losing sight of each other. Whatever we once shared has gotten buried in the muck of sadness and fatigue. Even the early days after the diagnosis seem touching in comparison, for then at least our memory was intact. Our shattered glasses and angry words were madness, but our embraces made us sane. At the end of every fight we still had each other.

Now there is nothing. We have learned so well to cope with our grief — he no longer rages, I no longer cry — that we can sleep in the same bed and live in the same house, as distant as strangers. It is only when I am hurrying home that my memory returns and I can feel, hidden deep within me, an achy spot of love, as sharp and bruising as a stone.

I race up the hill and see our house, all lit up from within, and I imagine, as I do each evening, catching him in my arms, and feeling in his embrace that we are together again.

His parents are in the solarium, hunched over a battered little black and white TV with a coat hanger for an antenna. I sit on the floor and watch the figures roam across the snowy screen, lips moving, a crescendo of canned laughter.

"How were the kids?" I ask.

My mother-in-law says, "Rachel was so unhappy." She seems reluctant to go on, and only after a long pause, during which we stare at the small screen, does she continue.

"Her little body ached no matter what I did. Most of the morning I held her in my arms, Dad can tell you. Then Charlotte came home, and she felt left out seeing me with the baby like that."

"I'm sorry."

I get up and my mother-in-law says, "Don't forget to give Rachel her shot."

"Where's Paul? She was supposed to have her shot at six-thirty."

"He was only home long enough to have some supper with us, and then he went back to work. He's had a hard day."

The outrage rises against my will. "We've all had a hard day."

I go upstairs and get a needle and syringe. The gel has to be kept in the refrigerator, and when I take it out, it is solid in the vial. I rub the vial between my palms to get the gel to liquefy, then wipe the rubber stopper with alcohol. After I work a needle onto the syringe, I stick it through the stopper. The plunger first must be extended, next pushed fully forward to get the air out, and then, with the vial upended, pulled out to the proper mark. The gel is still as thick as honey and seeps slowly into the syringe. Though I hate to give Rachel these shots, I get an odd kind of pleasure from the preparations. I have gotten quite expert at warming the thick gel quickly, in knowing exactly how much beyond the dosage mark to fill the syringe, and how with two well-aimed flicks, I can get the air bubbles out most efficiently. Then I change the needle — advice from Miss Theo, who told me that the needle gets a barb after going through the rubber stopper.

There it is, the jewel at the needle tip.

Rachel's eyes are open. I lean over the crib and wait for a response I know I will not get. My baby, I think as I lift her. She is almost unrecognizable beneath the layer of fat and fluid, her face so blown up that I cannot snap bibs beneath her chin; her belly so distended that nothing fits her except stretchies that expand to cover her girth. I hold her in my arms and imagine Dr. Klibansky flying by. I grab his white sleeve before he is past me and shake him furiously. *Why do you make me torture her this way? Why bother? For what?* Sometimes he is sitting in a heavy chair, surrounded by books, when I barge into his office and beg him to let her die, literally get down on my knees and plead with my palms pressed together. She's brain-damaged and in pain, it makes no sense to make her suffer this way.

I switch on the overhead light in our room, and smooth the rumpled bedclothes. As soon as I put Rachel down, she stiffens and cries. *Mommy = pain.* My whole body trembles. *Mommy hurts me.* Which leg? Left in the morning, right at night — a mnemonic Paul and I agreed upon for this chore. I unsnap her pajamas.

Her leg is like rubber as I work it from the suit, hurrying so that I can hold her in my arms. *Mommy hurt comfort.* I find a patch of clean flesh toward her inner thigh and swab it with alcohol. She kicks her leg feebly. I catch her knee with my elbow and stick the needle in — plunger back, no blood — then jam it in again.

The plunger feels wobbly when I push, and when I pull back, the needle remains in her flesh. Her thigh is slick from the gel. I don't know when the two pieces separated and how much ACTH has dribbled out. All? Some? Rachel mewls steadily like a cat. I hate her, I love her, I'm terrified. If I give her another shot, will she overdose? If I don't, will she have another seizure? Will we have to start the treatment over, at a higher dosage this time? I pick her up and rock her in my arms. I want help. I want someone to tell me what to do.

I give her a second shot with half the usual dosage. Then I get into bed. The visions keep me awake for half the night. I imagine tripping while she is in my arms, tumbling down the flight of stairs, crushing her with my weight. It is so real I can feel her broken body. I imagine giving her a shot, weary and despondent, so anxious to get it done with I never get the air from the syringe or pull back the plunger to check for blood. I inject air into her vein and kill her because I wanted her to die. I see her room, the chains of roses on the walls, the empty white crib, the toys she never played with in boxes, her clothing in bags, and I don't know if it's true that I want her to die.

Charlotte comes into bed at dawn with her dolls and blanket, settles beside me, stirs and kicks and sneezes in my ear. The bureau drawer screeches; the metal handles clank against the wood. Paul sits on the edge of the bed and pulls on his socks.

"Do you have money?" he asks when I open my eyes.

His shirt is wrinkled. The points of his collar curl under. What wells up inside me is so confused I feel as if I have been damaged in some fundamental way and can no longer distinguish between pleasure and pain, love and hate. He looks haggard and ghostly. I think of the shot that he did not give and I did disastrously.

"Didn't Rachel wake up?"

He gives me a puzzled look. "She was up at six and just went back to sleep."

He lingers for an instant. I try to move away from the shot, to the place where I was last night when I ran home from the train station, arms pumping.

"There's a twenty in my bag. What time did you get home?"

"One. How about you?"

"Eleven? I don't know." All of this very tentative, as if we are two acquaintances meeting in a dentist's office.

"How was the — uh —"

"It was a meeting — all the department heads got together to go over the script. We have some more to do, so I have to go back later on today. I . . . missed you."

The words are as hard to get out as the first "I love you," so intense is my fear of being shot down. I am not even sure that they are true, though when he says, "I missed you, too," I feel a tremendous relief.

He shifts his weight. Charlotte sits up, regards us, then pads into her own room. How accustomed we have grown to our children witnessing our private affairs.

"Maybe we could go somewhere on Saturday. Drive out to the reservation and have a picnic or a walk, do something normal," I say.

"I'm working."

"All day? We haven't seen each other for a week."

"Is that *my* fault?" he says.

"I wasn't talking about fault; I was making a statement. I'm disappointed, that's all."

"Well, I'm disappointed, too."

His words chill me. I watch him rise from the bed and pull a jacket from the closet. The hanger clatters onto the floor. *You leave me the dirty work.*

"In me?" I ask.

"In everything."

He is halfway out before I can finish.

"You were home, why did you wait for *me* to give her the shot?"

"I was home for an hour."

"And now you're going away for the weekend and leaving her with me. Well, I don't want her all weekend long."

"I'll take her. I'll take her and live somewhere else. You can have Charlotte."

I sit up and throw the pillow at him. "Get out. Get out and take her with you!"

The thought of being without her makes me weep.

She is sick, poor baby, so weak she can barely sit up, bloated beyond recognition. Her blood pressure is high, her liver is enlarged. She is spilling sugar. Her cry makes me ache with love and helplessness — please, anything to help her, anything, my life to save hers. Please let her die. I want to hold her in my arms until she is well. I want to strangle her to death. I want her better again no matter how damaged she may be. I want her dead.

My dreams disturb me all night long. I wake in terror so often that I begin to resist sleep. Awake, I clutch her tightly, hands wrapped around the back of her head because I am afraid of what may happen in my weariness and despair. My hand trembles when I prepare her shot. It takes me several minutes to find a clean spot on her mottled thighs and when I do I hesitate, afraid that I will miss a step, forget to swab her, forget to check that I am in muscle, afraid that the needle will separate again, afraid in general.

I go in to work less often, and when I do the days are shorter than before. Work takes me far away and gives me moments of peace, and yet for no logical reason, home is where I would rather be.

My mother-in-law helps take care of Rachel with a compassion that never seems to sour. She meets Rachel's misery head-on, with an unfailing confidence that her nurturing can mediate the pain, and yet sometimes it seems as if she has absorbed Rachel's cries and carries them around in her own body, for this once ebullient woman is numb and speechless most of the time.

Paul and I rarely talk except to convey domestic messages. His parents say nothing about our estrangement, though I know that they see how apart the two of us are. What do they think? Do they recall, as I do, our first visit to Florida, when we were newly married? Paul got sick on the plane and, feverish for days, kept me at his side so that I could read to him. We cuddled together on their long brocade couch, he with an afghan across his shoulders, a hot leg over mine, hot arms around my waist, while I read. Hour after hour we spent this way, breaking only for tea and light meals, until five books and seven days later, his mother said, "Leave her alone, you'll wear her out."

One night the Glynns begin to pack. I watch, frightened by the prospect, for although it would be unkind to ask them to stay any longer, I'm afraid of what we might do to each other when they're gone.

We go to bed early that night, and my sleep is long and unusually deep, a sleep born of fatigue. What wakes me in the morning is Paul jerking upright in bed. He rushes to the bedroom door with such alarm that I follow behind.

Charlotte is sitting with a tattered blanket at the top of the stairs, breathless, hiccoughy, cheeks glistening. Paul strides past her and throws open the door to where his parents slept. Their beds have been stripped, sheets, blankets, pillows in neat towers on the chest. Even then I cannot believe that they have gone without saying good-bye. Paul takes several more strides down the stairs and opens the front door.

"They left," he says. "I can't believe they left."

When he looks up at me, all the hurt drains from my body. He puts his arms around me and draws me close. Then suddenly he breaks away and scoops Charlotte off the steps. He holds her against his chest and presses her against mine to make a human sandwich, Charlotte in the middle, face wet with tears.

After the Glynns leave, Lourie comes over every day. She holds Rachel in her arms for hours and sings her lullabies. I am grateful beyond words, and terrified that one day she will tell me that she cannot take it anymore. I am also ashamed that I do not have it in me to sit with my own daughter this way, that I lack the gift to give and give that Lourie has. It is not so much the crying that I cannot tolerate, but rather the fact that nothing I do helps in any way. My feeling of uselessness makes me turn against her: I hate her because I cannot help her. It makes no sense, but there it is.

When Rachel's birthday comes, I want to mark it in some way. I buy a cake with candles that she cannot blow, put her in the only dress that still fits, a loose smock with ruffles at the bottom, and drive her to my parents' house. I know that it is ridiculous to go through these pains — Mickey Mouse plates for a blind, sick child. But she is alive and she is ours and marking her birthday is the only way I have of showing my love.

She sleeps through dinner, and when it is time for her cake and presents, Paul and I quarrel because I want to wake her up and he wants to let her sleep. He is adamant, but he is alone, and so I take her from her crib and work her into the high chair. Our birthday girl slumps in her seat and moans, lips clenched, hands fisted. She is so huge she looks as if she is wearing crinolines.

She will not touch her pretty packages. It is Charlotte who opens them and makes a fuss over each — a jack-in-the box, a pull toy with blocks inside, a plush bird with large, loose wings. Paul watches her inspect the toys, his face grim, and so I ask her to show them to Rachel. She piles them on Rachel's high-chair tray, then takes her sister's hand and moves it across the soft, bright bird. Rachel struggles, too weak to break free. At last she pulls away, and using all her strength sweeps her arms across the tray so that the gifts fly into the air. The bird's wings open, and for an instant, it hovers in the air. We watch, all of us expecting for an instant that a toy stuffed with foam and nutshells might soar above us. The blocks fall, the bird thumps after them, and the truth confronts us again: Nothing can reach her, and in this way, we are exactly like her.

*October*

My mother is the one I argue with these days. I argue with her because she says that Rachel will get better, and because she does not like my haircut. I argue because she accuses me of starving myself for fashion's sake, when in truth my appetite has been formidable, but grief has stripped the flesh from my bones. I argue with her because we are invited to a family party, and she says it's not nice to bring Rachel and begs me to leave her home from this gathering meant for adults and children alike. We quarrel over this issue for so long that I lose my voice.

The next day she has the misfortune to tell me what a fine man Paul is, how wonderful he is with the children, how unusual he is to not feel threatened now that I am away so often, how much harder a handicapped child is on men than women, and so we argue again. I know that she is telling me these things because she is afraid that I will leave him. Nevertheless, her words drive me up the wall. Does she tell Paul to be nice to me when I'm not around? Does she tell him how hard it's been on me? Is anyone on my side around here?

I argue with my mother because she wants to take me shopping, but when we go out, she hears Rachel's cry magnified hundreds of times and is convinced that we are disrupting the other shoppers, who wheel howlers of their own. Rachel writhes in her stroller and shakes her head from side to side, her body's way of saying, "No!" and my mother *shushes* her in an angry voice, as if my daughter is spoiled and needs to be reminded of the rules. My mother wants to go home because Rachel is crying, and I am reminded of children locked away in institutions, of jokes and restrictions based on fear, and I argue some more. I remember battalions of wheelchairs rolling through a museum, and how she dragged me away so I would not have to see. Don't mess up our perfect world with your writhing bodies, gnarled stumps, wasted limbs. Do not show us your respirators, prosthetic devices. In the mothers' group, I was warned that I would become an advocate, and so I have.

"She has a right to live!" I tell my mother, just then remembering a key phrase from childhood: It's a free world.

It's not, of course.

She cannot judge the depths of my fury, and says: "Please, let's just take her home. It isn't nice."

"Tough shit," I say.

We argue because she says I'm bitter.

"I have a right to be bitter."

"Don't," she says. "You'll end up alone."

I laugh bitterly. "So what's new? I am alone."

And it's true. I think of our first week, and how our phone rang nonstop. How quiet our house has been at night and on holidays since then; how silent our cousins and friends. Where has everyone gone?

"You expect too much," my mother tells me. And while I am pondering this, "People are afraid to call; they don't know what to say."

"They're afraid — fine; I understand. But if my own relatives can't transcend their fears at a time like this, then I don't want to hear another goddamn word about family and how important it is. Because there's no point if all family amounts to is yea for us and boo for you."

"You don't know how it hurts me to see you like this."

I'm a mother myself and can imagine how upsetting it must be to see the sweet baby, carefree child, giggly teenager turned into this sad creature. Nevertheless, my language skills have deteriorated, and all I can manage is another sullen "Tough."

I pack Paul off to Denver for a meeting, literally pack for him like the good wife that I am not, counting out underwear, folding shirts, choosing ties. And then it's the same old thing, can't wait for him to leave, can't stand it when he's gone.

The first morning I wake up alone, a thought burns in my brain. We are killing this child. She is going to die from this stuff that we are injecting into her mottled legs.

I have been overly fearful since the treatment began, beset by dreams of causing her death, and so for the next few days I do my best to suppress these thoughts. Then one afternoon when I return from work, Lourie says, "She's getting so much worse."

When I call Dr. Klibansky I learn that both he and Dr. Gutman are at a meeting, too. Dr. Klibansky's secretary gives me the name of a pediatric neurologist who is covering for him, and the next morning, I get through to him. I describe Rachel's disorder, and the regime that she is following. I tell him how weak she is, how she can no longer roll over or sit.

"And this is ACTH she's on?" he asks.

"Yes," I say. "Are you familiar with it?"

"Quite. And what you're describing doesn't sound at all drug-related."

He says he will see her if I like, but that it probably isn't worth my while driving her into New York when the best he could do would be to check her heart and lungs, the same as my local pediatrician.

I take his advice, and tell my story to our pediatrician instead. She does a routine check — eyes, ears, nose — tells me that Rachel is overweight, and that her ears are a little pink. There's nothing *really* there, though it could be the start of an infection.

She writes out a prescription for amoxicillin, which I know I will not fill, and jots down on another paper the name of a special school nearby where I might think of sending Rachel. "It's got an excellent reputation," she says.

The school is for the lowest-functioning children, the ones without hope. It is where Katie has been placed. I crumple the paper, drop it in her waiting-room trash, and leave.

On Thursdays I cry. As soon as I enter the infant stim room, I feel the grief well up. Pachelbel's *Canon* makes me cry. Rachel moaning. A child who takes his first steps at three; a child trapped in a body that will not work at all; the bright, awkward murals painted by volunteers — Raggedy Ann and Andy, a trainload of toys. The huge bear in the corner, with its massive, slumped shoulders makes me cry sometimes, and so does the child who screams "Momm-mmeee!" in fear. Sometimes I am discreet and no one notices. Sometimes I hide in the bathroom.

One day, after listening to Rachel moan for a solid hour, I break the way a dam breaks; one minute everything in control, and then suddenly a torrent, and no way of stopping it, though it is very embarrassing, nose running, hoarse achy sobs, mascara flaking beneath my contact lenses, a giggle, a dry laugh as if my crying is for joy. Thank you for the party, thank you all.

"I shouldn't bring her here anymore," I say.

"If you don't want to bring her, don't," Faith says. "But please don't think that she's upsetting us. Or that we expect her to perform."

"It's such a waste of time."

"Not for us. Don't forget, we work with children in coma."

I nod and sniffle and feel foolish, and when the session is over I take Rachel downstairs to see Dr. Goldstein.

He has not seen her since July, and although he is friendly and chatty, and addresses her in the same jovial way, I can tell by his manner that her appearance disturbs him. I tell him about the infantile spasms and the shots of ACTH, and when I am done with my recital, he says:

"I've never heard of a reaction like this. Maybe what we're seeing isn't the ACTH, but the brain damage itself. Often it becomes more evident when a child gets older."

"Who said that — Klibansky?" Paul asks, when I relay via phone this piece of news.

"Klibansky's at a conference and so is Gutman, so I talked to Dr. Goldstein —"

"Klibansky told us she might be sick, didn't he? And Gutman said, what? 'Some babies scream from sunup to sundown.' So don't tell me what some asshole said, because I don't want to hear it."

On the day of the family party, I can't find anything that fits Rachel. I end up going downtown to buy her a one-piece suit that is several sizes too big and needs to be rolled up at the ankles and wrists. Even this is snug around the middle.

I can't find anything to wear, either. I rip clothing off hangers, try something on, toss it on the bed, put on something else, the whole time arguing silently. She is part of the family, I tell myself, a cousin no matter what. Why should I hide her away? She's my daughter, she goes where I do.

Paul fumes; Rachel cries. I try on everything I own and still hate the way I look.

We are late, which improves no one's spirits.

All the way down to my uncle's house, while Rachel moans in her car seat, I continue arguing silently. Do I have to pretend that my daughter doesn't exist, when she is one of us, flesh and blood? Are these parties meant only for the able-bodied and not for her?

Inside me is such a pocket of rage that there is no way to admit that part of the reason I am bringing Rachel is because I don't have the heart to ask Lourie to take care of her for the sixth day in a row.

When we arrive, Paul carries Rachel into my uncle's house and I hurry straight to the bathroom. I sit on the edge of the tub and imagine climbing out the small window and running far away. Then I wash my face and leave the room.

Paul is standing in the kitchen bouncing Rachel in his arms and explaining about the spasms and the shots that make her sick. My family stands and listens, and when he is done speaking one of my cousins takes Rachel so that he can have something to eat. After a while, my aunt takes her from my cousin's arms; then my father holds her for a while. The afternoon passes this way. There are times when I hold her, and times when she is far enough away that I can almost forget her.

# ❧ 15 ❧

# We Wait

*November*

ON THE LAST DAY of the month, Paul and I hold Rachel down on the bed, slip a mottled thigh from her pajamas and give her the last shot. When it's all done, I take her into my arms and say, "No more, baby. No more."

Paul sweeps the syringes and needles into the trash, then tosses in the vial, with thirty dollars worth of gel left inside.

The next week we have our first snow, thick, linty flakes, and wind so strong it looks as if the snow is made upon the ground and blown into the sky. I find a snowsuit in the attic large enough to accommodate Rachel's girth. "My bundle of joy," says Paul, as he straps her into the car seat.

The road is beautiful, the upcoming car an ocean liner in the foggy sea. Just as the windshield wipers push the dry snow away, more splatters on so that Paul has to strain to see the way. I love snow. I love it stubbornly, the way one loves a worthless person, and so our last paltry winters have pained me.

Soon we are on city streets. A man sweeps his car with a kitchen broom; a woman walks past, enshrouded in a plastic dry-cleaning bag. Her dog wears earmuffs. Long before I see the tan buildings that make up Hospital City, I can feel in my gut that we have arrived.

We park the car and trudge up the steep hill past eye and cancer and brain. One year has passed, almost to the day, since the diagnosis was first made. One bad year. "I'll punch him if he's rude to us," I say. "I swear to God I will."

"Don't," says Paul.

The fact that he believes me capable of such a thing is enough to calm me down.

We hang up our coats in a waiting area shared by several doctors and are working the snowsuit off Rachel, each of us on one leg, when Dr. Klibansky signals to us from the corridor. He is just as I have seen him in dreams: small and scowly, with a headful of wild hair.

"Let's get her in here," he says. The tails of his white coat fly as he turns.

What a simple room this is: pale blue walls, a Picasso print of a handful of flowers, swabs, tongue depressors, Band-Aids, a chrome garbage can. Paul sits Rachel on the examining table and pulls her shirt over her head. His hands are trembling. I stand in a corner and watch him tug her overalls clumsily over her shoes. When at last he succeeds, he sits her up, and arranges her legs in order to balance her. She lists and weaves. Klibansky edges over.

He pushes her down and helps her up, taps her knees, and tickles her soles. He winds the tape measure around her head, and I hold my breath as if my stillness will change its size. When he measures again, I can see his displeasure. I want to know, I don't, I want to know, I don't.

"Dress her," he says at last.

We are sitting in his office when I speak.

"She can't lie on her stomach. She's too weak to sit. She moans all day long."

"I warned you about this, didn't I? I said some babies cried."

"I was told that her weakness had nothing to do with the ACTH, that what we were seeing was a result of the brain damage."

"Not by me."

"You were away."

"A myopathy is a very common side effect with this drug. She'll get her strength back shortly."

The need to know wins out. "Is her head size still normal?"

He shows us the chart that records her head measurements, and I see that a straight line could connect all the points except this last one.

"There's been a dip, but that's to be expected when a child has had infantile spasms."

"And it means —"

"There was an insult to the brain and the growth slowed down."

"What's the prognosis?" Paul says.

"The fact that she had infantile spasms suggests damage, and of course you can see what's happened to her head size. If you're asking to what extent there's damage, I really couldn't say. In all probability there'll be some intellectual impairment."

There it is again, those words.

"What exactly does that mean, intellectual impairment? Is it a euphemism?"

"I don't use euphemisms. It means just what it says, that a whole range of deficits may show up. You may know right away; you might not find out until she starts school and more is demanded of her. Maybe it represents a loss of thirty points on an I.Q. —"

"That's not bad if she had an I.Q. of one fifty," Paul says.

"— or it could be stubstantially more. Give her time to recover from the effects of the ACTH. Then what's important is how fast she catches up."

Snow is still falling when we leave, but there is hardly a trace of it on the ground. Paul cradles Rachel so that the flakes fall upon her face. "Snow," he says. "Cold white snow."

I remember him sitting on the couch with Charlotte, an open book between them, and how he had pointed from picture to picture. "There's bunny. Bunny's socks, bunny's shoes, his jacket, hat, gloves —" I remember the afternoon I walked past and saw him point to the pictures, and heard her say: "Bunny zhoos, bunny zocks, bunny 'at, bunny dacket . . ."

"Light!" he says now. "Curb! Taxi! Snow! Snow, Rachel, snow!"

## December

And so we wait.

This we do together. We wait for a change, or short of that, for a sign that change is coming. Waiting becomes my occupation. Paul goes to work each morning and calls each afternoon to ask, "What's up?" "Nothing much," I say, and he gets off.

When Charlotte was born, he told me that having a child made him aware of time passing as nothing before ever had. An infant is transformed from a sleepy bundle of needs into a sensate creature so quickly that it is like watching a time-lapse flower bloom. He called me every day after her birth and there was always some momentous news. She smiled, she sat up, she held her cup . . .

Rachel wakes up and we lift her from the crib. Her chin is chafed. She wants to nurse. Outside it is cold and gray, it is cold and sunny, it is cold and rainy. Paul calls and says, "Hi, what's up?" And I say, "Nothing new." "Any mail?" "Gas bill, water bill, junk."

We pick her up, kiss her moon face, change her diaper, careful with her bruised legs, and one day it is snowing outside, and a few days later it has thawed. We bundle her into the big snowsuit and take her to infant stim, to my parents, to the Y, where Charlotte has swim class, and one afternoon I can feel the cold in my lungs, and the next day I can go coatless.

We pick up toys and shoes, we pick up Rachel and kiss her swollen belly, and in the supermarket when she cries, we drop grapes in her mouth, like tokens into a slot. Paul calls and says, "Hi, it's me." And I say, "Hi, you." "Anyone call?" "Let's see . . . hmmm . . . a computer named Hal selling life insurance." "And?" "We didn't want any." "And?" "That's about it."

In those interminable days in which nothing at all happens, Charlotte goes to birthday parties and learns to read *Go, Dog, Go,* Paul grows cells and plots data, and I draft a story that I call "Giving Baby the Needle." Rachel wakes and cries and we change her diaper and hold her in our arms. The sun comes out so brightly one day that winter feels near an end. The next day sleet falls from a blackish sky, nasty stuff that wakens Rachel when I take her out. Paul calls, and there is never anything to say, so I report on the crust in Rachel's ear crevices, the length of her fingernails, the dark down that has grown along the sides of her face and the nape of her neck, another side effect from the ACTH. I say, "I cut her toenails and she didn't seem to mind." Or, "She sat in the bath without falling over," because in this case inane news is better than no news at all.

One day she smiles. She is still bloated and uncomfortable, but for the first time since before the shots, she is well enough to step outside her discomfort. And I realize that the onset of her misery was so sudden that it was instantly felt by us all, but that her healing has been gradual.

"She isn't crying," I say to Paul one day when we are all sitting together.

We aren't fighting, I might have said, if only I had noticed it at the time.

A smile, an interest in something other than food; a response to our voices; a willingness to play simple baby games that she had loved in the months before. ("Where are Daddy's glasses?")

Then one Sunday morning, the four of us are in bed together, and I am nowhere near ready to rouse. Charlotte and Paul whisper and shift and tug on the blankets and decide in loud voices that they want the kind of pancakes that only I can prepare. I am begging for sleep, ready to sell whatever privileges I have for an extra twenty minutes. The sun is high, and the others are hungry. I roll myself cocoon-style into the covers. Charlotte crawls on me and pulls at my eyelids, the way she did when she was two and would say, "Open eyes, Mommy, open eyes," prying at them with sticky fingers.

I open my eyes unwillingly, and what I see is Rachel, struggling to climb the mountain that is me. She grunts as she works her way up. She clutches at the blanket and pushes off with her feet, her face solemn with effort. She is working hard; she is giving it everything she has.

# PART IV

# ❧ 16 ❧

# Healing

WHEN THE SHOTS WERE OVER, our wishes were simple: All we hoped was that Rachel would get better. We wanted her to be able to sleep peacefully and wake with a smile and get pleasure from the world the way she had before she got sick. We were delighted by her first attempts to reach out from the pain that held her captive for so long, but we did not harbor expectations or think about her future. After all, we too had to heal, though neither of us was aware of it.

She cried less as the winter wore on, then hardly at all. The bruises on her legs began to fade and her smiles turned into laughter. One day when I was snapping a terry bib around her neck, I realized that the edema had begun to go down.

Our healing was as slow and subtle as hers. We spent easy hours together, laughed, spoke of other things. Step by step we began to reclaim our own lives, to remember the dreams we had before the diagnosis, my book, his dissertation. One night when Paul was talking to me from another room I realized that our voices had changed. Gone were the prickly tones that we used regularly, the jibes and accusations. We spoke kindly to each other again, the way a friend speaks to a friend, a lover to a lover.

Charlotte's healing was more dramatic. When Rachel got better and we began to laugh and speak in civil tones, she lost her meek subservience. She dropped her socks into the toilet, peed into the bowl, and then denied the whole thing. She shredded a carton full of Styrofoam slugs and dumped the entire load onto the solarium floor, spit her chewable vitamins on the floor beside the sink each morning, took Rachel's stuffed toys and hid them beneath her blankets. Although she was still charming when she was with Paul or me alone, she could not bear the two of us together, and when we hugged or kissed in her company, she drove her small body between us. She was so miserable seeing us happy it was as if she preferred the days when the two of us barely spoke.

The winter that Rachel's body began to heal from the effects of the ACTH, Charlotte began to have trouble with her eyes. We asked her anxious questions, and she admitted that, yes, the board in school was blurry and the big letters in her storybooks were hard to read and sometimes she saw two of everything and sometimes she could not see at all.

We made an appointment with an eye doctor whose office was around the corner from our house, and on a snowy afternoon she walked there with Paul. I was outside shoveling when the two of them strode up the hill, through fluffy snow that should have made her smile. Charlotte was several yards ahead of Paul, clumps of snow on her hair and sweater, jacket unzipped, tears streaming down her face. She slapped a coloring book and "I love my ophthalmologist" stickers into my hands and stormed into the house, refusing to tell me a thing. Paul delivered the upsetting news that her eyes were "boringly normal."

We gave her an old pair of Paul's frames and later, funny glow-in-the-dark frames of her own. She wore these for a while and quickly grew tired of them, and by the time she turned seven, when we began to suspect that eventually she would need glasses, she proclaimed them ugly and swore that she would never wear them.

I rarely thought about Rachel's sight the winter that Charlotte wept because her eyes were normal. Whatever visual deficit she had was so dwarfed by her other problems that it stopped being of prime concern to me. She was brain-damaged, though to what extent we had yet to find out. As Klibansky had told us: "You may know right away; you might not find out until she starts school and more is demanded of her." My memory tells me that I had so totally adjusted to her near-blindness that it did not upset me anymore. I suppose that wasn't quite true, because I can recall how I always sat close to her and smiled broadly. I was not testing her. I was too bruised to dig, and so was Paul. I think that I sat and smiled at her like that because I still missed the eye contact that tells a parent so much when no other communication is available, and because as hopeless as it was I was still waiting for her to respond the way most babies do, to light up at the mere sight of me.

One day I flashed a big toothy smile, and I could have sworn that my little girl scrunched up her face and smiled back. Or did she? Because for me nothing stings worse than false hope, I had learned that past year to doubt before I believed, and so I muted the excitement that had begun to well inside me, smiled again for Rachel, and got in return a big wrinkly-faced grin. I stuck out my tongue, and just as if she had known this game all along and had been waiting for me to wise up and play it with her, she stuck out her tongue in return.

Even Paul could not deny that she saw and mimicked my smile, that, therefore, she could see my face. Clear or hazy was irrelevant. She smiled in response to my smile, stuck out her tongue after I stuck out mine. Thereafter, other things began to interest her that for so long she had ignored — balloons and toys and mirrors. In infant stim I set her in front of a hinged mirror and she made monkey faces at her image. The light had to be in such a way, the mirror had to be close by, she had to be alert enough to try. But when she made faces in the mirror, it was so wonderful to behold that the other mothers turned and watched with awe and said, It's a miracle. All that grief . . . Those bastard doctors . . .

No, it was not miraculous, though it felt that way. In his initial diagnosis, Dr. Hines had suggested that her visual deficits would be significant — not complete. It was the long wait that had dimmed our hopes, nine months until she saw beans and bananas and a shaft of light. It did not seem reasonable to expect more, for the way she tilted her head suggested that the vision she had was peripheral, and as Paul had told me numerous times, there is no visual acuity in that part of the retina (nor is there color), and thus, no way that she would ever see clear, detailed images. Even so, she could interpret smiles and raspberries and saw enough of her own sweet face to enjoy monkeying around in the mirror.

I recalled Sharon telling me that children must learn to make use of the vision they have, and that even when their condition is static (as Rachel's is), their ability to see increases for years, and so after Rachel's first responsive smile, Paul and I went around like two buffoons, grinning and sticking out our tongues. I bought her picture books, a puppet with huge poppy eyes, a bright red ball with large white spots; I blew soap bubbles and gave her pot lids and pieces of foil to catch the light. Rachel cocked her head and scrunched up her eyes and reached out for things. She showed frustration for the first time in her life and whined when she wanted something or when we left her alone, for now she knew what was out of her reach. Her grating cry was music to us, and Paul would put his arms around me and say: "Ah. Just like a real baby."

Like a real baby, she began to crawl. She was not seven months or eight, however, but a year and five months. Like a real baby, she pulled herself to stand, not at eight months or ten, but at a year and a half. We took such joy in this real babyness — our own sweet, curly-haired child grunting as she reached, burbling, raspberrying, babbling, splashing in the tub, humming nun nun nun to herself in the morning, pursing her lips for kisses. A real baby. (So delayed!) Just like a real baby. (Why did it take her so long?) It was so unbelievably great. (Was she retarded?)

Toward the end of that winter, I got used to Rachel being well. This is not to say that I took for granted her splendid health, but rather that with time came a renewed awareness of her delays, an underside to our happiness. I did not live every second of every day with the knowledge that she was brain-damaged; the word itself and all that it meant crept up on me in vulnerable moments. I have always experienced what I call the dreads, dark fears of what the future might bring, and her brain damage was one of the dreads that descended upon me when I was weak, bored into my heart, filled me with fear, and then departed, leaving me nearly unblemished to enjoy her babyness again.

When Rachel was fifteen months old, Lourie left us. Mrs. Kaiser knew of her gifts and helped her find a job as an aide in a school for orthopedically impaired kids that paid more than I could afford. Not much more, since those who work with young children earn less than garbagemen and housecleaners, but enough so that she might save money for tuition and start a degree in special ed.

The hospital had a day-care center, a small structured program for handicapped children run by a warm and capable young woman named Robin. Two full-time caregivers, and in the afternoon high-school volunteers, looked after an enrollment of perhaps six children, most of whom spent part of each day in preschool. It seemed like the perfect place for Rachel.

I hated sending her there. I had always handed my babies into someone's arms, and now I would be giving Rachel over to a *place*; a room, furthermore, where orthopedic apparatus lined the wall, walkers and strange medieval-looking contraptions that strapped around waist and legs. Her first few mornings in day care I hovered around the room, waiting for her to show a sign of pleasure or unhappiness — for any sign at all. I scrutinized her at breakfast to see if she seemed anxious about leaving me, and in the afternoon to see if she was scarred.

At fifteen months Rachel was not a complicated child, with a range of likes and dislikes and moods. Because of this it was hard for me to leave her in someone else's care, for when I left I felt as if I had nothing more than trust to carry home with me. She did not have fear in her repertoire; nor did she tease or play games. She was never coy or moody. She could anticipate (and therefore had memory). When we approached her, she wiggled with pleasure, reached out and showed her delight with a whole range of utterances, and when we sat her in her high chair, she grunted and banged her spoon. She knew what it meant to be put in her crib, though never once did she protest. Only one thing upset her, and that was when Lourie sang "Lullaby," the song she sang when Rachel was so sick. Months after the treatment had ended, Lourie sang "Lullaby," and Rachel's whole face crumpled, and she burst into a strange silent cry that seemed based in remembrance.

It didn't take me long to see that Rachel was loved in day care. Robin and Karen did all the appropriate things in order to stimulate her; they taught her patty cake and played ball with her and tried to get her to stack rings on a pole. They put her in a cart with big wheels that she could push, read to her, sang to her, showed her simple pictures, encouraged her to move. They also styled her hair every day, so that whenever Charlotte and I came for her in the afternoon we found her with her hair parted down the middle with a barrette on each side, or in a bun on top of her head, or combed wet so that it fell into ringlets.

Picking up Rachel from day care became an important part of the day for both Charlotte and me. It always began the same way, with the two of us tiptoeing into the room, then kneeling silently a few feet from Rachel, and waiting for her to recognize us. She never did. Eventually Charlotte would tire of this game and join the day-care kids for snack time, and I would call Rachel's name, and when she shrieked with delight, come close for a hug.

Charlotte busied herself so happily in this room that it was hard to tear her away. Often an hour passed before I could gather my two girls and start down the long corridor. On our way out, people always stopped to greet us. The nurses poked their heads out of the clinic, the social worker put down her phone. I never despaired for Rachel when I was at the hospital. She was loved and valued, never judged, never seen as damaged or deficient. Here every gain she made was cause for celebration.

One sunny March day when Charlotte and I came for Rachel, we found her outside, outfitted in a white helmet, holding on to a metal walker and taking her first steps. She was so tall on those boxy little feet, so pleased with herself. I snapped a whole roll of pictures of her taking those careful first steps. (It would be another six months before she could walk alone, another year before she was comfortable on her feet.) The grandmothers hated those photos. They saw only the apparatus (just as I had seen only the medieval-looking contraptions the first week Rachel was in day care). If only they could have seen the child beneath, standing and laughing, her face lifted to the sky. If only they could have been with me when I carried her down the corridor, where everyone applauded her great effort.

We do not live in isolation, however. Other people's babies reminded us how delayed she was, children her age who ran, jumped, explored, demanded, tried their parents with their stubbornness, delighted them with their wit. Just because she was adored in day care didn't mean the progress reports from infant stim or the physiatrist would stop coming in — "Cognitive level 10 months, gross motor level 7–9 months, fine motor 7–11 months . . ." — this when she was fifteen months old.

A smile was no longer enough. What accounted for these delays? Was the brain damage responsible for everything? What about the fact that she had been sick for so long, the whole autumn in treatment, and long before that, the nighttime seizures that went unnoticed? "Give her time to catch up," said friends and professionals. These same people also told me that normal children whose development has been impeded by illness caught up very quickly once they got well.

How quickly? Did it take a month? A year? How much of a role did vision play in her delays? She could see faces and balloons, though she could not recognize me when I walked into the day-care room and knelt before her, ready to take her home. Could I still, in all fairness, study the charts that compared the motor development of normal babies with those who were totally blind or had "minimal light perception"? Were these charts applicable now that she could see her own reflection? Was her poor vision an excuse for her gross motor delays? What about her head size, which had dipped after the infantile spasms? A below-normal head means that there has been cell death. How much? Thirty points off an I.Q. of one thirty? Fifty off an I.Q. of one hundred?

"How can you worry about a child who feeds herself so nicely?" my mother said, because Rachel drank neatly and fed herself with a spoon well within the guidelines for a sighted child. Why could she do this and not other tasks that normal children mastered by her age — stacking rings on a pole, making a tower of blocks, turning pages in a book? A child gets proficient by practicing these tasks, and Rachel resisted doing them. Why? Because her poor vision made them empty for her? Or were they far beyond her ability?

Why, at a year and a half, didn't she have a neat pincer grasp, that is, a thumb and finger grasp used to catch a raisin or a ball of lint, something that fifty percent of all children show between ten and eleven months, according to the Denver Developmental Screening Test, and ninety percent show by fifteen months? This particular ability was a neurological milestone, not something learned. Why did Rachel continue to use her hands the way monkeys did, with the more primitive palmar grasp? Why didn't she say "Mama" or "Dada," something that ninety percent of all children, including those who are visually impaired, do by twenty-two months? Was she neurologically impaired? Were the speech centers in her brain damaged? Was she retarded? Was it possible that her delays were caused by her visual deficits, that even though she could make out our smiles and extended tongues and reach for balloons, she was a blind child who had been terribly sick and one day would catch up? Or were we deluding ourselves?

There were so many extenuating circumstances for her delays that I could not accept that she was really delayed, because to accept it felt like giving up, and she was making enough progress for us to keep believing.

I can remember days when I walked into day care and saw this child, who had once been nothing more than a pretty little lump, holding on to the walker with brand-new determination and taking careful steps across the floor, and thinking, My God, she's come such a distance, why do I worry so much?

I can also remember a day, when Rachel was about eighteen months old, and I was feeling heartsick about a report that I had received, meeting Kristin Peters, the teenager with optic nerve hypoplasia, who had been so harshly characterized as "a real mess." She was on her way home from an out-patient therapy session when I ran into her and her mother in the corridor, and she told me with great animation about a new school she would be attending in the fall, and how she would get to work with computers, and how she had not had a seizure for six months, the longest time she had been seizure-free since she was five years old. I understood why she had been called a mess, with her pale green eyes that roamed in their sockets, her empty gaze, and an awkward, lurching gait. She also had smooth auburn hair, and, dressed in shorts, she was lean and coltish and absolutely lovely to me, a young girl just blossoming into womanhood, bright and filled with energy. When I walked away I thought, She has her brains, she has everything. Seizures and blindness and all, I wished more than anything that my daughter would be like her.

The journal that I began to keep during this period of time is sparse, though within it I read that one day I am "happy, happy, happy," and that Paul and I "dare to believe."

Also: that we went to a party the next week where normal children gamboled, and Paul, as if noticing his daughter's difference for the first time, asked, "Is that what they're supposed to be like?" That night we quarreled over his grocery shopping, and I ended up in tears because of the overblown cucumbers he brought home. Later, when I figured out why I had gotten so upset he would not hear what I had to say, and I went to sleep realizing that "we are still torn apart by this."

Ten days later she is "sweet and responsive, a doll, an utter joy. She brings out the warmth and affection in even the crustiest of souls."

The next month an old friend who had moved to the West Coast saw Paul at work and asked about Rachel, and Paul got so upset in the middle of talking that he had to leave the room. When he told me I felt as if our sorrow would never end, that we would never stop crying.

It would seem as if we were much the same the winter that Rachel began to recover as we had been after the diagnosis, up and down with dizzying speed, despairing, believing, accepting, depressed. In fact, it was much different, for I was no longer completely in the grip of all those ups and downs; I was not drowning in woes. I had a child whose future was uncertain, and I had days filled with pleasure and moments of exquisite dread, and so many hours when I did not think of her at all that even now it surprises me. No, in the beginning Paul and I used all our energy just to stay afloat, and all of our promises to each other and all of our fights had Rachel's blindness behind them. Now when people asked how we were doing, I could say with honesty that we were well.

I knew that it was far from over — *it* being the problems that we had yet to face. There was this, however: Rachel was well and did not fill our house with her misery. She was cheerful and responsive, and often the dreads hovered far enough away that I could wake up and feel that the day would be a good one and take in the peace I felt, literally absorb it into every cell of my body because it was what I wanted with the greatest urgency. What I had learned, finally, was to live from day to day — sometimes.

Rachel's sickness was like a great storm that had blown us apart, and it took time for Paul and me to pick ourselves up and put our lives in order. There was no residue of bitterness, the way there might be after an unresolved battle. The storm was over and we were still together. I wished that we could have held tight, though I did not see this failure as a failure of love — who knew that our way of grieving would be so different? What was there to prepare us?

We learn to love by being loved and, later, by falling in love. We learn to raise children and live with another person in much the same way. Nothing teaches us about grief until we grieve, and then it is too late. The way I had always heard it, hardship brought families together or tore them apart, that those who truly loved each other came through, and those whose marriages were weak did not — just as simple as that. After the diagnosis I often recalled an article I had read about a couple whose child had Tay-Sachs disease, and their physician, who said that some couples sat on his office couch shoulder to shoulder, and others at either end, and that he could tell at first glance which ones would pull through together. I believed this and tried to picture us as the ones who sat shoulder to shoulder and was devastated when I was forced to concede that we were not.

How could we sit together? He was incapable of considering Rachel's future, and I could not let it go. I had an obsessive need to worry, cry on his shoulder, share sad visions, confront what appeared to be the truth — just what he could not tolerate. I wanted him to help cheer the progress that Rachel made that he, with his scientist's eye, saw as "unproven." Later, when I realized that before I went back to fiction I had to write this book to make sense of what had happened, I asked Paul for his point of view on specific incidents, and he was unable to give me help, for the past was gone and he could not plumb his memory for details.

What different styles of grieving we had! How can I look back and say if only we had loved each other enough, we would have pulled through, hand in hand?

I always knew that Rachel would walk, and if I was impatient to see her take those steps unaided, it was because the passing of days took us closer to a diagnosis I did not want to accept. The sooner she walked, the less impaired she would be — or so I felt. I studied the developmental charts the way astrologers study the stars, expecting answers in their bars and graphs, predictions of her future. If ninety percent of all children could do a task that Rachel could not, she was still okay; if the bar ended or the curve fell below her age and she was not yet capable, I worried. The fact that she was nearing two and still did not walk upset me. But I knew that she would get there.

I did not know whether she would speak; and this was what I wanted most. I was aching to find out who this child was, to get a glimpse into her soul, and so I was still ready to bargain with the little vision she had for intellect and speech.

At fifteen months, she did not speak a word, neither "Mama" nor "Dada." At eighteen months, the same was true. She was twenty months old when I felt for the first time that she was on her way to saying something.

*Buh* came first, one small sound, innate to all babies. Whenever I put her on the changing table to diaper her, her arms would fly, the fingers of one hand touching the small doll my mother had gotten her when she was an infant, and the sound would bubble at her lips — buh-buh-buh. "She's trying to say baby," I told Paul. He did not take me seriously. She had been babbling for some time, and what I was hearing was just a random syllable — mah, pah, buh — there were few enough so that the chances of her saying any one at a given time were high. Though I was sure he was wrong, I did not push it. Soon enough she would say the word that bubbled at her lips.

The progress that Rachel made seemed to take forever. Sometimes I thought that this was because I waited so intently, and a watched child never speaks. And I watched and watched until one day the lowly buh became a bah, and the bah a bah-bah, and from that a closer approximation to the real word — baby.

After that, there were others — Mommy, Daddy, zhoo, zock, ball, balloon, 'nana, and several more. She used them appropriately, there was no question at all. Shown a balloon — a particularly easy thing for her to identify — she would say balloon; touching her sock, she would say zock. But if we said, "Where's Mommy?" she would turn and point to . . . Paul, or Charlotte. "Where's Daddy?" we asked, and she would point to me, or her grandmother . . . as if she wasn't really sure.

"She's not going to give you a straight answer just because you want it — she's a *baby*," said my mother.

"She doesn't know the difference," said Paul.

"At that age they sometimes get mixed up — normal babies, too," the speech therapist told us.

Paul said: "She doesn't know the difference."

Later that same day I heard him on the telephone with an old friend. "She's doing really well — we've got our fingers crossed."

Was she?

Euphoric, I made lists of Rachel's words; despairing, I did the same. She knew *forty* words, I thought in utter amazement. I didn't know that she would ever talk, and here she was with forty words, which she spoke in such a sweet little voice, clearly enough for strangers to discern.

She knew only forty words. If she were normal she would know more than fifty words, be adding new ones all the time, begin stringing them together, and all she knew were forty words.

Charlotte began to have her own problems that winter. We had enrolled her in kindergarten before she was five, in a school system where the trend was to enter children late. Her nursery-school teacher had suggested that we consider giving her an extra year, but Charlotte's maturity and self-reliance allowed us to forget how young she really was. Kindergarten, with its heavy emphasis on basic skills, and homework every night, was hard for her.

In the winter, one side of her neck swelled up, and Paul and I panicked, thinking it was cancer. The day I spent waiting for her doctor's appointment, I realized how vulnerable Charlotte was, that Rachel's problems would not spare her sister from physical or mental woes. I could not depend upon her to be healthy or happy. Anything could happen to her, too. (The swelling turned out to be a gland, and went away. The problems with school went away, too, though they would return when Charlotte was in second grade.)

She was also beginning to show the strain of having a sister who commanded so much attention. I tried to give her permission to be angry with Rachel, but perhaps she still thought of us as delicate, for her behavior toward Rachel was touching, even when the two of them were alone. Her dark feelings came to the surface when she was with Lourie, however. With her once-beloved friend, she was quarrelsome and demanding, with an insatiable need for gifts and attention, and an inability to believe that Lourie could love them both.

In my own mind there was no competition between my girls, for I had ample room to love them both (and ample room to worry, I now found out). Charlotte engaged my mind and heart, and Rachel touched a soft nurturing side I had not known existed so strongly within me. Rachel was kissable and cuddlesome, while for Charlotte there were limits to such things. Charlotte had homework, long, thick hair she liked me to brush each day, major decisions she would not make alone about what outfit to wear, a decision that included undies and socks. She wanted presents and her parents as playmates. Because she was more complicated, she got the lion's share of my time, though she did not feel it. After all, we did not cry over her, anguish over her development, call doctors on her behalf, speak of her endlessly on the phone. People did not ask after her in the same detail.

The spring that Rachel was twenty months old, I planned a trip with Charlotte, two days to do whatever we wanted in New York, our own apartment for two nights.

It was still hard for me to leave Rachel. She did not cry when I was gone or hurry to see me when I returned. I could not read what, if anything, she thought about my absence, nor did I know if she had the mental ability to understand that although I went away I always returned. I had left her twice to go on brief trips and could not call her on the phone and say, as I did to Charlotte, "I love you, sweetie, I'll be home soon," and so I carried her image around, never able to fully shake my longing for her. Both times, she got sick when I was gone, as if her body sensed my absence. When I returned there was no special greeting, no change in behavior. We simply picked up where we had left off.

Charlotte and I traveled by bus (her choice). For the whole ride she sat with her nose against the grimy windows. She did not speak a word until we debarked on an upper level of Port Authority that reeked of exhaust fumes. Then, as we hurried for the stairway down, hacking and teary-eyed, she said, "*Mommy*. This is so fun. This is even funner than I thought."

Everything was fun for those two days. She liked having breakfast in the coffee shop that Paul and I had frequented when New York was home, where her daddy went the night she was born and cried from happiness into his beer, and where, on our second morning, the owner recognized me and said, "Don't tell me this lovely young lady is baby Charlotte Claire?" She liked the wind that blew her skirt up to her chin when we reached the top of the Empire State Building, and the way the Staten Island ferry fit without a bump into its slip.

She loved the Met, the mummies, the sculpture garden, the rooms of furniture from colonial times. Paintings were boring, she pronounced, though when we went to the Modern the next day and passed the Rousseau exhibit, she wandered like a sleepwalker from canvas to canvas, studying the gypsies and animal eyes. She liked the scale models of houses with tiny people and trees, and the cafeteria, where she could linger over all the things that she might eat.

Twice each day I felt a sharp longing for Rachel. In the gift shops that Charlotte adored, because I wanted to buy something for Rachel, and she did not care for toys or pretty things; and later in the evening when we called Paul, for he would say, "I mishoo" to both of us, and then hold the phone to Rachel, and there would be nothing on the other end except Paul's attempts to coach her, and if I listened very closely, her thick little breathing, for she had come down with a cold the day we left.

I have a photograph of Charlotte kissing Rachel when we returned from our trip. Rachel in the car seat, bundled in her pink parka, her flawless skin rosy. Her broad face was still fat six months after treatment ended, her lips pouty, her blue eyes completely blank.

Here she is a month later, cruising through the living room, from table to wall to couch to chair. Paul tiptoes toward her and she turns and cocks her head, as sensitive to sounds as a deer in the woods. Her eyes flicker as she tries to figure out just who it is. And when he draws close enough for her to guess, she pinches his arm, squeezing his skin with such force that she trembles from the effort. This pinching, hair-pulling, and biting has been a problem for us. She does it out of excitement, and not anger, almost as if she cannot fully take us in until our flesh is squeezed between her fingers.

"How about a kiss, Rae-Rae?" Paul asks.

She sucks in her lower lip and kisses his cheek and then, for good measure, turns, tottering, and puts her arms around him to give him a little "ug."

"Babykins!" he calls out, whisking her into the air. "Oooh, I love you."

Charlotte's eyes grow stormy.

"She's changed, don't you think?" he says when we are alone and can whisper our excitement away from Charlotte's jealous ears. "She's moving around a lot more. Exploring. She's coming along, isn't she? She's really doing well!"

Here she is a week later, passive and potbellied as a Buddha, sitting and sitting, undisturbed by the dreads that have come rushing in, shaking me to the core with their whispering. Use the word, use the word, use it. Retarded. She's retarded.

Sometimes she was so cute, so utterly normal that it seemed impossible for anything to be wrong. Sometimes the sight of her trying a new task would move me into believing that she would be fine. Sometimes she was so blank that whatever hope I had vanished at the sight of her.

Sometimes we would go out hand in hand for a walk and Paul would talk about how wonderful it was just being with his beautiful children, and ah, nothing was wrong, nothing, nothing. Sometimes he was upset about work and came home and said, "I've had it; I want out," and I would feel in my gut a raw fear of the future, an aching knowledge that her problems would never go away.

One day, a year after Paul had seen Rachel pick up a kidney bean from her high-chair tray and believed for the first time that she could see, we found ourselves stricken with a heady case of Maine fever. It was a Saturday and I had followed Paul to a variety of hardware stores to browse at post-hole diggers and table saws. Afterwards, as a treat to our tolerant children, we went out to lunch in one of the ubiquitous diners that on other days made me despair about living in New Jersey. We

were sitting in a booth dividing up French fries and sandwich corners
when Rachel suddenly became glassy-eyed and lifeless.

Charlotte used to stare into space at that age, often enough for her
Maine baby-sitter to say, "Charlotte's in Bolivia!" several times a day.
But she snapped out of it quickly. Rachel remained motionless while we
tapped her high-chair tray and stroked her face, never blinking or crying,
without change of expression.

For the minute that Rachel was still, all of the unhappiness of the
year before came rushing back, the fatigue that overcame us, a kind of
physical, spiritual weariness that I had never known before.

Then it was over, and Rachel swept her hand across her tray, discov-
ered the piece of sandwich, and began to eat.

It was over for us just as quickly. I realized how fragile our happiness
was, so much out there waiting to crush it. We had a brain-damaged
daughter and she had just had an epileptic seizure.

When I took her for an EEG, the technician who glued the electrodes
to Rachel's scalp said, "Dr. Klibansky! What a wonderful man."

"He is?" I said.

"He really cares about the children, not like most of them. He comes
to the hospital late at night when no one's around, just to look in on
them."

I searched for this caring side during our appointment and was unable
to find it in gesture or word. We did come away from our meeting with
a diagnosis of partial complex seizures and a prescription for phenobarbital, a drug that had been around for many years and was considered
safe because, in Dr. Klibansky's words, it did "nothing hidden" to the
body.

A week after she began treatment we left for Maine.

I thought that I would never shake free of my upset over Rachel. But
suddenly we were heading up the dirt drive to the cottage, and I could
see the bay glistening between the trees, and our little house stood, neat
and fragrant from pine needles. The first thing Paul did was string up
our Yucatan hammocks between the trees, and we piled into the biggest
one, which was roomy enough for the four of us. And as we lay facing
the sea, arms, legs, wiggly baby flesh, birds in the trees, the loveliness
around me calmed me, just as always.

It was a warm, dry, exceptionally sunny summer. Lourie stayed with us for the month of July and helped take care of Rachel. Charlotte went to day camp. In previous years I had worked inside the cottage in jeans and sweater under artificial light. This year I spent most of the day outside on a chaise, pad in my lap, binoculars at my side, and I never forgot, not for a second, the splendor that surrounded me.

I ran on the hilly roads and swam in the bay, which was unusually warm, this dry summer. The bluefish ran early, and for two days the bay turned silver with vast schools of porgies, some jumping from the water, so that even on a windless day when the bay was mirror-still, the water would break with leaping fish.

Paul bought a thirty-gallon aquarium, which we filled with ocean water and little creatures from the sea; hermit crabs, baby eels and shrimp, and inch-long lobsters. He was uneasy about the idea of a bunk bed for Charlotte, something she and I wanted her to have, so he built her one out of unhewn logs and used old crib sides to keep her from falling out. We called her new home Skycrib, and it became a haven for her with space enough at the foot of the bed for her to lay out her toys and doll villages and play in peace.

One day after Paul had gone back to New Jersey, I took Lourie and the kids for a canoe ride. We paddled out to the cluster of islands and chose one to explore.

The wind picked up while we were gathering sea heather, and by the time we started for home, it was so strong that despite my furious paddling, the canoe kept drifting back toward the island. Charlotte became frightened. I paddled until my arms burned, sang a round of "Row, Row, Row," to distract her, and paddled some more, until many rounds and strokes later, we were safely home.

That evening while I prepared dinner Rachel went from couch to windowsill to table to chair, singing, "Row, Row, Row," in a soft tentative voice.

I kept my fingers crossed and wrote in the Maine book:

> She has begun to explore and babble, sings "Row, Row, Bo" relentlessly, says mu-u-u-ck (milk), 'nana, ap-pul, bu-u-u-k (book), dur-dul (turtle), sings no no no no no, chants like a cantor, climbs on chairs, and on the bed, found her "button," which turned pink from poking. Can put man in car! Walks one step and dives into our arms — scary! Charlotte, seeing her wrapped in her hooded towel, says, "Mommy, she looks like a *dorf*."

Lourie wrote:

Ray-Ray is doing great — she's almost walking. At the beach she mistook a man with a big belly for a balloon . . .

And my mother-in-law:

Surprise, surprise, Ray Ray is doing great, speaking words, including Nana, Papa, turtle, row row your boat, mommy, daddy . . . She is a walking doll . . .

# ❧ 17 ❧

# Her Radar

RACHEL AT A FRIEND'S HOUSE, two years and two months old. She is not familiar with the room and stands at the periphery with her head cocked. Five other children are playing nearby, most of them younger. They fight over a rocking horse, play with blocks, eat grapes, throw cushions off a daybed, roll around like cubs, nuzzle in their mothers' laps, then jump back into the fray.

Rachel stands. She "attends," as Mrs. Kaiser would say, very attuned to what is going on. At home, she stands with her ear against the refrigerator to hear it hum; in infant stim she listens so intently to the taped music that she forgets to follow the singer's directions, and at my friend's house she stands and listens to the children play until we walk her into the center of the room. Although she is not steady on her feet (she has only been walking for two months), neither is she afraid, and so we let go of her hand and step back.

The children rush past and *boom!* she is on her diapered rear end. She hoists her body up — at two still overweight (a residue from the ACTH, and from her inactivity). She is up on her feet for only a moment when the kids run past from the opposite direction, and *boom!* she is on her rear end again. Up and down, like one of those heavy-bottomed birds.

She always got up again — it was (and still is) her nature. She was cautious and unsteady and eager to try no matter how many times she fell. It touched me, this drive she had just begun to show. It touched me to see, when I undressed her, that the skin on her knees had been abraded so often that after a couple of months of walking, it was scabbed and leathery. She shuffled and lurched, tripped over cracks and obstructions, or because of her own enthusiasm, fell and got up.

If you were to see her at home or at school, where she walked as freely as a child with perfect sight, you would swear that nothing was wrong with her vision. If anything was rearranged, however, if, for instance, the dining-room table was extended, she would walk into it, taking its corner right in the nose. A change of color on the ground was difficult for her, green grass to gray cement, for instance, or carpet that changed shade, because the darker area suggested a drop. On uneven terrain she inched forward, the way a sighted person walks in a darkened room, one toe extended cautiously, then the whole foot, then another careful step.

She could not get around all that well and did not see all that well, but when she talked she made contact wherever she was. Speech became her radar, her person detector. She knew everyone by name — the teachers in her room and down the hall, the children in day care as well as those in other classes — and when she came to school she called out to them from the distance — Nanda, Rob, Lewa, Doon. (She called Charlotte "baby" for months, then gradually "Dee-dee," then "Stister," then "Dadit," then "Sha-dit," then "Sha-wit.") She managed Laura well enough (Lewa), though for a reason I never understood, did not come up with a name for Lourie, who was now an aide in a preschool class across the hall and saw Rachel every day. She meowed like a cat (and often, a cow), stuck out her "dung," recited her alphabet, counted to twenty. She said, "How doo yoo doo too day," when greeting people, "thanks," and "wekum."

She said, "Tickle!" to Paul, then laughed uproariously, experimented with her voice by saying, "Mommy," in a crazy desperate voice, a hoarse voice, a whisper, a shout. She kissed dolls with big smackers and gave them "ugs," lifted up the shirts of teachers and friends to search for their belly buttons, grabbed the knees of sitting strangers, pried open their thighs and pressed them together, the whole time reciting, "Open! Cwosed! Open! Cwosed!"

The reports that came in after Rachel's second birthday were the most hopeful since the diagnosis. Her gross motor skills were nearly a year delayed, and her fine motor skills just as dismal. But her speech and language skills were only slightly below age level, and this, given the fact that "performance was compromised by Rachel's visual impairment." The speech therapist also noted that "she has shown significant improvement in picture identification and demonstrating the functional use of objects."

Of all the times since the diagnosis, this was when my hopes were strongest, this time when she was walking at last and using new words, when she would head down the corridor calling out to her friends, for her friends were everywhere, when she had begun to recognize pictures in books — a photo of an apple, an orange, an egg, keys — life-size pictures on plain backgrounds. It took good lighting and effort on her part to see these pictures, and often she would try to fake at first, by saying, "Cute!" when we showed her a picture, or "Baby doll," though it might be an elephant or a ball of yarn. Even this seemed a sign of progress, since six months ago she had no tricks at all.

There is a wide range of what is considered normal language development between the ages of one and two, with some children naming things at a year, and other perfectly bright children failing to speak until the age of two. A typical two-year-old has two hundred to two hundred seventy-five words in his spoken vocabulary, though most parents can tell you the same thing as a speech therapist, that there is no reason for concern if a child that age says far less.

It is between the ages of two and three that the huge spurt in language skills occurs. A normal child's vocabulary begins to take off, and when she communicates, it is with clear intent. I knew then that this was the most critical time for Rachel, that her vocabulary had to increase, and she had to start stringing those words together soon if we were to believe that her motor delays had another basis, and that her intellect was intact. Either she would continue to develop or she would slip behind, and whichever it was we would know in the next six months. Maybe she would think and read and have friends. "Maybe she'll go to college after all," said Paul. Oh please, please, please. She's doing so unbelievably well.

Rachel was two and a half when she began to use her radar in the outside world. Wherever we went, she would locate strangers and bring them closer with her odd little staccato:

"Hi! How are yoo too day?"

This whole sentence from such an unsteady curly-headed little girl, so startling and adorable that no one could resist saying, "Fine! How are you?"

"Gooooooood!"

"Such a little girl, she speaks so well! What's your name?"

"Rae-Rae."

"How old are you, Rae-Rae?"

"Doooooo."

"My goodness, do you go to school?"

"Hi!" she might say.

"Is that your big sister?"

"Ummmm. Hi! How are yoo too day?"

Even when the responses were out of synch with the questions, strangers found the little girl who was as small and round as a child a year younger, and the formality of her greetings, to be utterly charming. Everywhere we went people told me how smart and precious she was.

The winter Rachel turned two and a half Paul and I planned a ski trip. We struggled over what to say about Rachel to the people who worked in the nursery there. If we stressed her problems they might refuse to care for her, and this seemed ridiculous since she was so delightful and in many ways so normal. (And who knew? Maybe she'd be fine!) We settled upon explaining that her vision was poor and that she was delayed, young for her age.

"Oh, she's so *smart,*" said the sitter when we picked her up at the nursery. "I've seen a *lot* of children, but she's a smart one, all right, she does her ABC's and she counts."

Sometimes Paul and I turned to each other and shared a rueful laugh. Sometimes we explained what worried us the most, that she was very good at rote, but could not go beyond her patter. Sometimes I would hear this lavish praise and think, Why not? Maybe I'm so fearful I'm incapable of appreciating how bright she is.

Then a friend would come over, and I would hear what a normal, unremarkable child could do with speech, how much more there is than mimicry, more than the same phrases over and over again. It doesn't take most children long to put words together the way Charlotte did at Rachel's age when she called my breast milk "mommy juice," and named our house "Foodtown House," because of the big supermarket down the hill.

I watched the weeks pass after Rachel's second birthday and when I saw that her need to talk increased much faster than her vocabulary, I began to dread the passing of time. I did not want her to be any older than two because as long as she was two, she was still normal, despite her repetitions and her limited number of words. I called her two for as long as I could, and when March came, I called her two and a half. I felt the months pass and worried that her progress had not been fast enough. She was two and a half in March, in April, in May and June.

Two and a half was still a baby; three was nursery-school age. I was afraid to think of her as three.

As winter passed she struggled to go beyond her set pieces and took to interrupting our conversation and saying: " 'Scusky, Daddy. 'Scusky, 'scusky," until one of us was quiet.

"What?"

"Um . . . see . . . um . . . abadago bago."

"Do you want to sit closer to the table?" one of us might ask.

"Abadago bago."

"Bring her up," Paul might say, for the two of us struggled to interpret this strange thing that she had begun to repeat.

"Abadago bago, abadago bago, abadago bago . . ."

She used this phrase for several months whenever she needed to talk and had nothing to say or no way to say what was on her mind. Long after we had learned not to struggle to interpret it, she continued to get a lot of response in the outside world, for people are used to finding a baby's speech difficult to understand and respond enthusiastically with "Oh!" and "How nice!" and "Is that right?" Abadago bago puzzled but did not upset me, not until the next phrase came in, this one interpreted as "I want to go to school," "I went to school," "I want preschool," and "I want a bagel," and which persisted for nearly a year.

When Rachel started day care, her teachers had suggested that Charlotte visit when she had a day off from school. That started a custom that Charlotte loved, of "helping" with the children every month or so. She painted pictures, played with the toys, rode in wheelchairs, pulled one of the adapted chairs up to the table to join the little ones for snacks. Although it was true that this well-equipped playroom was heaven for her, with its vast array of donated books and toys, the dollhouse and carriages and musical instruments, it must also be said that she became attached to the children in day care, just as Paul and I had, and thought of them as her friends. She brought home books on signing so that she could speak to her friend Jenny, learned the sign for "cute" and "baby" and the letters that spelled out Charlotte, and talked with pride to her playmates about her friend Jenny, who was deaf. One day I came into day care to get my two girls and found tiny Jenny in her wheelchair, pushing Charlotte in a stroller.

Charlotte loved to build and at home often made houses and furniture and people from snap-together blocks. Her creations were fragile and often came apart. Once she was playing with her block people in my office, when I overheard the conversations between these little plastic amputees. "Oh, yes, well, my *arm* fell off . . . *I* have to ride in a wheelchair because my leg is gone . . . One day *I* was walking and my head came off . . ."

And yet she faced the children in day care without sadness or pity or fear. The orthopedic contraptions, braces, orthotics, carts, and wheelchairs — the only things I saw the first times I entered this room — did not seem to faze her. She spoke freely of those with "problems," a word she must have picked up from us. "He's like Freddy, he has a problem," she said of a janitor who was mute. Or: "He's going to a special camp for children with problems."

When she invited a child to play at the house after school, she insisted that her playmate come with her to get Rachel. As soon as the car was parked, Charlotte always raced ahead, waving her arms at the automatic doors to show what a great magician she was. Down the hallway she would run, stopping to introduce her friend to the social worker, saying hello to the nurses, then through the second set of doors, which led into day care. The playmate proceeded happily enough until we reached Rachel's room. Then, as Charlotte raced over to her friends, I would see the playmate step back and gaze with fear at the tiny girl in a wheelchair, the boy who rode in unending circles on a tricycle, the boy their age with turned-in undersized legs, the boy in a rigid body cast, his legs splayed, the girl who sat in the corner rocking and clapping her hands. They were children to us, Gregg, Freddy, Sean, Jenny, Jean; they were the stuff of nightmares to Charlotte's friends.

The playmate most often regained her speech when she was in the back seat of the car and would ask, "Why does your sister go here?"

And Charlotte would say, "Oh, she has a problem."

Only once did I see Charlotte pick up on her friend's discomfort, and that was when Sean, who was her age and interested in the girls she brought by, said, "Who's your friend?" Charlotte turned and saw her playmate standing in a corner, hand cupped around an elbow. "Who's your *friend*, Charlotte?" he said again. "Introduce me to your friend." She did not make the introduction.

It will end, I thought that day. The time will come when her pride in her baby sister turns to shame, and she will no longer bring anyone home. I promised myself that I would not be angry if this happened, but when I watched the two of them tumbling in the solarium, or when I saw Rachel search for Charlotte, calling, "Stister? Stister?" I knew that it would break my heart.

Rachel's infant stim class now met twice a week for two highly structured hour-and-a-half sessions each week. During circle time there were songs with gestures ("Open your hands, touch your knees, and turn around, turn around, turn around . . .") that helped the children learn to follow directions, and games that taught simple concepts. ("Okay, I want everyone to take *one* toy out of the sack. Just *one!*)

After circle time, the therapists arrived and the children went to various tables. Two might do fine motor work with blocks and puzzles, and another two tactile things, "art" projects with paint or beans and glue, or a cooking project with an instant batter that needed to be stirred and poured. The third group did gross motor play on the slide or air mattress or with big foam balls.

Rachel did not like to sit at either table and used her newly developed charm to avoid it. When we sat her down to build a tower with one block atop another, something most normal children can do by a year and a half, she would smile prettily, push the blocks away, and say, "All done!"

"Rachel has developed some avoidance behaviors, stating that she had finished a task to avoid doing it," it said in the next report, "but this was easily redirected."

It went like this: Rachel popping up from her chair and announcing, "All done!" and Mrs. Kaiser saying, "Oh no, you're not," and sitting her back down.

The same report describes Rachel as displaying "cooperative, happy behavior." And this: "She was very auditorily alert during group sessions and tried to participate . . . in spite of visual limitations. She knew the names of the other children in the group." Her verbal perseveration was also noted at this time.

*Webster's Third* defines perseveration as "continual repetition of a mental act usually evidenced by speech . . . . a spontaneous and persistent recurrence." It is not a normal functioning at any age.

Rachel, happy, cooperative, auditorily alert, stopped people on supermarket lines and in doctors' offices and stores and said, "Hi, how are yoo too day?"

And there it was again, this unusually friendly child, for most little ones are shy at this age and nuzzle their mothers when strangers speak to them, while this one approached strangers, played "open, closed" with their thighs, and spoke to them in a clear little voice.

Who could resist answering, "Fine, how are you?"

"Gooooood. Ummmmmm. I want to go to school."

And the person might say to me, "What a bright little girl," and to Rachel, "That's nice. Where do you go to school?"

"Um . . . I wanna go to school."

"Just like your sister, hmmm? How old are you?"

"Um . . . I . . . um . . . I wanna go to school."

I might say, "Tell how old you are, Rachel," because this was a question that she could answer. Often she would simply say, "I wanna go to school," and toddle over to the next person to say, "How are yoo too day?" within earshot of the first.

People laughed. Most still thought it was cute, though fewer than before. I tried to distract her by asking her to tell her name or getting her to count; I learned to tell strangers not to feel compelled to stick around, for Rachel held people captive for a long time, struggling to say something, with nothing to say.

One of her therapists told me to clap my hands sharply to stop the perseveration; another to ignore it. We did both of these things, and sometimes they worked, though more often it was as if she *had* to perseverate, and if we distracted her the phrase would come out over and over, like a verbal seizure, "I wanna . . . I wanna . . . I wanna . . ."

Once, Paul said: "It makes me sick when she does that."

Not disgusted sick, upset sick, for she was happy and steadier on her feet and played all the games in circle time, and woke in the morning, saying, "I want up!" And "I want ope," for open; and "Back up," with a big push when she wanted us to move. She used possessives for the first time, speaking of "my book," and "my baby doll," and called my mother "Dave," my father's name, though my mother calls for him so frequently it is a song that she sings, and thus her name, the way it is for the whippoorwill. And so we had not abandoned all of our dreams.

*       *       *

In the spring when Rachel was two and a half, and I had begun to hope that days would last as long as weeks and weeks as long as months so that Rachel would have enough speech to turn three, we began to be concerned about her eyes again. One of them crossed. Not always, though often enough, now that she was using her vision. Paul and I discussed taking her back to see Dr. Hines, then changed our minds before we made an appointment because he was a neuro-ophthalmologist, whose concerns, it seemed to us, were far more esoteric than dealing with something as simple as a lazy eye.

We ended up having her examined by a local pediatric ophthalmologist, who came to the clinic at Children's every month. After the exam, the doctor said it wouldn't hurt to patch her good eye twice a week, and — who knew? — it might even do her some good. We were to keep patching her until the fall, when we might see whether or not it helped.

We bought the patches, "optic occluders," at the pharmacy, put the box on her changing table, and chose a day to start. That day passed. We chose a second day and missed that, too. Then a third and fourth.

The truth was, neither of us wanted to patch her. To cover her good eye meant leaving her nearly blind, putting her back into the world of her infancy. We could not quarrel with the treatment, which after all was standard therapy for "strabismus," unequal ocular muscle tone, and of great importance, since in strabismus the good eye takes over in order to avoid the confusion of a double image, and the weaker eye is suppressed, which in time results in loss of vision.

Eventually we shot fingers. I lost and patched her eye.

Rachel cried and struggled weakly when I put on the adhesive patch. She went to school and got around her familiar room as well as before, blithe and gay as always, the same except when it came to identifying pictures. I loathed those patches. Even after I saw how well she adapted, covering up her good eye continued to upset me.

The only effect patching Rachel's eye had was that it alarmed strangers. Although strabismus is common in young children and so is patching, it suddenly thrust her into the world of the obviously handicapped, no longer so cute nothing could possibly be wrong with her. Now when she approached people and said, "I wanna go to school," they looked at me, suffused with pity, and it was no longer, "Isn't she adorable!" but,

"What *happened* to her eye?" All this made me realize once again how much beauty is valued, how much worthier she was in the public's eye when she was cute.

I continued to meet with the other mothers the year that Rachel turned two. Though I no longer had the need to spill fears or relay medical tales, the group remained as important to me as before. I still rearranged my schedule so that each week I could be with these women, in this place where I was known. It was like the need to touch base with childhood friends, the ones who know us as we are, stripped of all artifice.

Of the original group, only Steven's mother remained. Katie had turned three the year before and was placed in a school for the lowest-functioning children. Lauren and Alex were in preschool across the hall; Lauren making great gains despite her neurological problems, and Alex falling farther and farther behind.

Tory's family had moved. One of the mothers kept in touch with her, and periodically brought back news. Tory had made no progress at all, and at two and a half remained at a seven-month level. She had no object permanence; that is, no sense that people and things existed when they were not in her sight. She was cranky and irritable, and though her mother still said that Tory would catch up, she was having a hard time coping with a child who was so unrewarding. She was furious with the therapists and the program Tory was in, and with Tory's sister, who looked and behaved like a child who was two years older, so that there was no longer the need to explain to strangers why one twin was so much bigger than the other.

Now there was Steven, whose cerebral palsy had been diagnosed as mild, and whose mother waited, as Paul and I waited for Rachel, with all her fingers crossed. The doctors felt that he would walk normally, perhaps stumbling when he was fatigued, and that his intellect would be unaffected. At two and a half, strapped into the lightweight b.k.o.'s (below the knee orthotics), made of plastic and fastened with Velcro straps, he had begun to walk with a stiff, jerky gait.

He was also "tactilely defensive," hypersensitive to touch, and gagged whenever he touched anything soft, gooey, or wet. He hated the art projects in infant stim, gagged when the glue was set before him, and rejected so many kinds of food that mealtimes exhausted his mother. And he still did not say a single word. His mother wrestled with the reasons for his delay. Was he learning-impaired? Slow? Had there been damage to the speech centers of the brain? Would he talk in time? Was it possible that he'd never speak at all?

We were joined in the mothers' group by women whose children had never been in infant stim before. They had been normal at birth and thereafter, and only now, with their third birthday approaching, had certain delays begun to show up. Among the children was a lively, clever boy who did not speak at three, a girl of three who chattered fluently but could not make an X with a crayon or put pegs in a board.

No matter how mild the impairment, the mothers who were grappling with their children's problems for the first time grieved deeply and obsessively, while those of us who were old hands had a very different style. The old hands did not rail or weep; we sighed instead. Gone was the rage at insensitive doctors and strangers and claims adjusters at insurance companies; the old hands were busy learning to operate within the system.

We had one concern this year, one topic that we discussed week after week while we ate the homemade muffins one of the women brought. All of our children were either turning three or were three already. Three is not a baby anymore. Three is nursery-school age, and we were all grappling with decisions about schooling for the following fall.

Not long ago the goal of the federal government was to provide an equal education to all children. In recent years, thanks to advocates for the handicapped, the ideal is now seen as an education suited to each child's needs and abilities. Education for special-needs preschoolers of three to five has been law in New Jersey since 1983; now it is mandatory nationwide.

Because the responsibility for providing this "suitable" education falls on the school district where the child lives, the fate of a child with special needs varies from place to place. In an optimistic case, the child-study team in the town is responsive to the needs of the child, the desires of the parents, and the suggestions from therapists and physicians, and a program satisfactory to all is found. Or a town may have its own preschool handicapped program and aim to fill it with children of varying needs and abilities, because sending children to an out-of-district program can cost five to ten thousand dollars a year, while putting a child in the town's existing program costs much less.

Learn to be an advocate, we heard again and again over the year. Speak up for your child even if you have never raised your voices. A town cannot force a parent to put a child in a program that is unacceptable. All decisions can be appealed. You and your children have rights.

In September Rachel would be three.

Charlotte's abilities at one and two are not so clear in my memory, but three I clearly recall. She was a month shy of three when we took her on a camping trip to Yosemite and Sequoia national parks. It was September, and the bears were hungry and brazen. One night Paul slung our duffle bag full of food between two trees, not high enough, however, and at night, a bear came and boxed with the bag. Paul woke and saw him and yelled a hoarse "Hoo! Hoo!" from within our tent. Another morning, in another park, where all of our food was locked in the metal bear-proof box the camp supplied, we found our car with a missing window, a bear footprint on our suitcase, and nibble marks on Charlotte's bag of toys.

I mention these incidents because I remember that the bears were a thrill for Charlotte, and that she spoke about them constantly and asked Paul to "Hoo! Hoo!" for her. I remember how we explained to her that the bears were not bad, that they broke into things because "they did not know any better," and also her telling us that a *baby* bear had broken into our car — she knew because he had played with her toys.

Whenever I thought of this I was staggered by the difference between Charlotte and Rachel. Charlotte, who was not precocious and did not speak early, was asking us to relate family tales and applying the "didn't know any better" explanation to those who left garbage in the parks or camp fires smoldering. She was talking about baby bears. She was toilet trained.

Well before I talked with our town's child-study team, I knew I wanted Rachel to be in the preschool program at Children's. I felt sure that being there would benefit her most, though I had only my gut to back me up, and no hard, clear data. The social worker warned that I could not tell members of the team that I wanted my daughter at Children's because I knew and trusted the staff or because the social worker kissed Rachel when she walked for the first time and the nurses in the clinic applauded. It was irrelevant that this place had been her second home from infancy.

Nevertheless, when I spoke to the team's coordinator I said these things, naively hoping that they would suffice. He listened respectfully and then told me about the preschool handicapped class in town.

I made an appointment to sit in on the town's class in order to make cogent comparisons between that program and the one at Children's. In the meantime, I asked a lot of questions.

I learned that the children enrolled in the public school program had only mild delays in various areas, and that most were eventually mainstreamed; that there was a speech therapist and an occupational therapist, but no physical therapist, and, therefore, no children with serious orthopedic problems.

Several of the teachers and therapists I sought to provide me with solid, unemotional reasons why Rachel should stay at Children's asked me to reconsider. Why be so adamant that she stay at Children's? Why not think about sending her to a program with children who were more advanced? It wasn't as if she needed therapies that were offered only at Children's. "It might be good for her. It could really push her ahead."

A vision appeared to me with a clarity I never allowed myself to see. Rachel in a regular classroom. My little girl in kindergarten in Charlotte's school. I could see her standing in line with the others, small, as Charlotte had been, her name spelled out on a wooden apple. Rachel with neighborhood friends, at birthday parties, running home with artwork in her hands. I allowed myself to imagine these things, and when I did I understood that *I* needed Children's, that the support I got might be clouding my vision. By the time I visited the town's class, my mind was wide open.

It did not matter that the day I sat in on the preschool handicapped class the aide was impatient with the children, that all the tasks the children performed had a strong visual component; it did not matter that speech therapy was given in half a room and behind the accordion divider the junior high band was practicing, cymbals and all, or that an inept substitute led the class, and that I never met the teacher who had been hired for the following year. I sat and watched the children and all I could see was that they were not handicapped, at least not to me.

They were doing the kinds of things Charlotte did in nursery school, tasks that I could not imagine Rachel doing a year from now no matter how much she progressed.

There were never any negotiations. The child-study team evaluated Rachel and agreed that Children's was the best place for her.

"Why are you crying?" Paul said when I told him the news. "It was just what we wanted, wasn't it?"

Three stories from Maine, the summer that Rachel stayed two and a half for four extra months.

1. Just before we left for our trip, Rachel had a seizure. When Dr. Klibansky saw Rachel he said, "Well, she certainly is a pretty child, *that* isn't one of her problems."

He told me to increase her dosage of phenobarbital to three times what it had been at the start. Then we went away.

I had recently learned that although phenobarbital does nothing *hidden* to the body, it depressed the sensory cortex, decreased motor activity, and altered cerebellar function, that it frequently caused drowsiness and sedation and learning problems, which, in a child as young as Rachel, could be permanent. I no longer had a benevolent view of the drug, therefore.

Early in the summer Rachel's perseveration increased. She seemed to have more trouble than before in communicating in even the simplest way. I called Dr. Klibansky from Maine to ask about the high dosage of phenobarbital, and he assured me that there was no reason for concern "as long as she's her usual perky self."

I nearly let it go, but the word "perky" was so inappropriate for Rachel that I said in an annoyed way, "I wouldn't exactly describe Rachel as *perky.*"

At that, he suggested lowering the phenobarbital dosage and starting her on a second drug called Tegretol that did not cause learning problems but came with a series of warnings and cautions that rivaled those of ACTH.

Now we had some difficult choices. Should we risk learning problems or physical damage? The literature warned of such things as "serious and sometimes fatal abnormalities of blood cells," serious skin problems, congestive heart failure, abnormalities in liver function tests, pulmonary hypersensitivity, cortical lens opacities, and aching joints and muscles.

The drug company did not recommend this product as the drug of first choice in seizure disorders, nor was "safety and effectiveness" established in children below the age of six.

We decided to start her on this drug, however. One reason was that Dr. Klibansky maintained that no patient of his had suffered from any side effects from Tegretol. Also, as long as she was on Tegretol she would have her blood levels checked weekly at first and then monthly, so that we would be able to monitor her health.

Shortly after we lowered the phenobarbital dosage and started her on Tegretol, she indeed began to perk up.

2. Linda came up to Maine with me so that we could begin work on another project. The past year, she had been traveling a great deal, showing the film we co-wrote at various festivals. Home between these trips had shifted to Los Angeles, so we had seen little of each other. Whenever we spoke she asked about Rachel and I told her whatever I was feeling at the time.

She had been living with us in Maine for a few days when she said, "Why didn't you tell me she was so bad?"

I was devastated. She was so bad and I didn't even know it. So bad when I had been reveling in her prettiness and did not see. What was so bad about her?

She perseverated and said, "You know what? I wanna go to school," several times a day. She could not initiate any play. She never touched the laundry basket of toys. If I spilled them out she might choose a rattle to shake, at most.

She wore an eye patch two days a week, was that so bad?

Also: She could not answer questions, simply could not process even the most straightforward ones, and when we asked her something like, "Are you hungry?" she would say, "Whaaaaaat?" although she knew the words and could tell me herself that she wanted to eat.

Linda's words resurrected a fear that she would not communicate with me, for a child who chatters mostly nonsense phrases, who can make simple statements but cannot answer the easiest questions does not fully communicate. Her words filled me with the fear that Rachel would grow up to be a strange creature, whose speech was made up of snippets of overheard phrases and nothing more, like the man who approached me on the train platform, dressed in a workman's shirt and jeans, an ordinary fellow until he stepped too close and rumbled in my face, "DON'T you think the Rrrrrrraritan Valley Line is the best line in the state of New Jersey?" And then veered toward a group of elderly women to ask, "DON'T you think the Rrrrrrraritan Valley Line . . ."

3. The days passed, many of them rainy, it was true, but it was Maine all the same. My household responsibilities here consisted of sweeping pine needles from the cottage, washing the dishes by hand, and once a week bringing my wash to the Laundromat. I had time to lie in the hammock, take the kids to the islands in a canoe, and to the Topsham fair to see prize pigs and sheep. I baked muffins and made jam and, removed from the doctors' reports, lessons, responsibilities, and chores of home, I had time to be aware of how much I loved my children. In Maine my love for Rachel was separate from her problems. I loved all that was sweet and soft and charming about her, and celebrated all of her steps with no obsession with where she should be, none at all, so Linda's words stopped resonating, and she was no longer so bad, but just my very own.

The woman I hired this year to take care of Rachel was a retired woman, a young great-grandmother, one of several sisters, all of them strawberry blondes. Every day Gerry came by in her little tan car with Evie or Charlotte or Betty or Mary. I had been quite candid about Rachel's delays when I had hired Gerry, but the sisters would hear nothing of them. No, she was a quick little thing, who learned the games they taught her and made them laugh, the way she said, "How doo you doo too day," in gruff and squeaky and whispery voices, and stood at the door, yelling, "Mittens, go home!" at the cat, just as they did. She knew all the words to "One Lonely Oyster," and lay on her mat at nap time singing "Alone, tee-hee, alone," and the last "Sssssss — BANG!" from "Dynamite." No, she was as smart as a whip.

She was patched two days a week, and even on days when she had both her eyes to use, the hills, with their knobby roots and rocks and stumps, made her cautious when she walked, and so the sisters were always aware of her poor vision.

One of them took me aside and said that it was good to have Rachel around because her grandchildren would now understand that some children were less fortunate than they were. She said this to me a second time, and later to Paul. I found it odd, and rather shocking — the way I had when a friend of Charlotte's had asked her, in a rather sneery tone, why Rachel's eyes looked funny. "Her eyes?" Charlotte had said, genuinely puzzled. "Her eyes don't look funny."

"Do you think of Rachel as 'less fortunate'?" I asked Paul.

"No," he said. "Do you?"

"I don't," I said. "I really don't."

# ❧ 18 ❧

# Loving Rachel

I CRIED THREE TIMES the fall that Rachel turned three. The first time was the morning I put her on the van that took her to preschool at Children's. She was all dressed up in little overall shorts, new shoes with striped laces, and a blue backpack that had once been Charlotte's, just big enough to hold a change of clothes and a notebook for her teacher's daily comments. At eight o'clock the horn bleated and Paul, Charlotte, and I walked Rachel outside, letting her take the front stairs in her cautious sideways fashion, hand against the railing, toe edging out to feel for the end of each step. Paul helped her onto the van, and the driver's aide strapped her into her car seat. Then the van pulled away, van of all my fears, taking my daughter to a special school, just as I always knew would happen, knew more deeply and fully than Paul, and never knew at all. I put my arms around Paul and wept, and heard in the background Charlotte ask in a small voice, "Why is Mommy crying?"

"She cried when you went off to your first day of nursery school, too," he said.

"I didn't cry when Charlotte started nursery school," I told Paul later.

"You didn't? I was a little misty."

"But not with Rae-Rae?"

And Paul, who still sometimes says, "Who knows, maybe she'll make it after all," and sometimes, "She's really delayed, isn't she?" said, "I thought she looked cute with that backpack, like a little mensch."

The second time I cried was on Thanksgiving. I had come into my parents' living room, where my father sat with Rachel and an old friend, and heard the friend say, "She's a beautiful child," and my father, ". . . such a pity." I turned around, went back upstairs, sat in the bathroom and cried one of those inside-out cries I had thought were in the past.

Then I washed my face, went downstairs, joined my family for dinner, toasted everyone's health, and helped myself to all the trimmings.

While I ate I composed a letter to my father that said how much I wished that he would love Rachel as she was and not see her as pitiful, that if only he could stop thinking of all that she was not he would be able to see that she was charming and lovable. Try to stop thinking of her as our bad fortune, *she* isn't suffering, I wrote in my head. *She* doesn't feel deprived. Her vision and intellect are her own self, all that she has ever known.

In the letter I told my father about an evening I spent with a childhood friend, and how in talking about people we knew in common, we mentioned a lonely woman, incapable of love, a bright man compelled to destroy his career, the son of a mutual friend, paralyzed by depression, and how when I got home and Rachel greeted me at the door, I wondered why we thought of her life as tragic.

I believed what I was writing in my head, believed it absolutely. Why then had I cried that evening? Why did I cry four months later, when a woman from Tennessee, a stranger, called to tell me about her little girl, diagnosed as having optic nerve hypoplasia, who at seven months had been completely blind? They'd had her prayed for, and the Lord God healed her, and now she could see twenty-twenty. She was Rachel's age and fine in every way. And the mother wanted me to know this so that I would remember that "He is the same God as in the Old Testament, and still performs miracles."

I got off the phone and relayed the message to Paul. I was just about to apologize to him for spouting like a geyser when he began to cry, too.

Three times is not so bad, not when I compare it to the months after Rachel's diagnosis, when I cried so often I felt as if I would end up permanently desiccated. Or to the next year, when I cried less over Rachel, but was easily set off by other things, a canister from an animal shelter with a photo of a white dog and beneath it, THIS PUP BORN WITHOUT EYES. Starving Ethiopian children made me cry, the sound of a screaming baby, a conference with Charlotte's teacher in which I was told in somber tones that my daughter had poor scissors technique, a story of a retarded child lost in the woods, a dead possum mother and babies lying in the road, a PBS feature on childbirth that had a shot of a mother holding her newborn baby, a frail great-grandfather cutting challah at my cousin's wedding. I could go on . . .

This year when I see pictures of stray dogs I no longer cry. Now I want one very badly. The fact that I am allergic to dogs is nothing. I want that stray dog so badly I'm ready to drive out to that dog shelter in south Jersey, take that little puppy in my arms, feed and care for it and bring it back to health. When I read about foster children, I want to take in a foster child; when I saw a Vietnamese child standing on the seat in the train singing, "Mary Had a Widdle Wamb," at the top of his lungs, I wanted to adopt a child instead.

Birds, guinea pigs, dogs, kittens, children. Once I was a brackish spring gurgling forth with tears, now I am in a maternal phase and want to nurture in a queer compulsive way. I want to give back, to help someone needy, to tape broken plant branches, feed ailing robins, nurse a child back to health. This past winter I drove my family crazy with my fervent desire to start medical school so that I could care for those who suffered and rid the world of all disease. All I can say is that I no longer cry as much.

Rachel liked preschool, not that she could tell me so. I knew by the pleasure she took getting ready in the mornings, by the way she called out, "Kathy's here!" when she heard the bus driver beep the horn outside, and by the fact that when she lay in bed at night, she recited her classmates' names, as if to recall them, and sang the songs that she had learned in class.

Her preschool room looked the same as Charlotte's, cubbies filled with toys, an easel and sand table, construction paper cutouts on the walls — colored leaves when I visited in autumn — and a chart with each child's name and birthday. Also on the wall were lists of each child's objectives, for example, "Count to twenty. Write name." Or "Copy + and o. Work on 'same' 'different.' "

It was a heterogeneous group. One child had brain damage as the result of an accident, another cerebral palsy, a third spina bifida. One child was bright, one had severe neurological problems that impeded his learning, one was delayed, one hyperactive. This isn't to say that each child had one problem only. Once you get into the world of special-needs children you begin to see how complex are the problems, especially for those many who are brain-damaged. When Rachel's "active problem list" was set down in the first report I received that year it was as follows:

poor vision
delayed fine motor skills
tendency toward perseverative language
mild cognitive delays
very short attention span

This last item on the list — very short attention span — proved the trickiest to handle, for Rachel's early "avoidance behaviors," her habit of saying, "Baby doll," when she was shown a picture of a shoe, or "all done," when she was given a puzzle, was a big stumbling block to her learning. During story time that fall, when the other children had gathered in a circle to listen to the teacher read, Rachel would speak out and shift in her chair. When she was told in a firm voice to be quiet, her face would crumple slowly, mouth turning down and down in a silent cry, and she would rub her eye with her fist or curl into a fetal position on the floor. How would she learn if she could not pay attention?

And what of the second item, delayed fine motor skills? Her hands and shoulders were so weak that she could not pull apart snap-together blocks. She also had trouble integrating her tactile and visual systems, and used one or the other separately; so that, for example, she might be able to identify an object on the table but not be able to tell you what it was when it was placed in her hand. She did not have a clear sense of where she was, and her occupational therapist, who saw her individually once a week, and had been one of the initial evaluators when Rachel was three months old, was still unsure whether this was because she was dyspraxic — that is, had a subtle motor-planning dysfunction — or because of her limited vision.

I visited Rachel's class that fall and saw how hard it was for her to share her teachers with the other children and to sit and focus her attention on the tasks given to her. And yet despite the adjustments she had to make, I was amazed at how independent she had become.

She hung her jacket on her own hook in the cloakroom and carried her chair to the table to join the others for a snack. When snack time was over, she put her paper plate in the garbage and her cup in the sink. (No wonder she threw away her dishes at home!) She could tell the functional use of objects; that is, if asked what a cup was for, she would say "to drink" and scissors were "to cut." She understood prepositions such as "in" and "under," and could tell her speech therapist where an object was. She had begun to use her finger to locate a hole in

a pegboard and to be able to work the peg into the hole (though sometimes she worked her finger in one hole and struggled to put the peg in
another). She could also make a vague approximation of an *0* with a
crayon and had begun to identify big and little objects by pointing.
And if it was hard to get her to attend, and if she perseverated and
showed avoidance behaviors, her teachers were learning to help her break
through by cuing her, reminding her of the task at hand, several times
if necessary. "Where is the big one, Rachel? The *big* one. Show me the
*big* one."

I realized after that day in class that she was a different child at school
from the one she was at home (as all children are) and that in her structured class she was learning things, making progress in her own way,
while at home, where we could not sit and work with her all day long,
she remained a strange child who still got lost in her own repetitions.

At home she at last took toys from the top of the basket and wheeled
her dolls in a carriage, yet remained unable to initiate anything more
complicated than that. When I was busy in the kitchen, she wandered
around, opened cabinet doors and slammed them shut, jiggled the metal
bowls that hung inside, asked a dozen times for something to drink,
said, "You know what? Sandy's coming over . . ." a dozen times.
Whenever I tried to read the newspaper, she would bash her fist into
the paper and ask me to watch her jump. She might ride on her trike
or pick up her toy phone and say, "Hello, Grandma? This is Jane.
I'll call you on Friday . . . ," then hand me the phone and say, "It's
for you."

Her speech was still concocted of learned phrases and polite overheard
niceties and so she retained what a friend described as the manners of a
schoolmarm, saying, "Hello, how are you?" to strangers, and "Excuse
me, can I ask you a question?" (though she had no question), and "Have
a good day!" before she walked away. Sometimes she said, "I'll call you
on Friday," which always left them laughing. (Would she still say these
things at forty? Will I laugh if she does?) If she picked up a pencil at
home, she asked, "How do you spell Rachel?" or "What's two plus
two?" just what Charlotte and I said when we sat with pencils at the
table. "I have homework," she announced when she came home from
school. Sometimes when we were walking, she leaned way over and said,
"Stop for a second, my shoes are untied," though her laces would be
knotted tightly.

The fall that Rachel turned three I decided to scrape the wallpaper off the dining-room walls, five layers of paper, none of it strippable, on old plaster walls. For those who congratulated Paul and me for having raised such a polite child with her ready thank you's and excuse me's, I report with regret and amusement that Rachel learned to say "Oh shit" that winter, and said it with the perfect, irritated tone she heard me use. She would travel along the walls with a putty knife, saying "Oh shit" every few feet. If I was atop the ladder and dropped the sponge, a little voice below would tell me, "Say 'Oh shit,' Mommy."

At home no one could sneak a snack without Rachel finding out. This child, who held a cup early and fed herself neatly at a very young age, knew the names and odors of a bewildering array of food at three. Poor vision was no impediment. Rachel could spot a grape a mile off, distinguish between a blueberry and a raspberry in her own mouth. One afternoon I opened the refrigerator when she was two rooms away and she asked, "Are you opening the refrigerator?" And, "What are you eating?" as I took out a jar. "Is it a pickle?" when I unscrewed the lid. And then, hurrying toward me, arms flying, "Excuse me. May I please have a pickle? Thank you very much."

By winter we had begun to notice that sandwiched within these overheard phrases were words that came from her own head and heart. Just at the point when she would be driving us all a little buggy saying, "You know what? Sandy's coming over!" she might say, "You know what? My ummmmm . . . my shoe is off." And it was true! Or, "You know what? Sandy's coming over. Annnnnnnd . . . I played with Buddy and Kristy and Adrian. In school. It was so fun!"

A social worker from the Commission for the Blind sat in on Rachel's preschool class every few weeks. After her winter visit she told me about an optometrist who did work with low-vision kids. "He can get measurements that no one else can."

Nothing conclusive had been gained from the patching, and Paul and I had again been wondering what steps to take next. Should we go back to Dr. Hines after all? Find a pediatric ophthalmologist who had more experience with children who had optic nerve hypoplasia? This recommendation from the Commission, for an optometrist in a small town west of us, did not seem particularly compelling. What was he doing in this little town if he was so good? Why an optometrist, who was not a medical doctor, instead of an ophthalmologist? Who was he?

An unusual man, it turned out; a sculptor and tinkerer, who began his career in optometry working with low-vision adults, who had been told time and again that nothing could be done to help them, that they had to learn to accept their limitations. The situation was even more dismal for infants, because they had no advocates, and no way to speak of their frustrations.

Pediatric low-vision work suffers from the same problems as conventional medicine, with far more effort spent describing syndromes than working on interventional strategies. Eight years ago, when parents of low-vision children were still being told that nothing could be done, Dr. Siwoff began to devise methods that might enable these children to get the best possible use of whatever vision they had.

In an eye chart, acuity is measured using an object of a certain size at a certain distance. (What object and what distance is "a matter of convenience," according to Dr. Siwoff.) Letters can be used, or pictures for younger children. In order to measure visual acuity in infants or in children who cannot speak, their eye movements must be carefully observed. Dr. Siwoff found that two tests used together turn out to be extremely reliable.

In the first, he relies on something called opto-kinetic nystagmus, which is the involuntary response of normal eyes that makes them flutter, and "do a little dance." Using a series of stripes on a drum that moves against the visual field, Dr. Siwoff will back away and watch the opto-kinetic nystagmus. When there is no "dance" he measures the size of the stripes and their distance from the child.

In the second test he uses white plastic spheres against a black background. Acuity is measured by the size and distance of the ball, and by studying the child's "purposefully guided visual eye movement."

After Rachel's acuity was measured this way, and it was determined that she had no significant refractive error (she was not nearsighted, farsighted, or astigmatic), Dr. Siwoff checked her external eye health and did a neurological evaluation of her extra-ocular muscles. A prism bar was used to measure eye deviation. If eyes are straight, a penlight shone at them will be reflected in the center of the pupil; if not it will be displaced. Dr. Siwoff believed that many low-vision children "learn" to turn their eye not because of a muscular problem, but because of a sensory one, so that their eye will deviate or turn to the area of best seeing. With Rachel this appeared to be the case. Her eye crossed so that she could make use of a window of vision.

Dr. Siwoff tried prismatic spectacles on her that repositioned retinal images — literally putting the world onto a functional piece of retina. Then he asked her to reach for a small bright ball that he held first in front of her and then to either side. Each time she reached out and took the ball without pause. She did not cock her head in order to catch sight of it, nor did her eye cross. Furthermore, she could see the ball when he held it to her left, whereas without the prismatic glasses, that part of the world simply did not exist for her.

Next he took off the glasses, threw the ball, and asked Rachel to get it. She walked crabwise to retrieve it, head cocked, eye turned, toeing in with her left foot. He put the glasses back on and threw the ball again. Rachel straightened her head and body and got it without delay.

Why did the glasses change Rachel's gait? Without them, she had to turn her head in order to get the best field of vision. By doing this, she tightened her body.

As Dr. Siwoff explained, "We're designed to get visual information head-on when we walk." When Rachel turned her head in order to find the window of vision, her brain got confused. "The eyes say they're going straight, but the head is turned, so the body tightens."

Our visual system affects our ability to walk, to take in information, to relate to space. Dr. Siwoff believes that it is not uncommon for a visually impaired child, in searching for an area of clearest vision, to tighten one side. He believes that sometimes the gait problems in low-vision kids that are diagnosed as orthopedic tend in fact to be visual.

Without prismatic glasses, some children never find out that they have a window of vision. Many appear not to have vision because they don't know how to use it, which is why stories like ours, of infants who are completely blind for so many months, are not uncommon.

We expected Rachel to reject her glasses, and imagined that we would have to keep them on with a special band around her head, but when, two weeks later, Dr. Siwoff gave her the little pink glasses, she touched them once and left them where they were. She quickly learned to adjust them when they slid down her nose by pressing her palm against the lens, then straining to look through the splotches of lunch that she had mashed into the glass. We got so used to seeing her with them that when they were off she had the unfinished look that longtime eyeglass wearers get. Later, she would take them off whenever she was tired. (Much later, she began to fling them off, leaving them in couch cushions or on the floor. She bent the earpieces, nearly snapping the frame, and when, on her teacher's suggestion, we had her eyes reexamined, we found that her weaker eye had begun to do more work, and that most likely she had been seeing double images.)

The glasses were the first positive thing that had been suggested for Rachel. All we had heard before our appointment with Dr. Siwoff was never, impossible, irreversible. Now that she had glasses we waited for something miraculous to happen.

At first the only change was in her gait. Because she no longer cocked her head in order to see, she walked more upright from the first moment her glasses were on. Her feet did not turn in as much, and if she still lurched, she walked with more confidence, indeed, took to running whenever possible, calling, "Run, run, run!" her arms flying in all directions. "Run, run, run" in her own unique style, which her occupational therapist aptly described as "chasing after her center of gravity."

Her teacher thought she did better with picture books and attended for longer periods of time, though she wasn't positive it had to do with her glasses. Her occupational therapist didn't see much of an improvement and suggested that perhaps Rachel hadn't gotten used to her improved vision.

I should have known that the changes would not be sudden, that they would be so gradual time would have to pass before we saw that she was different. It was only toward spring that we noticed how much more tuned into the world Rachel was now that she had glasses. She noticed people. She was more interested in the other children in her class, and sometimes brought those who weren't ambulatory books or toys to play with. In a store, she looked up and pointed to an umbrella mounted over our heads; outside, she showed us a tree. We had never suspected she even knew what a tree was or could see something so far away, and now she was reaching her arms out and telling us to look at the pretty tree. The glasses had enlarged her world.

She had never explored and now she did. She opened drawers, took knives off the kitchen counter, jumped on the couch cushions. The summer before she turned four she threw a comb and finger puppets into the aquarium Paul had set up in Maine, and on another day stood by the large tank, drinking teaspoons of the murky salt water. Before she had glasses she was unaware of combs and finger puppets, of the fact that water burbled in the large tank, and so these things would have been unthinkable.

Around the same time that we began to see how much bigger Rachel's world had become, her preschool teacher recorded in her book that Rachel was "inconsistently identifying colors." She suggested that I test her myself, and so each afternoon I gave her a pile of plastic pegs and asked her to give me one that was green or yellow, the colors she seemed to identify most often at school.

I was supposed to work regularly with Rachel at home, to "follow through" with the tasks she was learning in class. I found this increasingly difficult, for she was so distractible, collapsing on her back or asking me irrelevant questions in the midst of a lesson. When I tried to teach her, I was reminded of her deficits and disabilities, of everything she could not do. It also brought back all the afternoons I lost scrutinizing charts, weighing her delays, trying to figure out exactly where Rachel fit and what her future might be. For three years I wanted truth in all its grimness, fact, no matter how bad. I didn't want to do that anymore. I knew that Rachel was delayed, but I had reached a point where I wanted to celebrate her progress rather than mourn her delays, where I preferred uncertainty to a verdict that would tell me what her limits would be.

It was different working with colors. I never expected Rachel to be able to see colors, so there were no pressures for either of us. "Which is the *green* block?" I asked her day after day. "Rachel, look, the *green* block. Give me the *green* block."

Sometimes she would pick up a green one. Sometimes she might go for an orange and take the green only after I repeated the instructions. There were days when she picked out her colors effortlessly followed by days when she seemed to have no sense of color at all.

It took until late spring for her to become consistent enough for me to tell Paul that she identified colors. He refused to believe, but I no longer desperately needed him to see what I saw, believe what I believed, grieve when I grieved. I did not hysterically insist that she could see color, then waver in my convictions when he disagreed. I gave him the pegboard with thirty-six pegs and told him that during his free time he should get her to pick out the green ones and that he would see that she could pluck those few from among the thirty-six. As I turned away, I thought with dismay that she would not do it for him.

She did, and when he came upon me that night he said, "You know what this means, don't you? She's got some central vision. I never would have believed it. She's got some central vision!"

That was the second time he cried after Rachel turned three.

I don't want to end this story. I want to tell about the day in June when I visited her in speech therapy, and how she sat for thirty minutes without squirming, identifying large lifelike drawings of clothing and saying, "It's a . . . shirt. It's a . . . pants," and then, when drawings of food and clothing were placed side by side, telling the therapist which she would wear and which she would eat. That day she also followed the two-part commands she was given, clapping her hands, then putting a yellow block on her head, touching her nose, then clapping her hands, touching her head, then opening her mouth. I want also to tell that in occupational therapy, she lay on her stomach in a swing suspended from the ceiling, and, as if to prove a controversial theory that weight bearing and movement helped integrate tactile and visual systems, she swayed and snapped together large blocks.

I want to hold on to this manuscript (the way I want to hold on to the clock hands) so that I might continue to record her gains. By ending now I must report that she spent the warm months asking everybody's name and age, including those she knew best, and that she stopped strangers to say, "My dad said," a sentence that remained incomplete for four months, until finally she arrived at, "My dad said . . . hi!" Also, that she could not play alone and was still hard to engage in anything other than the stacking and sorting exercises she learned in school. She sang nursery rhymes and songs, made simple observations and statements, followed directions.

She could not recall for me anything that she had done that afternoon, even if it was something exciting, like taking a pony ride. When Charlotte or Paul were gone, she never asked where they were or when they would return; she could not tell me anything about them, or about her classmates, though she still recited their names at night. She could not dress or undress herself. She was not toilet trained.

We did not know whether she would ever be able to read or reason or live on her own, if she would stop perseverating or continue for her lifetime. Some children who are delayed in infancy catch up, others continue to progress in their own slow way, others lag further as the skills they must perform become more complex. Rachel's preschool teacher was pleased with her progress and had hopes for her, but her occupational therapist was unimpressed by her abilities and felt that she could handle little besides rote learning, that she could not work within a body of information or use information to solve problems.

*Why don't you cry anymore?*

Because she's ours and we love her. We're more accustomed to living with Rachel and all that her life entails. If she were like Katie it would be different, I suppose; if her luminous eyes were all that bound her to us; if she got bigger and heavier but grew in no other way, so that all we could say about her was, "She's so heavy I can hardly lift her," we might, like Katie's mother, begin to speak of a residential facility, an institution. Then perhaps we would still cry.

Rachel's struggle is her own, her life is destined to be different from any I have known. Once her future obsessed me; my fears of who would love her and what kind of life she would have were so strong that I could not see much else. But nearly four years have passed and it is normal to let go. Time lessens the anxieties, smooths the edges: Time does heal.

*How have you changed?*

I seize the moment, and wring every bit of happiness from it, and at the same time I feel more vulnerable than before. When I go out on a morning run, and the air is crisp and cool, and my stride long and effortless, I feel vigorous, strong, connected to the earth and heavens, kissed by fortune. Life is sweet, and I am so unbelievably happy, and . . . one day I will never feel like this again; one day I will be old and it will all be taken from me, one day I will die.

So what else is new? My closest friends might say that I have always been this way, *always*, a hand-wringer since adolescence — but then again, I don't happen to believe that hardship ennobles us. Grief makes us aware of how fragile we are, how powerless to determine our own fate. It is not like chicken pox, with guaranteed immunity after one bad case. No matter what has happened in the past, something worse can happen in the future.

*What have these characters learned?*

On one hand, nothing.

On the other hand, the following: how to give shots, how awful it is to be unable to alleviate someone else's pain, how rotten life can be, how exclusive an emotion grief is, how many ways there are to grieve. My vocabulary has improved. Listen to me spout these specialists' words and speak with ease of adaptive skills, partial complex seizures, developmental delays, cognitive deficits, perseveration. I can make cocktail party chatter with ophthalmologists, physiatrists, speech therapists, special-education teachers, neurologists, Braille teachers, social workers. If having a baby enabled me to speak to other babies, having a handicapped child has enabled me to feel comfortable with the handicapped.

In one of the I-overcame-bullies-and-prejudice autobiographies that I read after Rachel's diagnosis was an incident that enraged the blind author, in which a man took his arm in an airport and said, in essence: I am comfortable with your blindness because my grandson is retarded. I don't think he meant that all blind people are retarded, as the author felt, but rather that a voice inside him had been released that allowed him to speak with ease, to relate to others who were handicapped. (And this is one of the strongest arguments for mainstreaming, that familiarity minimizes suspicion and fear.)

Is that all?

I ran into Steven's mother at the supermarket one night. Our children had been in different preschool classes and we hadn't seen each other since the summer before. She said, "How's Rachel doing?"

And I said, *"Fine!* She's got glasses with prisms in them, so her vision has really improved. But she's got a lot of learning problems, and . . . she's pretty delayed. How's Steven?"

"Oh, he's coming along really well, but . . . He still doesn't talk and now they're starting to say he probably never will. He's been so frustrated not being able to tell us what he wants, and for a while he was biting everyone. Then about a month ago we started signing with him, and he's really been responding."

I hurried home and climbed the stairs to look in on my girls. Maybe I'm lucky after all, I thought as I tucked them both beneath their covers.

Then I imagined Steven's mother going home and stepping softly into her son's room. I could see her kissing his forehead and feeling lucky, because her love ran so deep. I might come into her mind and she might think, "God, she's got her hands full, the kid doesn't see well, she lurches, she repeats herself all the time, she has epilepsy, she's retarded." The other mother might say that because to the world that's what she is.

To me she is Rachel. My love for her is not the dumb, gut love of mother for her baby rat, though that is part of it. Nor is it a sorrowful love. I love her because she is warm, charming, and responsive, because she loves in return, because she wakes up calling our names, and tells us to tickle her, because when I ask Charlotte what she wants to eat, Rachel, three rooms away, calls out, "Ummmm cream cheese olive onion mustard fish sticks apple juice," and when I kiss her she says, "*I'm* so sweet!" I love her because when I go to the bathroom, she follows behind me and says, "Excuse me, excuse me. May I come in?" and then opens the door and says, "I am in!" with great glee. She steps into the shower and says, "I am in the shower!" and, "You're taking a pee-pee? I can hear it. That was good, that was very very *very* good. *Yeah!*" I love her because she is mine.

She makes me laugh. She learned how to jump in July, and now jumps at the slightest provocation, arms clenched, elbows bent, springing high. Often her feet don't leave the ground, but she is pleased and proud anyhow, and so are we. She gives her dolls big wet smackers and tells them when she's alone, "Are you my tootsie pie? Hmmm? Hmmm?" and kisses us, never blinking, right on the lips. Inside is a pure, sweet spirit.

I'm not saving for her college education.

I cannot live through Rachel or expect the world to applaud me for her accomplishments, for once she grows up and loses all vestiges of babyhood, whatever her ultimate handicaps, she will never be valued by the world.

It would be a lie to say I do not care. If there were a magic pill that would rid her of all deficits, I would give it to her, but I don't love her less for her imperfections; nor do I love her in spite of them, though there are times when my love is still tainted by sadness and fear.

She is my little girl, and she has such a long, tough road ahead. I have seen her fall and pick herself up so many times; I have run my hands across her leathery knees and marveled at her drive, and her body's way of adapting to it. But there has never been a time when I have not had to stop myself from holding her in my arms so that she will never trip again.

I am with you, Rachel. These last four years have prepared me. I have learned to introduce you to the world, and to be proud of you in the face of pity or ridicule. I have grown to love you so deeply that I can truly say that I can no longer imagine my life without you.

August 1987